THE FARROWS
OF HOLLYWOOD

THE FARROWS
OF HOLLYWOOD
THEIR DARK SIDE OF PARADISE

MARILYN ANN MOSS

Skyhorse Publishing

Skyhorse Publishing books may be purchased in bulk at special discounts for sales promotion, corporate gifts, fund-raising, or educational purposes. Special editions can also be created to specifications. For details, contact the Special Sales Department, Skyhorse Publishing, 307 West 36th Street, 11th Floor, New York, NY 10018 or info@skyhorsepublishing.com.

Skyhorse® and Skyhorse Publishing® are registered trademarks of Skyhorse Publishing, Inc.®, a Delaware corporation.

Visit our website at www.skyhorsepublishing.com.

10 9 8 7 6 5 4 3 2 1

Library of Congress Cataloging-in-Publication Data is available on file.

Cover design by Kai Texel
Photo credits: All photos are from Wikimedia Commons or publicity still handouts.

Print ISBN: 978-1-5107-6883-3
Ebook ISBN: 978-1-5107-6884-0

Printed in the United States of America

"So we beat on, boats against the current,
borne back ceaselessly into the past."
—F. Scott Fitzgerald,
The Great Gatsby

CONTENTS

A vagabond, he came out of nowhere, and blossomed literally overnight into one of the highest salaried writers in the film colony . . . [and] a real social light. Wherever there was an elite dinner or a grand opening or a Blue Blood revel, he appeared escorting some of Hollywood's most famous beauties. He was everywhere: The Mayfair, the Cocoanut Grove, the exclusive Academy dinners. A handsome young man of teutonic features, with light hair clipped short, steely gray eyes, and something Prussian in his erect bearing. He always impressed one as being cruel. No one seemed to know much about him. No one does now; although there are vague rumors of a deep, dark past.

"Hunted Men of Hollywood,"
Modern Screen Magazine, July 1933

INTRODUCTION

Director John Villiers Farrow came into Hollywood the same way he went out: a mystery, an unsolvable puzzle whose pieces never fit together into an understandable whole. Yet between the time he showed up in Los Angeles, in 1927, and the year he died of a massive heart attack in 1963 at the young age of fifty-eight, the Australian American Farrow wrote and directed over fifty films, most of them memorable, even classic—great sea chases and high seas adventures, westerns that were quirky in their boots, and most famously, some of Hollywood's greatest film noir classics of the 1940s and 1950s, including the masterful *The Big Clock*, the shadowy *Alias Nick Beal*, and the psychotically tinged *Where Danger Lives*.

But John Farrow left something else behind: a nearly thirty-year marriage to actress Maureen O'Sullivan that produced seven children, including actress Mia Farrow, who would go on to keep the family name public, something John Farrow would never have wanted or imagined. For him, there were reasons to stand far back from the limelight of a gossipy town, shrink from the glitz, the glamour, and the seduction of the spotlight and instead stay behind the camera. He had secrets: dark parts of his soul that he kept hidden from others even as he made them suffer for them.

John Farrow, a tormented soul who had little idea of the extent of his psychic pain, had little awareness of the pain he caused his family or the legacy of trauma he left his children when he departed their lives. But his daughter Mia, closest to John Farrow in spirit and love, made them public without intent, without malice. Father and daughter hold between them the gamut of the Farrows' fascinating and conflicted lives that played out over several decades in Hollywood.

This book, a biography of the Farrow family, charts their double lives: As Hollywood royalty, the family created a fairy-tale public existence. But behind that exterior lay an often dark world touched by psychological turmoil, pain, even tragedy. When John Farrow died, few people outside the family knew the interiority of the man, the inside narrative of his family. It wasn't until his daughter Mia Farrow accused her partner of many years, Woody Allen, of sexual misconduct that the Farrow family secrets slipped into the public eye. In telling a story about Woody Allen's behavior with his children, Mia unwittingly revealed her own relationship with the father who left a legacy of pain, trauma, even tragedy to his children years earlier that continues to affect their lives and the lives of future generations of Farrows. To understand the story Mia tells, we must first understand the teller herself, Mia. Yet, in order to understand Mia, we must first understand her father, John Farrow. This biography of the Farrows takes up the task of looking fully into their lives—for history's sake, and for the sake of stories we tell, the stories that keep us all connected to and implicated in each other's lives.

I intend neither accusations toward nor support of Mia Farrow, the Farrow family, or Woody Allen in these pages. My interest lies with understanding some of the psychological warfare that embraced the Farrow family. This biography addresses the phenomenon of psychic trauma, meaning the psychic wounds that, unfortunately, occur all too often in our human condition. We are vulnerable souls, lest we ever forget that.

In this book I also discuss two distinct kinds of facts: historical facts, which are facts, feelings, behaviors that exist in the social world, that can be documented (as I have done throughout the book). The other kinds of facts are those that stem from an analysis, an interpretation of the unconscious life of these family members. They are true to the narrative in someone's mind but they are not required to be historically accurate. These I do not document with notes. Instead, they are part of the language of the unconscious; they are notable but they are not necessary consciously intended by the people I discuss. Yet they have more truth to them than anything consciously said, done, or felt. The language of the unconscious has a logic of its own, a truth of its own. It is the most accurate means of understanding anyone. I have not created these facts, have not imposed them on the family or mistakenly credited them to the family. I have instead recovered them by knowing the people I describe.

PART ONE

One

A HOLLYWOOD FAMILY

History, like trauma, is never simply one's own. History is precisely the way each of us is implicated in each other's traumas.

—Cathy Caruth, *Unclaimed Experience*

In February 1992, actress Mia Farrow let herself into boyfriend Woody Allen's apartment with her key and entered his bedroom. Glancing at his dresser, she discovered something that no doubt shocked her: photos of her nineteen-year-old adopted daughter, Soon-Yi Previn, naked and smiling for the camera. Looking at her daughter's naked body on display was enough to crumble Mia. But who was Soon-Yi smiling for behind the camera? Of course, it was Woody.

If the shock didn't topple Mia, what would? Woody was not Soon-Yi's father; then, again, he was. Although not yet in the picture when Mia and former husband André Previn adopted Soon-Yi, Woody was now Mia's partner of twelve years, a reluctant participant in Mia's strong desire to create family around her. The way Mia (and most of society) saw it, if Soon-Yi was Mia's daughter, was she not also, by proxy, Woody's daughter? Living with unspoken yet well-defined social codes, were they not as good as carved in stone? Woody had just made a huge mistake, a wrong turn; he'd crossed the line.

Worse still, he'd betrayed Mia. That kind of betrayal breaks your heart, pulls the ground out from under you. You don't recover from this one.

As it turned out, that day was just the tip of the iceberg under Mia and Woody. Mia's private discovery became everyone's public information—but not without her help. In August 1992 Mia Farrow held a press conference and accused Woody Allen of molesting the child they had adopted together, seven-year-old daughter Dylan Farrow. According to Mia, this news came straight from Dylan's mouth. No coaching, no interception from Mom had occurred.

This news story thoroughly captured the imagination of men and women everywhere, so completely seduced the global media that it was nothing less than the creation of another universe in which all Mia-Woody news junkies could coexist peacefully while taking one side or the other. Thirty years later, since closing out one century and ushering in the next, little has changed.

Various events and "disclosures" helped to blow it up in 1992. Woody soon announced that he was having an affair with Soon-Yi and that they were in love. Time and again, Woody denied that he'd done anything to Dylan; his denial never wavered. One investigation after another failed to find any evidence that Woody ever molested Dylan. Was this true? Was this retaliation for Woody's betrayal of Mia with Soon-Yi? The news gathered steam, then grew larger than life: these were celebrities, after all, soon to become legend, as their sad story eventually gathered momentum from the mood of the soon-to-be #MeToo movement. It was an issue that now fed itself on the demand that centuries of female suffering be recognized and that retribution be doled out to males everywhere to compensate for their long history of physical and emotional crimes committed against women.

The Never-Ending Circle

Eventually the Woody-Mia fiasco established boundaries between warring neighborhoods of thought: Mia's supporters (of which there were many) on one side, Woody's supporters (mostly nonverbal) on the other. For years, darts and arrows, damning accusations, exploitive headlines, and endless photo ops flew from one camp to the other. Through it all, Woody was never legally charged with any crime. Now and again, larger events popped up to breathe new energy into the battlefield. In 2014, for instance the Hollywood Foreign Press Association bestowed its prestigious Lifetime Achievement Award on Woody for his body of work.[1] Ronan Farrow—Woody and Mia's biological son—took offense and then took to the media to voice his outrage that a "child molester" such as his father be rewarded for anything in this life. Then, Ronan himself made headlines after publishing an investigative piece in the *New Yorker* in 2017 that outed movie mogul Harvey Weinstein's sexual harassment of film industry women that had secretly taken place for years. Ronan won a Pulitzer Prize, and Weinstein went down, taking with him a huge assortment of other "male sexual predators" in the #MeToo movement that swept across the globe, "catching" every powerful male in every variety of business who could be named as an "abuser" of women.

Then, in 2021, HBO aired a documentary, *Allen v. Farrow*—five years in the making—that once more pumped new life into the Mia-Woody fiasco. The producers kept their work under wraps for those five years: when small-screen audiences first heard about it, airtime was in no time: the documentary seemed to have suddenly appeared out of nowhere.

But *Allen v. Farrow* turns out to be a full-fledged work of *art*, heavily armed with weapons of mass conversion. Looking more like a romantic melodrama feature film than a documentary, it pulls out every possible conceit of fictional film: seamless editing that makes the spectator feel as if he or she is in an alternate romantic universe that is just as real as the one outside the screening room; lush romantic background music; impeccably plush background and homey foregrounds (Mia's Connecticut home called Frog Hollow). Most importantly, sitting front and

3

center most of the time, Mia herself narrates a woeful tale: how Woody Allen, a sophisticated manipulator of all media tactics, duped her, Mia, an unsuspecting innocent who hadn't a clue of what was going on behind her back. Daughter Dylan, seven years old at the time of the alleged molestation, supposedly needed no coaching from her mother or any other of their friends who confirm that Mia's tale, her accusation, is the whole truth and nothing but.

Despite the documentary's huge, seductive, and beautifully crafted arsenal—the weapons of mass persuasion, the narrative tilted toward Mia's innocence—no drumroll was heard after HBO aired its five-part piece of propaganda. No mass conversion to Mia's side of the court could be felt: her people had always been on that side of the net.

No matter the ratio, it still remains that, after thirty years of verbal warfare along with the chill of a cold war (even as the players grow older and move on with their lives), there is still no closure, no conclusion to draw about Mia and Dylan's accusations or Woody's ongoing claims of innocence. No formal investigation has turned up any evidence that Woody molested Dylan. What's more, no verdict looks likely to be coming around the corner. There is no new evidence or information, no change to be seen on the horizon.

Has the evidence pointing to Woody's guilt been stolen? Has it been so expertly manipulated by his handlers that it looks to have disappeared? Or, has it never existed? Have the last thirty years been nothing more than one person's narrative, and a fictive narrative at that?

In 2018, Mia and Woody's adopted son, Moses Farrow, one of Woody's staunchest supporters, went viral. He put his blog on the large map of social media and reiterated that his father, Woody Allen, is innocent and has been from the get-go. He went even further, claiming that, in truth, his mother, Mia Farrow's, story is fakery. In fact, he says, Mia is the abusive one in the family and has been so for years. And, once asked by a slightly slanted news reporter how he could *not* have seen anything at all between Woody and Dylan, Moses answered, "How can you see something that never happened?"

Well, you can't.
But, it's not quite that simple.

The storyteller never lives separately from, or even far from, the story. You can try to separate the two, but you can never sever one from the other.

Going further, what if the teller of the story sees no difference between the facts and the story. They are very different from each other.

Mia Farrow is the progeny of a family of gifted storytellers. Living inside a narrative, a story, was natural to them. There were always facts, but they made stories from them. Telling stories, and performing them in public on the movie screen, or on the stage or for television, was no less familiar than writing or directing one. If life were a script, the stuff of stories, it would be understandable. Both her parents were Hollywood storytellers: Her mother Maureen O'Sullivan acted them out on the big screen, her father John Farrow spent his life's work, his lifeblood, in the act of creating stories, as a writer and film director.

John Farrow grew up inside his imagination. He never had a choice about it. Abandoned as an infant by his father and his mother torn away from him, he grew by any means he could: he lived his life in stories and adventures; he had to create a foundation and context of his own making, mixing fiction and fact, to replace the family he did not have. This suited him well when he arrived in Hollywood. But for some it's too easy to confuse the real and the fictive, to fail to distinguish between the two. It might be entirely possible that John Farrow, having grown up so isolated in his own imagination and the world he by necessity had to invent in absence of a familial one, created the narrative of his own life to tell others (no less than himself), replacing the fictive story as real, replacing the facts themselves with stories.

Farrow's failure to distinguish between the two seemed compatible with his wife Maureen O'Sullivan's instincts as a movie star. Her long relationship to the Hollywood publicity machines was by nature based on telling public stories to shield private, personal lives. Talking to Hedda Hopper or giving an interview to a popular woman's magazine was, by definition, a performance. It would be complexly understandable if her life with John Farrow quickly transformed into three decades of posturing as happy, when in fact living with the woman-chasing John Farrow was often tormenting for her. In turn, the Farrow children were mostly silent about their homelife. But, as Mia later wrote, Hollywood thought the family lived a fairy-tale existence; in truth, a nightmare often lived there too.

Complexity ruled. John Farrow could easily be his daughter's intellectual mentor, teaching her by example how to master the art of storytelling. She loved this father who told stories, who filled her mind with adventure. Yet he was also a father who beat her and placed his Catholicism on the family like a great burden.

Just as every Hollywood movie has a script and a backstory behind it, so too does every story, no matter who tells it, have a prewritten script and backstory. More often than not, these remain unseen, unspoken—and unknown. In the myriad of stories, and scripts, that emerged from, and that have flown around Mia Farrow's accusations against Woody Allen, one story has remained left untold—the possible backstory to, and connection with, Mia's own childhood. Her childhood, much like all of our childhoods, could very well color the way she sees now, and the way she lives her life and talks about it.

The Farrow home was hardly a fairyland. In truth it was a tense, rigid, tightly wound and religiously bound environment where the children hardly saw their parents and spent many hours at parochial school and later Catholic boarding schools.

Play became urgent, a lifesaver. It hardly numbed the pain of John Farrow's frequent and unpredictable anger; it hardly numbed the sting of his physical and emotional abuse of his children, but play became part of the landscape, as we shall see.

Yet, the man who would eventually beat his children was also the man they looked up to time and again. His frequent absences from home when directing a film on location, coupled with his emotional unavailability when he was present, only made him seem more urgently desired. For Mia especially, who followed him into show business, who remained closest to him in spirit and in emotional likeness, John Farrow, who died when Mia was seventeen, was Mia's closest emotional mentor—even ally. Keeping her father alive in her life, while it might have been unconsciously played out, could very well have been the undercurrent in her storytelling, perhaps even her life's work. Mia is irrevocably tied to her father. John Farrow shaped Mia's life. She is his manufacture. To understand Mia and her childhood is to discover the untold backstory, even perhaps the psychological motivation, behind her accusation against Woody Allen. Yet to gain any understanding of Mia, to know Mia, it is first necessary to understand John Farrow.

Where Fairy Tales Begin

The story of the Farrows as a family begins in postwar Los Angeles, a city whose particular landscape and lifestyle directly influenced their everyday existence. It was a time when many World War II veterans left the East Coast and brought their families west to take advantage of the city's still wide-open spaces, rapidly closing in. Los Angeles was experiencing a housing boom, attracting people from all parts of the United States who now took up residence in the City of Angels. The biggest draw was of course the movie industry, which had long ago taken over the city and by now defined it. The industry continued to attract a nonstop flow of people from all around the United States and Europe, anyone who wanted to taste the glamour and excitement of Hollywood. And as glamorous and exciting as the movie industry might seem, its real business was to perfect the art of dreaming. You could dream, imagine, and then create any version of yourself and the world around you that you desired. Eventually the two might even merge into one coherent space and become the reality that never faded.

Beverly Hills, the birthplace of all the Farrow children, was the emerald of Los Angeles, a city founded by famous movie people such as Mary Pickford, Douglas Fairbanks, Charlie Chaplin, and Will Rogers. By the time the Farrows became a family living in Beverly Hills the city had long enjoyed the reputation of being home to the wealthy, the successful—and, of course, the famous. More than anything else, the enclave housed the stars who appeared in the movies. How so many lives with so much imagination could fit inside Beverly Hills's small parameters was a marvel.

But famous faces were only half of the city's stories. Some West Coast families had roots going back generations, families having built lives as farmers, merchants, and cattle herders. Still others were transplants who came to see if they could build a life on little more than a dream. Some stayed only as long as they could. Others could think of no better place to be as new decades descended on the city and the simpler days faded forever.

Life in Beverly Hills in the 1950s felt more intimate, seemingly more innocent, than any time since. This was a family town, and the warm climate brought people outside where connections between people seemed easier and more casual. But change would, of course, descend on the city. Innocence would be more difficult to claim.

As more tourists came to visit each year, the city always gave them something to look at. If you turned south of Beverly Hills proper, you'd find the Celluloid Monument, a large piece of marble with the likeness of eight Beverly Hills citizens carved into it. The eight were famous movie people who, in 1928, fought the big, bad city of Los Angeles, which was swallowing up this small patch of heaven. These citizens, like the majority of those to settle there, were movie stars, celebrities, famous names with plenty of money. They were film industry pioneers like Douglas Fairbanks, Mary Pickford, Charlie Chaplin, and the city's first mayor, Will Rogers.

The Celluloid Monument sits at a busy and auspicious corner, Olympic Boulevard and Beverly Drive, where the light turns red and seems to stay that color for five long minutes, making drivers a captive audience, forced to look at the figures and the words carved at the bottom. But it's not a glitzy monument, so it leaves little impression on tourists and errant locals.

The same cannot be said of the many locals who are members of the film community. The monument reminds them of who they are, what dreams live inside them, and how they spend their lives: making movies, worshiping movies, even feeling fed up with movies after spending so much of their lives with them. They *are* the movies. It's no mystery. It's just a fact.

And so it was, back in the 1950s. During weekdays, not unlike any other city with business on its mind, Beverly Hills's streets bustled with board lunches, corporate handshakes, and harried jaywalkers trying to get to them. But on weekends the locals could take time to think of themselves as regular folk. On Sunday evenings, as dusk descended on the city's palm trees and bougainvillea vines, washing the city with romantic pink and red hues, entire families would walk out their front doors, past their impeccably manicured front lawns, and take to the streets. You'd see them enjoying a leisurely stroll, maybe window-shopping along Rodeo Drive or Dayton Way, as many of them made their way to Sunday-evening dinners at a favorite restaurant. To a visitor passing through town, this flow of friendliness, the warm sense of community and family, could rival any heartfelt sentiment an MGM *Andy Hardy* movie could cook up in the 1930s.

At this hour, restaurants welcomed their regular customers as if they were family. Cuisine from any country could be found. If you wanted to eat spaghetti, you'd find yourself waiting in line on almost any street in the area. If you happened to like more exotic dishes, you might find a table at the famed and pricey Trader Vic's or brave the crowd at the popular Luau restaurant on Canon Drive and Brighton. Despite its small radius, Beverly Hills seemed to offer a plentiful bounty.

On Sunday evenings you'd walk down any of its avenues and see families entering the numerous eateries that dotted the streets, each unique in atmosphere and cuisine. If you went inside one of them to wait for a table, you might look around the dining room and spot a number of recognizable faces you'd seen on movie screens or on television. Families took up many of the larger tables. The atmosphere was relaxed; the patrons chatted to each other as they ate. If you gazed more closely, your eye would undoubtedly stop at one particular family of nine sitting quietly reading their menus. It might have been the Farrow family: their faces were handsome, even beautiful—you wouldn't be the first to notice this.

The seven children and their mother, actress Maureen O'Sullivan, might have waited for director John Farrow to call the waiter to their table and order. And they paid little attention to stares from others in the dining room. They were called the pretty ones, the beautiful Farrows. For many, especially those who knew them from a distance, the family must have lived a fairy-tale life. After all, they had looks, money, and movie star prestige.

Yet the real facts can be very different from what we imagine them to be. Looking at the beauty and reserve of this family, who could have guessed that the Farrows, now sitting quietly in a Beverly Hills restaurant, lived in a world that could hardly be described as a fairy tale? And who would have ever anticipated the sadness, the trauma, the tragedy that awaited this family in the years to come?

John Farrow was one of Hollywood's busiest directors; he'd worked in pictures since the late 1920s, rising to prominence very early on. Yet, even though many of the people seated in this restaurant had worked with him at one time or another, even frequently, during those thirty years, probably no one could tell you they knew much about him; who he really was. His coworkers at the numerous Hollywood studios around town could not say they understood him, even if they'd worked with him regularly.

Nor did any of John Farrow's immediate family truly understand him. Farrow was a mystery—to the Hollywood community, and even to his wife, Maureen O'Sullivan, and to his seven children. He may as well have been the king of a magical yet distant place in a fairy tale from a time long ago. Of the myriad of publicity photos taken of the Farrows, in one after another, one can look closely at his face to see a distant look in his eyes, as if he were caught up in a different place or unreachable state of mind, where no one else could enter. Actor Tab Hunter, who worked with Farrow on *The Sea Chase*, described Farrow's face as "creepy," with his "beady eyes" that looked like "two piss holes in the snow."[2]

It might have been that the distant look in Farrow's eyes indicated how much trouble he had being present for suggestions his coworkers offered on the set. He had a reputation for being difficult, to the point of not getting along with these coworkers and eventually being called, as actor Robert Mitchum, among others, had said, unfeeling to the point of being sadistic.

Regularly clashing with people he knew and worked with, Farrow seemed unable to decipher the codes of the social world he lived in. He often resisted that world. It was a mystery, but no more a mystery than Farrow was to himself. Something in the man was off-kilter, out of whack. How could the family not feel the brunt?

Yet the Farrows presented a picture of pitch-perfect, even idyllic, family life. Just earlier that morning, and exactly like the Sunday before and the one before that, they marched from their home on Beverly Drive, headed down to Santa Monica

Boulevard, and then walked three blocks west to the Church of the Good Shepherd. As if performing a ritual, the Farrow children marched in a straight single line behind their father John, and their mother, Maureen. For those who lived nearby and could look out their window at this parade, the family's presentation was nothing short of a spectacle. "The Farrows looked like a mighty army," one neighbor later said, "and a mighty handsome one at that."[3]

The family John Farrow created looked as if they were made in Hollywood and just now stepped off the screen. They seemed made from a studio mogul's imagination of what America should look like: beautiful, better, cleaner, whiter versions of human beings than those in the real world. They looked like perfection, if you looked at their faces and no deeper. And American moviegoers took their lead. What viewers imagined while looking at these Hollywood stars looked far better than the blemished lives they had in the real world. They were incarnations of Fitzgerald's beautiful Jay Gatsby after he'd shed the cheap bookies and the fixers on his way up the ladder of success. If anything, they seemed untouched by the swarming mess of filthy and frightening unconscious darkness that ordinary human beings could fall into, that very swamp Hemingway's Nick Adams refused to step into as he breathed fresh air on the American landscape.

With their physical beauty, their blond hair, blue eyes, and their dignified, measured steps, the Farrows seemed to emerge from a Hollywood big-screen creation—the one no one ever questioned because they wanted so much to believe it. Yet, just like the movies that could have created them, their lives were partly truth and partly fiction. The entire family lived in a privileged world, not for a moment questioning it or considering that it might be different from the world of many other families. With the household staff, not their parents, attending to the children's care, with their mother's habitual retreats to her bedroom in order to be alone, and with their father's arbitrary emotional and physical outbursts, even abuse of them, along with their strict Catholic upbringing, it could be that hell hung over them relentlessly. There might have been something off in this home.

When the city returned to work Monday morning, John Farrow most likely walked onto the set of his current movie and slipped into his usual director mode: that of a martinet, dictating to what he might have considered his subjects. Farrow demanded absolute precision and commitment from his actors and his crew. He set the goals for each day and seemed to expect that everyone would take the same route he took to get there. Everyone knew the penalty for taking an alternate route or stepping outside Farrow's boundaries: one would suffer humiliation before an audience of one's peers, often followed by a twinge of regret for showing up to work that morning. The biographies and autobiographies of many well-known actors who worked with Farrow—for instance, top box office names Robert Mitchum and Glenn Ford, along with beauties Lana Turner and Maureen O'Hara—recount those "unforgettable" moments they or one of their colleagues dared cross the line on Farrow's set.

John Farrow had already earned a number of reputations in Tinseltown. They didn't mix well but rather collided into each other. He was the rude perfectionist as well as the angry perfectionist—all the while keeping his emotional distance from others.

At home with his children (when he was not off on location or isolated in his office working on a book), his need for perfectionism could create fear in his children that, experienced once or repeatedly, could be traumatic for them. Farrow's complexity, his contradictions, coalesced into a great story that Hollywood kept hidden until it no longer could.

When Farrow arrived in Hollywood in 1927 he needed a story of his life to tell others—to make himself known. The more adventure he brought with him, the taller the tale, the better. Anyone who sought a big career needed the right ingredients.

John Farrow disseminated a whopper of a fish tale, replete with romantic escapades, high-stakes sea adventures, and travels to exotic islands. Farrow's prose described a sensual, lush lifestyle and endless sexual escapades with beautiful women he met on those islands. He invented a beautiful fiction that displaced Farrow's real life (a talent his daughter, Mia, would inherit).

The truth of his sad childhood was something different: a boy abandoned by his parents, left to fend for himself. Disguise was essential. If writing his life meant exaggerating, even out-and-out lying, so be it. The story came from him: he owned it. If any part of it were untrue, no one would find out anyway. The story of John Farrow was a beautifully crafted work of self-invention handed to a town where inventing big dreams were and still are a way of life. Had it hit the big screen itself, the story of young John Farrow's road to Tinseltown, in all its romance and adventure, could have been one of Hollywood's greatest fictions.

But Farrow's life ultimately proved a tragic one. A talented director with a unique vision, a gifted writer and scholar, Farrow kept himself a secret to the end. Most likely, he didn't see himself as tragic or fully realize the damage he hoisted on the lives of those close to him.

The family that lives in this biography inherited all that John Farrow never realized he was passing on, the double life (part fairy tale, part nightmare) they had to live. No matter how beautiful the Farrow family looked to others, their days in Hollywood were marked by affliction, psychological turmoil, and tragedy. Their narrative shapes itself into a saga that never ends: a tale of sadness, of one generation damaging the next and each moving forward by means of the same broken wings. In the end, the story of the Farrows is the tale of a Hollywood shakedown, the biography of a beautiful clan psychologically hijacked by a gifted yet tragic figure of a father. John Farrow and Maureen O'Sullivan lived very different childhoods—his an isolated one; hers stifled by an overbearing mother. Their disparate experiences nevertheless led them to a city where you could find fiction to make real life bearable. John and Maureen shared a love of telling stories. They could help create them and live in them at the same time. Their tale might be the greatest story Hollywood never told.

TWO

DIRECTOR'S CUT: JOHN FARROW GETS A REPUTATION

We tell ourselves stories to stay alive.
—Joan Didion, *Slouching Towards Bethlehem*

John Farrow was made for Hollywood. He was a born story-teller, a buoyant adventurer, and (for extra credit) a gifted wom-anizer whose sexual conquests were tantalizing enough to make headlines on every scandal sheet in Tinseltown. His male beauty was enough to make a moviola swoon—not to mention a young starlet or two—or three.

Farrow and his handsome face arrived in Hollywood in the late 1920s, just when movies began talking. But they couldn't talk any better or longer than Farrow could. There was no short-age of drama in the story of John Farrow he brought with him, the backstory he liked to tell. His life story (so far, at least) was so full of pathos that it could move kings and studio heads to weep.

Farrow wrote the story of himself that every newspaper colum-nist, every reporter, and every gossip writer picked up and printed throughout his years in Hollywood. And he was ready to talk. According to Farrow, his Australian childhood was pure Dickens: the best of times, yet the worst. He lost both parents soon after his birth in Sydney on February 10, 1904. An aunt (whose name he seemed never to remember) raised him until he ran off at fifteen to join the Merchant Marine, eventually landing in the South Seas. So taken was he by the people and the landscape that a sudden urge to write about his adventures swelled up in him—and never let go. Later on he traveled to San Francisco where he found work as a theater critic for a local newspaper. Depending on the day and the version (there were many), it was then that Farrow probably met producer David O' Selznick, who told Farrow to take his movie star face to Hollywood and become an actor.

He went.

But Farrow became a Hollywood writer and director instead. Noir was his natural palette; sinister his zone. He sent Ray Milland scrambling for his life in the noir thriller *The Big Clock*; he set fireworks (as much as anyone could) under John Wayne and Geraldine Page in the western *Hondo*; and after Jane Russell and Robert Mitchum smooched it up in *His Kind of Woman*, he took half an Oscar home for cowriting *Around the World in 80 Days*. He was ornery and hell to work with—more than he was ever nice, but Hollywood kept him anyway.

And he could *write*—from the voluptuous (the ripe, robust imagery in his 1930 script and book *The Bad One*) to the voluminous (and much lauded biographies of religious icons and papal histories of the Catholic church). John Farrow liked to put pen to paper more than anything else; writing was John Farrow as his most authentic self. You could say he lived on the page before he lived anywhere else. In fact, much of the time he lived there *instead* of anywhere else.

Farrow kept journals brimming with his stories and poems: he'd wrestled with more than one blank page, filling each one with sea stories, romances, and tales of danger and adventure. But the best story Farrow ever wrote was the one about himself, the heart-pounding romantic adventure of his life so far.

He gave the story to anyone in Hollywood who would listen. Part fact, part fish tale, his story seduced journalists, studio publicists, and gossipmongers alike; they followed his lead down to each breathtaking word. It was clear: no one, not Valentino,

Barrymore, or Errol Flynn, the Tasmanian devil himself, had anything on John Farrow, traveler of the high seas and seducer of women around the globe. Hollywood loves an adventure story and always has—especially one that confuses fact and fiction, truth and embellishment. John Farrow's story obscured the line between what is real and what is imagined. The two lay hopelessly entangled, a story playing on some distant movie screen where the picture is forever out of focus.

Farrow claimed that, as a youth in his native Australia, he hated school vehemently, so he skipped out, stowing away on a ship with the Merchant Marine and sailing the Southern hemisphere. He landed in Tahiti where (to put it mildly) he tasted the charms of all the native girls on the island. He'd return to the island repeatedly throughout his life.

Behind Farrow's wanderlust lay an unsettling childhood he ached to leave behind. His was anything but a happy entrance into this world. Farrow's father, Thomas, left his wife, Lucy, but not before committing her to an insane asylum for post-partum depression (noted as "lactation" in hospital records). He put the baby, John, into the care of his sister, Ethel Lavinia McEnerny, who raised John until he ran off while still in his teens. Lucy Savage died in the asylum in 1907 of pneumonia and "tubercular ulceration of the intestines." She never knew her child. John Farrow had one keepsake of his mother, a small oval portrait of her that he carried with him the rest of his life.[1]

Farrow's story changed regularly. One version had him considering an accounting career after finishing high school. But that plan didn't pan out, since he never finished high school, running off instead when he was fifteen to join the Merchant Marines. His other notion, to become a writer, was a much better fit for Farrow; traveling the globe with the Merchant Marines he'd accumulate plenty of experiences to put on paper. All these plans, including the idea of eventually having a naval career, became fodder for storytelling. He later wrote that he joined the

Merchant service as a cadet, a tale that conflicted with another narrative, that he ran away to sea after jumping an American schooner, sailing "all over the Pacific," and fighting in revolts in Nicaragua and Mexico. Either way, he was on the water, where, eventually, he felt the safest. "The ship in which I served voyaged from Sydney to New Zealand, the Fijiian Islands, Honolulu and Canada," he later wrote. "Sometimes an alternate run would take us to Tahiti and various other islands."[2]

He continued, "During the tropical peace of the night watches I had ample opportunity to keep alive my ambitions of becoming an author and, in the off-duty hours of the long voyages, I had the time to read and study the great books." On those many voyages he wrote poetry and short stories.[3]

While in Tahiti, Farrow learned the story of the young nineteenth-century priest, Father Damien, who worked to aid lepers. He then contracted the disease himself and ultimately died of it. Farrow never forgot the story of Damien, who was later venerated as a saint by the Catholic Church and who became for him a model of charity. To show his admiration for Father Damien, in 1937 Farrow published a biography, *Damien the Leper*, still taught in Catholic schools today.

Also while in Tahiti, he also compiled an English-French-Tahitian dictionary, and was inspired to write a romantic novel, *Laughter Ends*, finally published in 1933.

Farrow eventually reached US shores—some reports have it that he arrived on an Australian windjammer or, according to Ray Milland, as "a purser on a Matson liner."[4] He enrolled at the Jesuits' St. Ignatius College (now the University of San Francisco) in 1923 but left after one month.

For Farrow, telling stories was a way of life, and writing fictions about other characters was fulfilling. Composing "stories" or "fictions" about himself was that and more: an artful means of compensating for what he didn't have as a child. Perverting the truth eventually led to larger acts of perversion resulting in far more serious consequences.

Carrying a slew of stories he'd written about his South Seas adventures, Farrow talked his way into writing theater criticism for one of the city's small newspapers. But, not all pleasures being equal, Farrow also found time to enjoy the charms of a local beauty, seventeen-year-old Felice Lewin, the daughter of a San Francisco mining millionaire.[5] He also began showing up at the offices of local newspapers, offering stories he'd written. They were either fact or fiction, whichever he fed the press. His stories impressed; he was already comfortable on the page:

> Jack Farrow is the young man's name during business hours, when he scrubs decks, polishes brass and does other humble tasks on the U.S. revenue cutter Shawnee, in San Francisco Harbor. John Neville Burg-Apton Villiers Farrow is his name during his off time, when he lives in San Francisco's arts colony and writes free verse, dedicated to Miss Felice Lewin of San Francisco, and enjoys a remittance from home. He explained his dual role by declaring he is the grandson of an English Earl and is studying to become a navigator.[6]

Felice was the most courted girl in San Francisco society, and she fell head over heels for the "mysterious, monocled youth (who) came out of nowhere" and claimed to be the heir to the imposing earldom of Westmoreland. After Felice decided to marry him, the senior Lewin began to investigate Farrow, contacting the British consul-general, who could not find the name "Farrow" in the Westmoreland line. Farrow was promptly arrested (for contributing to the delinquency of a minor) and after his release, was promptly thrown into the brig for "for breach of discipline."[7]

Still, in August 1924, they married, and Felice and Farrow had a daughter, also named Felice, born in December 1925. But like his father before him, Farrow chose not to stick around. According to a story in *Variety*: "John Villiers-Farrow, Hollywood scenarist, admits that his wife, Felice Lewin Farrow, former San Francisco society girl, is contemplating a divorce action. According to Farrow, incompatibility led to their separation two months ago. He declared a property settlement has been effected."[8]

He and Felice divorced in September 1927 and Farrow returned to the South Seas. While there, a chance meeting with documentary filmmaker Robert Flaherty, then shooting his 1927 *White Shadows in the South Seas*, sparked Farrow's interest in writing for the movies. That same year, he found his way back to the United States, allegedly jumping ship at San Francisco and traveling south to Hollywood.

Farrow arrived in Tinseltown ready to put his talent—and whatever else he had—to work. Had studio heads and producers, whom Farrow solicited for work, heard the tale of Felice Lewin and Mr. Monocle, they might have either shooed him away from their desks or chased him down the street throwing hundred-dollar bills at him, bidding Mr. Farrow to return and jot down a few tales for them to tell.

The factual story of Farrow's arrival in Hollywood was more straightforward. He first arrived in the United States on November 1, 1920, in Fort Townsend, Washington, as a seaman aboard the vessel *Samar*.[9] He returned again in 1924, on the US Revenue cutter *Shawnee*, in San Francisco, where he wooed and married Felice Lewin; when the marriage soured, he left again, traveling around the Pacific. He returned again in 1927 to start his career as a screenwriter. He carried no passport with him during this time.[10]

Farrow jumped into the movie business at a tumultuous yet fascinating juncture. Silent pictures were just on their way out as words began tumbling, sometimes clumsily, from actors' mouths. It seemed as if Farrow had brought the words with him, as if he and the talkies flew into Hollywood together.

But the advent of the talkies separated the velvety-voiced from the not-so-pleasant vocals, the mechanically adventurous from the more timid. Not everyone in pictures was still standing after the takeover. For those who'd survived the transition to sound—actors whose voices didn't shock audiences; directors able to operate confounding new equipment—talking pictures offered bold new forms of expression.

One of these directors, Raoul Walsh, who'd already built a sizable career and reputation in silent films, could hardly contain or put into words the excitement he felt after hearing sound for the first time. Winfred Sheehan, his boss at Fox, suggested he take in the latest picture playing at the Beverly Theatre in Beverly Hills. Walsh attended a matinee and could hardly believe the hackneyed picture he saw up on the screen:

> I got up to leave but turned back at the top of the aisle, when a burst of sound from the newsreel caught my attention. There before my eyes a Fox MovieTone News truck was filming a dock strike. The shouting came from a man who was evidently a union leader. His exhortation did not interest me but the open-air news shot did. I broke the speed limit all the way back to the studio.[11]

Sound pictures would quickly reinforce the grip that Hollywood and the movies already had on the general public. Tinseltown in the 1920s had already come to symbolize "the new morality" of the decade—mixing extravagance, glamour, hedonism, and great fun. By 1929, there were 25,000 cinemas; an average of a hundred million Americans went to the movies on a weekly basis. Stars made millions of dollars and became American royalty. The East Coast Edison trust that had dominated the motion picture industry had long been broken and filmmakers once cloistered in East Coast cities branched out to the West Coast. Its warm climate invited longer production days; its variety of landscapes inspired the imagination.

The beginning months of 1930 were both opportune and perilous times for the motion picture industry. Over time, the stock market crash of 1929 sent audiences to the movies in increasing numbers as a way to escape the stifling reality of economic depression. But it also caused the studios to tighten their belts and production costs. The studios were skeptical about using sound under a number of circumstances: for example, western films as a genre still embraced simple storytelling that often translated to very little dialogue, the exact opposite of what using sound implied. Equally problematic were the large, clumsy cameras that had to be enclosed in boxes to keep their whirring sounds away from the likewise clumsy microphones. These cameras could not be moved around easily on soundstages. Still, many directors loved the fact that audiences could now hear authentic sounds coming from the movie screen.

Given time, the new frontier called "the movie industry" grew a bit too wild, too loose, for some, and by 1934 the Production Code rode in to tame the town and its movies—by keeping an eye on what audiences saw on the screen. Will Hays and his posse kept vigil over what actors could or couldn't say (God's name was a "couldn't"), how characters looked (both breasts back in, ladies), and how they behaved (murder *always* got you payback; if you didn't meet your bad ending in an alley somewhere, you'd end up in the Big House for sure).

Yet, in spite of (or because of) trespassing over the line of decency, more men and women came to town to remake their images or become someone else completely. Even if you were Theodosia Burr Goodman, a Jewish girl from Cincinnati with little to recommend you other than a mouth like Clara Bow's, you could take yourself and your chutzpah to Hollywood and become Theda Bara in a couple of weeks. No matter what skills you had (or didn't have), if you dreamed big enough and had enough drive and chutzpah you could transform yourself into whomever you wanted to be. Men and women with ambition could either unleash their creativity or make a bundle off those who already had. More than one director in early Hollywood—such as a George Stevens or a Buster Keaton— jump-started a career by literally jumping a fence into the backyard of a production company, picking up a pencil, and starting to write a script.

New technologies in film certainly widened and deepened its scope; when Greta Garbo first "spoke" in *Anna Christie* in 1931, she gave her own humanity a voice and deepened her emotional impact. But she voiced only what writers gave her. The storytellers who came to Hollywood remained the bottom line and always would. They created the soil from which everything grew. Writers imagined the words that transformed into scripts that could make magic. Writers sent moviegoers to distant corners of the world—into the wild, out to the Arctic pole and the seven seas—or straight into the human heart.

Hollywood took everyone. When novelists William Faulkner and Ernest Hemingway saw their book revenues drop, they dropped into MGM's writers' bungalows for several years to make ends meet. F. Scott Fitzgerald, who actually loved the movies—whereas Faulkner and Hemingway found writing scripts demeaning work—wrote his last novel, *The Last Tycoon,* while living in the Hollywood Hills; he saw Los Angeles, the West, as the last frontier in the United States, a landscape of golden dreamers. Fitzgerald never finished *The Last Tycoon*; he died of a heart attack in 1940. Much like Hemingway and Faulkner, these great novelists were celebrities in town more than successful screenwriters. Hollywood proved a tougher town than expected for writers of such renown. They garnered fewer screenwriting credits than their glamorous aura might have indicated.

Still, if you were a pilot or a seafaring man or explorer and wandered into Hollywood, you could find work as a consultant in an instant. And if you were John Farrow, back from the sea and having already earned some notoriety as a storyteller and adventurer, you could also parlay your nautical expertise into work as a script consultant and technical adviser. Farrow did just that, and landed a job working for Cecil B. DeMille—eventually taking his talents to RKO and Paramount Studios.

The way young Farrow told it, he lived for adventure. He lived his life undaunted, taking risks when he had to and jumping into the unfamiliar if he could. Perhaps it wasn't all bunk, after all. Long after Farrow's death, Maureen O'Sullivan described her husband of twenty-seven years in similar terms. Nostalgia may have tinted her words. But, Maureen knew John Farrow as only a wife (and perhaps a few other women) could, right down to the snake tattoo wrapped around his right ankle before traveling straight up his leg to his groin.

"John was a *larrikin,*" she told her good friend, Mark Montgomery, with all the Irish in her. "He was mischievous, even rowdy at times. He was good-hearted but simply disregarded social conventions." His bad-boy reputation grabbed her attention long before she'd met John Farrow. When he moved from screenwriting to directing films, he showed his adventurous side. He was an adventurer and a poet to Maureen. Changing the details of his life story as often as he did, John was, in her eyes, "a master of invention."

This gifted writer who didn't think twice about going out on a limb (for an adventure and a story to tell) now climbed onto Hollywood's fast track and went places and took up its pace. Farrow was looking at a bright future. He could do wonders with a blank sheet of paper. Soon enough he'd direct films that still leave their mark decades after their initial impact. In the years to come, he'd be a father to seven more children, some of whom would find fame in their own way. Farrow was as much a Hollywood mythmaker as the city itself. But he also had demons, and would be tarnished by them.

Farrow took on almost any assignment that came his way, even writing intertitles for the occasional silent film. He wrote the title cards for *White Gold* (1927) and then for *The Wreck of the Hesperus* (1927) at DeMille Productions.

From a 1928 write-up in *Variety*:

> In the writers' class are to be found John Farrow, who was a poet in Australia. He got a job doing odd work at DeMille's. Then he sold Rupert Julian [a New Zealand actor, director, writer and producer, who directed sixty

films and acted in over ninety] the idea he should supply the titles for 'Yankee Clipper' [1927]. That put him over as title man and writer. He wrote [the] screen version of 'The Wreck of the Hesperus,"' [1927; the original of 'The Blue Danube' [1928], 'Menace' and 'Toward the Moon.'[12]

Farrow began selling his own stories and screenplays to the studios. He built up a reputation as a talented screenwriter with few limitations who wore many hats. So, of course, he soon left DeMille and joined the Paramount writing staff.

"John Farrow, only 23 years old, but who has several stories to his credit," quickly began writing screenplays and adaptations for the studio; he was tapped as scenarist and was sent to St. Martins, Maryland, to work with Gary Cooper and Fay Wray on *The First Kiss* (1928). He subsequently renewed his contract with Paramount.[13]

From *Exhibitors Herald and Motion Picture World*: "Paramount has just purchased the film rights to 'The Haunting Melody,' a novel by John Farrow, soon to be published by Putnam and Sons. Fay Wray and Gary Cooper will be co-starred in the film, which will have dialogue and sound. It is said that the recurring of a 'haunting melody' will play a large part in the picture."[14]

By the end of 1928, Farrow had even taken out a costly, half-page ad in the *Film Daily Yearbook* touting his stature as an author-scenarist for such films as *The Blue Danube, The Wreck of the Hesperus*, and *The Bride of the Colorado*. And in January 1929, an advertisement announcing the exclusive management of John Farrow by Myron Selznick (brother of David O. Selznick and one of Hollywood's top agents) ran in *Variety*.[15]

At Paramount, Farrow worked on a series of "woman's pictures": *Three Weekends* (1928) with Clara Bow; *The Woman from Moscow* (1928) for Pola Negri; *The First Kiss* (1928) with Fay Wray and Gary Cooper; and *Ladies of the Mob* (1929), also with Bow.

After writing titles and scripts with true staying power—*The Showdown* (1928), *The Four Feathers* (1929), and *A Dangerous Woman* (1929)—Farrow scripted a United Artists adventure yarn, *The Bad One*, released in 1930. Its two leads, Hollywood heartthrobs Dolores del Río and Edmund Lowe, who had helped increase box office revenues for several earlier pictures at the studio, were by now more than good friends. But Farrow, undaunted, found del Río as alluring as most other men did, and the two began an extended on-again, off-again romance.

Del Río was the latest on a growing list of Hollywood beauties Farrow bedded down now. As the years went by, the list grew longer. Eventually, the sheer number of women Farrow took to bed became almost (and permanently) dizzying. If Farrow began making a name for himself as a talented scenarist, and later as a director, neither measured up to his infamy as a gifted womanizer. One can only imagine the amount of energy it took to take so many rolls in the hay; to keep track, let alone keep up the schedule. Telling one woman about another would cause sheer exhaustion—requiring energy better put to use in another capacity. It would be understandable, then, that Farrow might have neglected to tell del Río about his erstwhile "engagement" to Diana Churchill across the pond. This was of little consequence, however, as the news would soon be readily available to anyone soon enough, and would surprise more than a few Hollywood beauties. The engagement was not simply a fiction of Farrow's fertile imagination. When it caught the attention of Diana's father, Prime Minister Winston Churchill, he told the press, in no uncertain terms, that his daughter, Diana, and Farrow were not engaged and never would be. Actually, he said, they were little more than good friends.[16]

When not busy being vibrant with del Río, Farrow was busy being vibrant on the page. When Farrow's novelization of the picture *The Bad One*, was, published simultaneously with the film's release, all of Hollywood could see Farrow's stunning prose style. His descriptions of Marseilles are vivid, even voluptuous—there's enough life force running through them that the reader almost feel their pulse:

> Marseilles is a city of the world, full of the smells and sounds of many races . . . It is a city of the present, of the people who live while there is life, a cosmopolis in which adventure still is lurking behind crazy doors, up slanting alleys . . . women accept each other and everything else with a ready candor born of rich experience, mellowed tolerance of the human spirit in its eternal conflict with the flesh.[17]

Farrow's language is strikingly cinematic, beckoning the camera to move around streets splashed with color and shape. The prose captures the fullness of life, and the animation invites readers to move freely and experience all the activity.

Working as a gun for hire at the studios and doctoring others' scripts gave Farrow hands-on experience recognizing genre and story structure. In doing this, he joined some of the great directors of his generation, such as George Stevens, Frank Capra, and Billy Wilder, along with those from a generation earlier, such as Raoul Walsh, Howard Hawks, and John Ford, who also learned it all by doing it for others first. But unlike the others, Farrow then turned 180 degrees and, after another visit to Tahiti, compiled an English-French-Tahitian dictionary.

By now, the whole town was talking, not about Farrow's vibrant writing style, but about his infamously vibrant sexual life. As Hollywood's number one playboy and womanizer, he lived in infamy. On this front, Farrow seemed tireless. He bedded down women from one corner of Hollywood to another. This kind of career required some skill in parting company with the truth in order to keep the peace and his women at the same time. He had to balance the women he slept with with the ones he didn't bed down but merely dated.

By 1930, his two most frequent lovers were his future wife, Maureen O'Sullivan, whom he met in late 1929, and the woman he'd been on-again, off-again with for several years previous to Maureen: his erstwhile fiancée, silent actress Lila Lee, whom he met in June 1928. Farrow knew that both women knew about each other. He never actually lied about one to the other; he more or less kept silent and let Hollywood gossip do the talking. *Modern Screen* printed a story in 1930 that offered some dirt:

> Maureen O 'Sullivan and Johnnie Weissmuller were seen dining and dancing together [courtesy of MGM publicity] . . . to counteract bad publicity Johnnie had . . . [but] you know Johnnie was telling [girlfriend] Lupe Valez all about it . . . Maureen is back with her old love, Johnnie Farrow, who was once Lila Lee's sweetheart.[18]

Lila Lee had recently ended her engagement to Farrow. More news on Lila Lee's relationship to Johnny would emerge soon enough.

Maureen knew that John Farrow was a "bad boy." She knew he needed to have more than one woman in his life, this despite his love for her. But Maureen had developed a strategy. She decided that she would be different than the other women who became jealous and angry. She wanted him and that was it. It didn't hurt that she also had patience—and determination. His womanizing didn't come between them now at the beginning of their relationship, and she would not let it ruin their future together. "Everybody knew that Farrow ran around and chased with this one and that one," Joseph Youngerman, who would become Farrow's assistant director in the 1940s would later say: "Maureen O'Sullivan kind of chased him all over hell" (information she might not have wanted made public). "He didn't run after her," Youngerman also said. "Finally, they got married."[19]

Farrow's appeal apparently had such a wide reach that it didn't end merely at women—or even humans. Animals found him irresistible too, at least in one version told about the time

Maureen O'Sullivan worked with Cheetah the chimp in the 1930s Tarzan franchise. Maureen told conflicting stories about her famous costar. She swore to David Letterman on his late-night talk show in the 1970s that Cheetah hated the sight of her, hissing and trying to attack her time and again until one of them had to be removed from the set. Years later, she changed the story, saying that the chimpanzee was so protective of her that he'd try to claw any man who came near her. Then John Farrow showed up on the set one day. Cheetah abandoned Maureen in minutes flat and stared at him with love in his eyes. Farrow mesmerized the chimp so completely that Cheetah's handlers began to wonder if the chimp wasn't homosexual.[20]

We can't know what purpose Farrow's womanizing served. He left nothing resembling a paper trail that would reveal the slightest personal thought. Other than daughter Mia Farrow's mention of other women in his life in her memoir, or Maureen's words about it quoted in her biography, the family still keeps silent about John Farrow. Friends and colleagues who never failed to discuss his womanizing at length in their biographies and autobiographies never questioned his seeming obsession. We know enough about human nature to understand that repeated behaviors often compensate for a loss, or a supposed loss. And we know that Farrow suffered great loss as a child. But as he repeatedly refused contact with the press, averting even his face from a microphone or news camera, he succeeded in shutting off any access to his interior life. While we can't know intimate facts about his childhood, we know enough about human nature to look at the adult behavior and find in it a scratchy picture and an understanding of Farrow the child.

Since childhood, growing up without the human intimacy and contact of parents, it might very well be that Farrow was forced to create his own values, his own rules, his own context, his own world. And only Farrow lived there. Living by the rules and values he created, Farrow might never have considered that they would collide with the world around him. But eventually they did. Many times, his sense of his own omnipotence proved difficult to censor.

In June 1927, Farrow saw a screening of fellow director William Wellman's landmark film *Wings* and sent his friend a telegram. The two had become friends when they both worked at Paramount Studios a few years earlier. He might have been accustomed to Farrow's "individual" style of humor, the kind that opens the floodgates to a man's soul. Farrow wrote:

UP TO LAST NIGHT I'D ONLY RECEIVED ONE BIG THRILL IN MY LIFE THAT WAS FROM A PORTUGUESE LADY IN SHANGHAI STOP I THOUGHT THAT WAS THE CLIMAX OF EMOTIONAL THRILLS BUT LAST NIGHT I SAW YOUR PICTURE WINGS BUT THAT BEATS ANY LADY OR BOY WHITE OR COLORED WHEN I SAY THAT YOU KNOW WHAT I MEAN OLD BOY.[21]

Farrow liked *Wings*; he more than liked it: It thrilled him enough that he breached his own self-censorship and expressed himself freely, giving away a hint of sexual aberrance that already may have extended beyond talk. Farrow's Tahitian adventures may have aroused sexual curiosity and behavior considered taboo in 1927. It was an innocent, unconscious slip. As much as Farrow wanted to be in control of himself, at times he failed to make the distinction between himself and others, failed to see his thoughts and desires as unacceptable in the social world around him. He had grown used to being alone; he didn't know himself in relation to the larger world the way someone else might—surely not to the extent that he knew only himself *as* the world. Even if he had, he may not have always been able to stop and censor himself. In this instance, a certain aspect of his psychological makeup, secretly held, probably for years, reached only a friend and, for now at least, remained private.

By the early 1930s, Farrow wanted to direct films, not just write them. But he had no offers yet and, in 1931, when the US immigration service advised Farrow to leave the United States under the threat of deportation, he traveled to Tahiti and England. In 1932, he was signed by England's Associated Talking Pictures to script *Woman in Chains* (1932) and several other films; he wrote *The Impassive Footman* (1932) for Basil Dean and worked as a writer and assistant director on G. W. Pabst's film *Don Quixote* (1933).

He then returned to America with papers that described him as an "assistant consular attaché of one of the Balkan countries" in early January 1933.[22] Farrow, of course, omitted that information in his biographies, saying that, after writing a score of screenplays, he became convinced that "a scenario writer had too little to do with the actual making of a film, so I left Hollywood and went to the Society Islands, in Tahiti, aboard a trading schooner."[23]

When he returned to Hollywood, he found himself in the middle of a federal government drive against "aliens" in the industry and, while enjoying a good dance at the Cocoanut Grove nightclub with Argentinean actress Mona Maris on January 27, 1933, he was arrested. He was placed on five years' probation for violating immigration laws. According to his passport, Farrow was a Romanian consular official with an expired visa (he became a US citizen in 1947).[24] This only reinforced his bad boy image.

The controversy didn't affect Farrow's Hollywood career, but he found other ways of getting into trouble. In 1934, Harry Rapf at MGM offered him a chance to be second director (uncredited, as it turned out) on their upcoming film, *Swamp Woman* (later changed to *The Wicked Woman*) starring Viennese temptress and actress Mady Christians. When Mady and John Farrow got together for a few evening flirtations, Farrow devised the idea of making a trailer for the upcoming picture. The two went a bit overboard, however, and, after too many cocktails one evening, went over to wardrobe and inadvertently left with more than a few dresses belonging to lead MGM actress Norma Shearer. The next thing Farrow heard was a few words from his agent, Myron Selznick.

"There's a plane ticket waiting for you at Burbank," Selznick said. "It'll get you to New York. From there on, you're on your own, but I'd advise you to change your name and book passage for Cape Town or somewhere equally remote. You spent exactly $27,500 of Harry Rapf's budget last night and Mr. Rapf is a trifle impatient."[25]

Still, Rapf and MGM offered Farrow a chance to be a full-fledged director. "His first effort will be a two-reel musical, 'Beauty and Truth,'"[26] which was later released that September with the title *The Spectacle Maker*. Exhibitor newspaper *Motion Picture Daily* gave it a glowing review, saying "A colortone musical well directed by John Farrow . . . Entire short is beautiful . . . should be a good asset to any program."[27]

After directing only one major film, *Five Came Back* (1931), and several rather insignificant pictures before that, Farrow discovered how much he loved the camera. He could manipulate it to get close-ups of actors' faces, and then suddenly pull far back for a long shot of the scene. He loved mixing the two.

Yet he'd never considered how difficult it would be working with others. A director controls a set full of actors, crew, and studio staff. As a man who saw himself as more omnipotent than interactive, who didn't always recognize others' needs and opinions, directing a film would require many skills he didn't have. Isolated in a room with nothing more than paper and pen, Farrow felt safe, free to soar into his imagination. But he turned on a dime into someone else when he controlled a movie set. Farrow didn't so much interact with his cast and crew as much as collide into and agitate others to get what he wanted.

In almost no time, Farrow earned a reputation as a mean-spirited bully. For the rest of his career, the reputation stuck. For good reason, he'd never shake it off. He was often demanding, short-tempered, and contradictory on his film sets, unable to tolerate the moments when someone crossed him or strayed outside the lines he'd set in place. His reaction to this trespass could seem cruel, even perverse, to the person on the receiving end. He wanted perfection, Dennis Sprague wrote in a newspaper story. Eventually he earned the moniker "the most disliked director in Hollywood."[28]

According to Ray Milland:

> John was one of those directors who got phobias about people . . . he'd deliberately bitch up the scene, because he didn't like the actors in it . . . Consequently, we had to make up our scenes ourselves, more or less. He had a touch of masochism about him.[29]

John Farrow could claim many reputations in Hollywood, a few of them flattering ("a gifted screenwriter and director" and a "master of the long take"). "The meanest director in Hollywood" seemed to stick, long after his career faded. His bouts of perverse behavior colored him dark; his reputation with actresses in Hollywood preceded him to a film set as if he had created a steady, unbreakable chain of events, many sexual in nature and just as many with a sadistic edge. Seemingly uncomfortable with both men and women, he stood outside the social loop. And his perversity would intensify as the years went by.

Farrow was also the "most hated man in Hollywood" and the "biggest heel,"[30] each popular, depending on the day, the set, or the victim. His verbal abuse on the set could sting his actors and crew members regularly. Robert Mitchum called him a sadist, even though the two were friends and drinking buddies. "I mean, he was a sadist," Mitchum loved to emphasize.[31] Farrow's behavior, and the complaints they incurred, remained consistent no matter the picture, no matter the studio. "He was cold, arrogant, and superior," assistant director Herbert Coleman said after working with Farrow, adding also that Farrow's affectation, the cane swinging from his arm, only lowered Coleman's estimation of the man.[32]

That didn't stop Coleman from shielding Farrow now and again from the suits when one walked onto Farrow's set asking where he was. Coleman would shrug his shoulders and say he didn't know, when in fact Farrow was in the back room having sex with a newly arrived ingénue.[33] Of course, that backroom session didn't protect the young woman from episodes of verbal abuse should Farrow happen to be in a foul mood anytime in the future.

The source of Farrow's rancor remained a mystery to those who knew him; it could be hellish for his actors and crew and often for himself. Seemingly at odds with himself, he might jump fences between moods, going from sullen, to hyperactive, then to standoffish. For those with the humor and stability to tolerate it, there was never a dull moment being in the presence of John Farrow, even as new manifestations of his psychology unfolded into the future.

Three
SWINGING ON A STAR: MAUREEN

Maureen O'Sullivan flew into Hollywood on an ambivalent note. Being a movie star was not the issue: she never wavered on her desire to be a popular actress on the silver screen. Something else put her on the fence. After failing to set the town on fire with the "good girl" persona Fox Pictures gave her, she landed at MGM and made a huge splash as Tarzan's sexy but definitely half-naked mate, Jane. Did she mind the "exposure"?

Maureen was grateful that the *Tarzan* franchise gave her lasting recognition in Hollywood. Not surprisingly, though, years later, Maureen remained convinced that Irving Thalberg and MGM made her into a harlot with the Tarzan series. Words are one thing (albeit contradictory at times), but actions are another. Over the course of her long career, no matter the role she plays—Maureen seems to be much less chagrinned than those words would suggest. The characters she played throughout that career—from Tarzan's Jane in the 1930s to the heartbreakingly jaded ex-Broadway actress in Woody Allen's *Hannah and Her Sisters* in 1986, Maureen has displayed a woman whose sexuality peeks out more often than she herself might have known. And when it did, she seemed none too worried about it. Despite her long reputation for fleshing out women both sweet-natured and serious, Maureen O'Sullivan might have wanted to play it sexy as well. She just couldn't admit it. In an interview she gave in the 1960s, she was characteristically "ambiguous" about the subject:

> Recently my [eighteen]-year-old son Pat came home from visiting friends to tell me they had been watching an early Tarzan film, in which I romped through the jungle in a brief animal skin costume. He confided that he didn't dare tell his school fellows that the jungle girl they were whistling at was his mother. 'The things they said, Mother,' he told me, 'I couldn't repeat to you, but you looked wonderful.'"[1]

If Patrick and his friends couldn't ignore Maureen's sexual allure, made even more tantalizing by the amount of fabric missing from her skimpy attire, they weren't alone. Nor was the loincloth alone in hitting its mark, no doubt working in cahoots with all of Maureen's other attributes: perhaps the sweetness in her face, the large blue eyes, along with the raven red hair. This much sexual energy displayed on the screen would seem enough to embarrass any teenage boy who suddenly came face-to-face with his mother's sexuality on full display.

While Maureen's breakout moment in *Tarzan* in 1932 was startlingly refreshing, it wasn't her first swing onto the big screen. She'd appeared in a few unremarkable films at Twentieth Century Fox in the last couple of years. But Tarzan was the first time audiences truly saw her and took serious notice. Years later she'd come to regret the teasing sexuality that Jane invited, courtesy of MGM's ingenious head of production, Irving Thalberg. But she now showed audiences that she had enough chutzpah to help shield her not only from the harsh jungle weather cranked out by machines on MGM's soundstages but also to navigate her way through the more hazardous world of the Hollywood jungle.

And Maureen was a dish, all right, enticing enough to give her buff costar, Johnny Weissmuller, a run for his money in the looks department. He Tarzan—She Jane. With this first outing, the two became instant movie icons and reigned at the box office for six years, raking in plenty of bananas for Cheetah the Chimp, and piles of jungle money for Louie B. Mayer.

The Tarzan franchise hit movie theaters just at the right time. Shortly after Edgar Rice Burroughs's magazine series (and then novel) *Tarzan of the Apes* in 1912, Hollywood jumped on the jungle bandwagon with a silent version, *Tarzan of the Apes,* in 1918, starring Elmo Lincoln, followed by several more silent Tarzan features and serials. They were solid adventure yarns on their way to something bigger.

But the franchise finally hit the big drums in 1932 when the sound version, *Tarzan the Ape Man,* brought the jungle to life. W. S. Van Dyke directed and MGM's boy wonder, Irving Thalberg, produced, showing off his latest find, Maureen O'Sullivan, as she took to the ropes with Weissmuller, an Olympic gold medal–winning swimmer. Johnny would make twelve Tarzan films, six of them, from 1932 to 1942, with Maureen, now the studio's hottest young ingénue.

Maureen O'Sullivan first came to Hollywood on the arm of Fox Pictures' noted director Frank Borzage after he'd discovered her in her hometown in Ireland. To have Mr. Borzage himself as her escort, it might have seemed that she already wore a royal crown. But the word "savvy" was yet to enter her vocabulary. It took a while before Maureen realized that Fox Pictures was not that gracious. Fox released her after one year. She was now an out-of-work actress—and it no longer mattered how many times Frank Borzage escorted her into a room. What Maureen didn't know, and which she doesn't mention in David Fury's biography of her (a text so controlled by Maureen's interjections, it's her autobiography as well), *Maureen O'Sullivan: "No Average Jane"*, is that Fox had hired Maureen as bait to gain leverage over their main star Janet Gaynor, who wanted a better deal and more money.

According to *Motion Picture News,* "Janet Gaynor took a 'boat' vacation to Hawaii over a salary dispute with Fox (she wanted an increase to $6,000 a week from $1,750) and did not show up for work. When she returned, Fox made no overtures to her and Sheehan even did not keep an appointment with her in his office. In the meantime, Fox is grooming Maureen O'Sullivan for stardom—and is exploiting the Irish girl more intensively than any player that has arrived on the lot in years."[2]

After Fox and Gaynor came to terms in their contract negotiations, the studio simply dropped Maureen's option. They didn't need her anymore; she'd served her purpose and was now out the door, condemned to freedom. This had to be especially difficult considering the fanfare that accompanied her first moments in Hollywood. Not every girl (practically no girl) made an entrance on the arm of one of Fox's hottest directors. Losing her contract left her feeling "lonely, forsaken and unwanted."[3]

Luckily, her freedom came to a halt when MGM boy wonder Thalberg took notice of the beauty and put her under contract. MGM put Maureen deep in that African jungle and wrapped her in that scant piece of loincloth that thrilled audiences. Though the Tarzan adventures made her a star and paved the way toward a long association with MGM, neither the loincloth nor the studio's public relations tactics fit very well with Maureen. Years later, she said:

> Between the violent reactions of an Anglo Saxon puritanical public because of what they termed my "nude" scenes in the first couple of Tarzan films, and the equally intolerant reaction of MGM executives who then clothed me in virgin white swim costumes which looked like they came off the rack at Macy's, I was thoroughly disgusted with the whole scene.[4]

Olympic gold medalist Josephine McKim's "bottom" showed up in those scenes, not Maureen's. But, in her opinion, audiences still saw her as "a promiscuous harlot." She added, "Irving Thalberg and Mayer were behind most of this harassment. I disliked both men intensely. . . . I still have a sour taste in my mouth about the studio system in those days . . . they were really nothing more than tyrants who controlled every aspect of the lives of their employees and star or not . . . you were nothing more than that to them, simply an employee to be used and discarded at will."[5]

Despite Maureen's resentment, she wasn't angry enough or foolish enough to leave a top studio such as MGM, where she was the center of attention, at least for the moment. Who knew what it might lead to in the future?

As it turned out, MGM liked its plucky young star well enough to let her out of the jungle now and then to appear in other films. In fact, the studio cast her in some of its most prestigious releases of the 1930s and 1940s. She didn't get top billing, yet she charmed filmgoers in screen adaptations of classics ranging from Charlotte Bronte's *Pride and Prejudice* to Charles Dickens's *David Copperfield*, adding in Dashiell Hammett's detective thriller *The Thin Man* and, for comic relief, the Marx Brothers' *A Day at the Races*.

Maureen's star was on the rise. Marsha Hunt, who played one of the Bennet sisters in *Pride and Prejudice* but who, unlike Maureen, received no credit, later said, "I never understood the reasoning behind that, since Maureen and I had the same amount of on-screen time." Yet Hunt hadn't put in jungle time the way Maureen had. The two actresses never mentioned the discrepancy until years later when they became friends. "At the time we made the film, nobody was really friendly. We were too busy doing our jobs . . . and competing."[6] Yet, Hunt hadn't factored in Maureen's doppelgänger, Jane of the Jungle. Maureen had already put in her share of profitable screen time.

Other than her unhappy year at Fox Pictures, her star rose so quickly that it might have looked to many as if Maureen O' Sullivan never paid her dues the way so many other actors had.

Yet that would be far from the truth.

Maureen O' Sullivan paid her dues, all right—she paid them in spades, and for a longer time than many. By the time she came to Hollywood, she'd already paid with her childhood, having left Ireland for the United States at age eighteen with enough emotional damage to ensure her a permanently broken life. Then, after a few good years in Hollywood, she would begin paying again, this time with her future as it rolled out before her. She would pay heavily, and in ways she could never have imagined when Hollywood first embraced her. And she'd pay to the one person she least expected she would owe. Yet her childhood prepared her for that. Maureen O'Sullivan grew up in a harsh emotional landscape that, unfortunately, she would always call home.

She was born on May 17, 1911, in the small town of Boyle, County Roscommon, Ireland. As a small child, Maureen already felt as if she lived in an unforgiving world. She adored her father, Frank O'Sullivan, a military man, and learned to depend on him more than anyone in her young life. His steadiness was the only solid foundation beneath her; she knew it wouldn't crumble. Her father provided the fleeting moments when Maureen might feel whole and unconditionally loved. She needed the measure of safety her father gave her in order to cope with her mother's increasingly erratic behavior.

For her mother, Mary O'Sullivan, simply being in the world was difficult enough; but motherhood made it almost unbearable. Mary found it impossible to love her children. And she made no secret of that. That was the one aspect of Maureen's childhood that never wavered. Everything else did. With such uncertainty all around her, Maureen counted on her father all the more. Her attachment to him was her lifeline. In a 1994 story published in *Hello! Magazine*, Maureen recalled that any happiness in her childhood was spotty at best. She was close in age to her brother, Daniel, who died an infant. Maureen never forgave herself for his death. She had bumped into him by mistake as he lay in his bassinet. He died shortly after and Maureen was convinced that she had killed him, even though the two events were unrelated.[7]

Yet Mary could not comfort her daughter, too distracted and exhausted by attending to her own needs. The self-absorption it took to give her "illnesses" her first priority left Mary little energy for anything or anyone else. Losing an infant might have shocked Mary but it did not dismantle her. Maureen was never told that in addition to her mother's inability to tolerate everyday occurrences in her life, she never recovered from seeing Maureen's father return from World War I with injuries severe enough to cause him physical and emotional pain the rest of his life. Upon seeing her "crippled husband," Mary O'Sullivan suffered her first nervous breakdown. Recovery was never to come. Illness, in all its forms, pervaded the O'Sullivan's lives from then on.

It would make sense that Maureen's childhood years were anchored to, and shaped by, her mother's illnesses, determining where Maureen would live, or who would come to the O'Sullivan house to watch her and her siblings. While Mary's "episodes" created a chaotic mental calendar for the family, details of what actually was wrong with Mary were never revealed to her children, no doubt amping up their fear of whatever it was that kept their mother away from them—and as child psychology teaches us time and again, the first culprits that came to mind would have to have been themselves. It could have seemed as if the two of them not only made their mother ill, but also, whatever the illness was, it was horrible enough that it could not even be named. They lived most of their childhoods controlled by a destructive force. Little was said; Maureen heard only that her mother was "ill"—then she'd be gone for long periods of time. "My mother spent most of my childhood in nursing homes, and when she did come home, I didn't particularly like her. She was strange and eccentric, and I felt she didn't like me very much either."

Years later, Maureen's daughter, Mia Farrow, also spoke of a mother, this time, Maureen herself, who would sometimes have to leave the family home to "take a rest." Her children didn't know her whereabouts or "whatabouts." Either trauma can find a child by means of one terrific blow, a catastrophic event, or it can chip away at its victim over a period of time, dealing smaller blows that add up to an overwhelming psychic wound that does not heal.

Mary O'Sullivan's inability to love her daughter throughout her childhood coalesced into years of trauma—not a sudden overwhelming blow, not as a sudden shock, but a constant gnawing at her, a perennial chipping away at herself, a daily confrontation with what she may have believed to be her hideousness, only one of many responses a child would have to a mother such as Mary. Eventually, of course, that the disapproval Mary constantly hurled at Maureen became a pervasive self-hatred would seem the only logical response from a child if her mother didn't love her, was unable to love her. It chipped away at her ego daily, creating a wound and enlarging it as it continuously reopened. And Maureen didn't need her mother to continue the onslaught; she eventually became an expert at taking up where her mother left off, even replacing her. She could do damage to herself *by* herself.

It seemed that Mary found more than one way to attack Maureen. Mary could also be cruel to her daughter. "She would make careless remarks about me and tell jokes at my expense which often made me cry," Maureen later told her biographer, David Fury. "Then she'd try and hug me which I didn't like either.[8] "One particular incident in Maureen's childhood always haunted her. She'd invited a young girlfriend over to have a tea party in the family's garden. As she showed her friend around the grounds, trying to be the proper hostess, she overheard her mother say to her father, "Oh, look at the poor little thing trying to entertain. Isn't she pathetic?"

The collateral damage from a trauma accumulates, gathers, and settles in, finally taking up permanent residence in the body. She would never find a way to repair the wound that damaged her; there is no cure. Maureen might look for replacements for what she lost, and for the wound that grew at the site of that loss. As an adult, she sought out religion to heal her wound, to soothe herself. But with trauma there is only what was once there and no longer is—the original and its loss.

Loss creates its own aesthetic, an unconscious design for coping, determining how the psyche will behave so as to survive. No longer the unharmed, original self, it is now the self, repurposed. Once trauma interferes, there is no putting Humpty Dumpty back together again.

As trauma goes, this was an absolute condition of survival.

Yet it isn't uncommon for children of trauma to believe, somewhere in their hearts, that they deserved that punishment. The fact that Maureen would come to endure John Farrow's mistreatment of her would certainly put her in that category— even beyond the couple's Catholic faith that prohibits divorce. Maureen may not have known what she could have done to deserve punishment from her mother, but Maureen could more than likely be primed for it for the future. Perhaps, in her mind, it was only a matter of how soon and how much.

Maureen was able to escape Ireland for a bit when her parents sent her to Paris for a year of high school. As pleasurable as it was, she returned to find life in the Irish countryside small and tedious—not to mention limited at best. Although she appeared in several local theater productions, she began to dream of an acting career. But, given where she lived, and given the mundane existence that stretched out before her everywhere she looked, a career as an actress, much less a Hollywood acting career, was less than a remote thought. Little did she know how lucky that year, 1929, would be (how bizarre it would have seemed had she even dreamed it). Some fairy dust, some strange bit of the uncanny, must have fallen on Maureen. Whatever it was, she was more than ready for it.

That magical dust that touched her was nothing less than the tinsel sent all the way from Hollywood. One of Fox Studios' most renowned film directors, Frank Borzage, happened to be in the Dublin area to shoot his upcoming film, *Song o' My Heart*. Fortunately for Maureen, Borzage stuck to his habit of looking out for local talent he might bring back to Hollywood. When he saw Maureen O'Sullivan dancing at the ball, he wasted little time in asking if she would take a screen test the next morning. She would—and did. Borzage knew, just as the camera knew, that he had something special in Maureen. Set to take her with him to Los Angeles, he hadn't counted on Frank O'Sullivan's resolute refusal to allow his daughter to go to Hollywood and live among movie actors, a group of humans he despised before any others on earth.[9] After finally smoothing out her father's objections, Borzage took the young beauty with him when he returned to Hollywood.

New to Hollywood, Maureen was picked to costar in Will Rogers's *So This Is London*, about a British-hating American whose son falls for an English aristocrat's daughter. The film was released in June 1930, three months before Borzage's *Song o' My Heart*; and although her performance is subdued due to inexperience, the movie was a success. Her next outing was *Just Imagine*, followed by a pairing with Charles Farrell in *The Princess and the Plumber*, a comedy about a derogated prince who hopes to restore his wealth and power by marrying off his daughter to royalty. Unfortunately, she has fallen in love with a young man who has been hired to fix the plumbing in their run-down castle. Her onscreen romance with Farrell was mimicked off-screen as the pair was often seen around Hollywood in each other's company.

Maureen's popularity with moviegoers must have pleased her enormously. That kind of mass approval might soothe her ego and help to boost her self-esteem after so many years of being the target of her mother's verbal and emotional abuse. But the public applause would never heal the actual wound of childhood trauma itself—and would always define Maureen the adult.

But popularity with movie audiences had its rewards since it could translate to large box office receipts and, like a domino effect, keep the rewards coming, such as better scripts and eventually more prestige attached to Maureen's name and reputation. The wider her name swept across Hollywood within these terms, the more rewards she might earn. But how long would this kind of luck hang around? Nothing, especially being famous in a fickle business, meant forever.

In the back of her mind always, Maureen probably knew the path she would inevitably take. How many young women in 1930s America, for one, could go against the grain, take an alternate route instead of the one that lead to matrimony? The path, and the life it led to, was written all around her. She knew instinctively that, as a woman, sooner or later she would take her rightful place in the society that molded her. She would marry and create a family. It was just a matter of time until she traveled there. She'd been raised in a culture and in a generation that assumed a woman's goal was clear: to find the husband she needed to start the family that was her feminine destiny.

In any case, Maureen was not the girl to question a received idea. She was, after all, her mother's girl—damaged by her childhood. With all the injuries she carried, amassed from all the bullets her mother shot at her, it would not be surprising if Maureen's idea of healing, of compensation, would hinge upon having a husband and a family of her own. What else in those years could be more assured of winning the Good Housekeeping Seal of Approval than a husband and a family, bestowing on a woman the coveted code for "normal"?

There was also the matter of Maureen's particularly traumatic childhood. It would make perfect sense if she also believed that a husband and a family would fill the aching hole in her heart, would provide the intimacy that she had yet to know.

And so, perhaps Maureen wasn't thinking about loneliness as she started out of her apartment on a particular day in 1929. It might have cheered her to hear birds chirping loudly in the trees as she walked down Sunset Boulevard and made a left into a dark building at Western Avenue. She might have awoken early that day, wanting to get to the studio before rehearsals began. As she later told her biographer, she now found herself venturing down the dark corridors of Fox Studios' executive offices, looking for David Butler, the director of her current picture, *Just Imagine,* a screwball science fiction tale set in the future year of 1980.

The darkness made it difficult to read the numbers on the office doors. She decided to take the plunge and now opened one of them—only to find herself in the wrong office. Sitting at his typewriter in the tiny, overstuffed room, one of Fox's newly hired screenwriters, John Farrow, looked up at her. The first note she jotted down on her mental scribble sheet was "Handsome." Farrow's leg rested on the chair next to him, and Maureen couldn't help but take in the tattoo wrapped around his ankle displaying the Latin phrase, "Semper Fidelis—Always Faithful." But the irony in it wouldn't have hit her yet.

Maureen probably figured out John Farrow right away. He would never be faithful to her; he would sleep with other women but not tell her. He would be selfish; he would put his needs first, even, at times, be unaware of hers. He would probably be all kinds of absent no matter where he was or what he told her.

In like manner, John Farrow no doubt saw Maureen coming. When she opened his office door and looked in, he had to see not only her beauty but all of the loss she carried in herself now coming at him. Most likely, he couldn't look away. In the depths of his unconscious, the most unknowable part of himself, he needed her. He needed her this way; he needed her damage and her vulnerable soul—her complete unawareness that she needed something and someone to fill her, to send her back to her once whole self.

Maureen O'Sullivan and John Farrow were not necessarily a good fit, but they were the right fit—the sad-hearted young woman and the writer, overflowing with a sense of himself, grandiose, overloaded with purpose. Maureen needed to fill the empty place in her heart. John Farrow was so fully loaded and ready to shoot that, if he'd had his way, he would have filled all the earth's empty spaces with himself.

The truth is, Maureen knew John Farrow had demons, but she didn't know their depth, the strength of their hold on him. She didn't know all he'd already been, or done, or even the half of what she was about to get. But, at this moment, she looked straight at him, and she saw pain. It felt right.

Four

GOING HOLLYWOOD:
JOHN AND MAUREEN
MAKE HEADLINES

When Maureen O' Sullivan first met the dangerous Mr. Farrow, he left a lasting impression. She later said:

> I had only been in Hollywood a little over a year when I met John Farrow . . . I thought he was wonderfully exciting and dangerous. He was twenty-six and without a doubt the most colorful character in Hollywood, having earned himself the worst reputation in town as far as women were concerned. Sexually, his prowess was legendary and there was even a rumor he had brought a new sex cult to America.[1]

John Farrow and Maureen O'Sullivan knew they were a match the moment they met, but instead of moving in closer, each moved in the other direction, then back again. They kept this pattern going, sparking a six-year run of hide and seek that played itself out in the pages of newspapers and magazines throughout the country and then some.

Over the years, the story of how they met grew to six or seven versions: perhaps at a nightclub, perhaps on the Fox lot when Maureen entered the wrong office, or maybe on the set of a Tarzan movie. Behind the flashbulbs and tabloid narratives, they were most likely more in love than not. But their courtship was as much fodder for gossip columns as it was the real deal off the page. No one really knew where reality ended and fantasy took over.

But Maureen and John both knew that, if you wanted a Hollywood career in the 1930s, you had to live part of your life splashed on the cover and inside pages of the fan magazines. Moviegoers couldn't get enough gossip about movie stars. Nor, at the time, could they get enough of John and Maureen's on-again, off-again romance and ate up every word of it. The two were a traveling circus of contradictions that followed more twists and turns than the snake tattoo running up John Farrow's leg.

John Farrow never let his feelings for Maureen O'Sullivan interfere with his reputation as being one of Hollywood's greatest womanizers. He wanted Maureen—and he wanted other women too. He had no specific plan; he never put great thought into it. He simply assumed he could have it all: Maureen on the right, other women on the left. Throughout their courtship, and later, in all their twenty-seven years of marriage, Farrow believed he could have any woman he wanted. Since he didn't always bat a thousand, he made sure to chase every woman he could. And Maureen stood by, patiently. She knew from the start that he had little intention of being faithful to her. As uncomfortable as he was with publicity, he accepted the fan magazines pursuing him repeatedly and let his love life go public.

Maureen, on the other hand, welcomed her growing fame. She played in the Hollywood jungle as if it were her natural habitat. Being a movie star just came easily to her, no matter how many times she feigned nervousness at just the prospect of giving an interview.

Being seen around town was a side career most of the film colony was eager to take on. While Maureen took it to heart, John Farrow seemed indecisive, hardly ever giving interviews during his entire time in Hollywood. Although looking more content when left alone, when he did make a splash for the public eye, it was in a big, bizarre fashion.

In the late 1920s, when both John and Maureen arrived in Hollywood, fan magazines were quick to notice each of them as they mingled socially and climbed ever higher toward successful Hollywood careers.

As early as 1927, while he was still married to Felice Lewin, Farrow's name was linked with budding starlets. He was among a group of Australian members of the film colony greeting Miss Australasia on her arrival in Hollywood to "break into motion pictures" at DeMille.[2]

By the end of 1927, he was again making the gossip columns as an unattached single, hanging out at the Hollywood Montmartre Cafe with the likes of popular film stars Marian Nixon, Billie Dove, Mervyn Leroy, Sid Grauman, and other Hollywood luminaries of the day.[3]

At the end of 1927, *Variety* reported that "he jumped in less than a year from $50 to $1,000 a week."[4]

A month later, as *Motion Picture News* noted, Farrow showed up at Paramount Studios as well. Although he was practically a youngster, the blurb read, Farrow was someone "Only 23 years old," but who had "several stories to his credit."[5]

In the early 1930s, Maureen took an apartment at the famed Garden of Allah up on the Sunset Strip, the shining jewel in Hollywood real estate. If you wanted to play where photographers' cameras flashed every night of the week, the Garden was essential living; there was hardly a star in Tinseltown who had not lived there or visited regularly. Though John Farrow was on his way up to these stars, he didn't yet enjoy the same celebrity she did. So Farrow lived around the corner from her at a place called the Ronda Apartments; that way he could spend a good deal of time at the Garden making his presence known—in one way or another.

And he did get attention. "Mr. Farrow had a snake tattooed on the upper part of the inside of his left thigh," columnist Sheilah

Graham later noted for the record. "He posed for long periods at the end of Garden's diving board wearing short swimming trunks and the snake appeared to be emerging from his reproductive organs."[6]

Written for effect, Graham's prose is short and direct in order to emphasize the bizarre scene taking place before her. What an odd sight this must have seemed to anyone who knew Farrow, who revealed nothing of himself if he could help it.

Graham makes mention of John Farrow (though not by name) at the Garden again, this time in a less humorous account of what he was up to during the time he split his affections between Maureen and Lila Lee. Graham, given her respect for her friend Marion Marx, at the time married to Harpo Marx, shields her along with everyone else in relating a very disturbing incident that occurred at the hotel.

"A wife of one of the Marx Brothers was called from the Garden at four in the morning by an actress who had been a statuesque silent-film star and was then working infrequently in talkies. 'I'm dying,' she moaned. 'You've got to come over; I'm dying.' Mrs. Marx hastened over. She was far from dead, but her bed, her gown, and her body were covered with blood. The sadist, who is now dead—the father of a famous current young film actress—had made little cuts all over her with razor blades. Cutting soft flesh was his particular hang-up. There was lechery at the Garden, but nothing as cruel as this. The same man was always pretending to commit suicide. They would take bets at the Garden on whether he would surprise himself one day and succeed. He died of natural causes two decades later." Writing in 1969, Graham knew more about Farrow's suicide attempts and cuttings than most.[7]

John Farrow and his tattoo were a package deal. Maureen learned this when both were on display the day Maureen walked into the wrong office at Fox Studios to find John sitting behind a desk, his leg perched on top of it to expose the tattoo. Farrow was happy to oblige as Maureen's eyes followed alongside the snake until they reached a divide in the road further up. Maureen dared not look too closely but nevertheless made a mental note of it all. It wasn't until much later on that she discovered where the snake actually ended—at his genitals.

Though Farrow and Maureen were a match made in Hollywood heaven, both played the Tinseltown field of celebrity dating. Farrow was romantically linked to young starlet Lila Lee, and was seen escorting her around the nightclub and party circuit.

From *Screenland* in 1929: "That amusing Matty Kemp was dividing his attention equally between Lila Lee and Bebe, though John Farrow was concentrating, whenever he got a chance, on Lila. 'Lila is looking so pretty these days that I suspect she is having a fresh romance,' remarked Patsy, as we noticed the adoring looks of Mr. Farrow, who just then was devotedly offering her dinner on a plate."[8]

Farrow was part of the "Mayfair Stock Company" at the ballroom in the Mayfair Room at the Biltmore Hotel in Hollywood, and he and Lila hung around with a litany of Hollywood celebrities.[9] And when Louis B. Mayer's daughter, Edith, married producer William Goetz in May 1930, "John Farrow and Lila Lee were among a list of attendees made up of the elite of Hollywood."[10]

With just four films under her belt, Maureen was already becoming a regular in the gossip sheets. "Maureen O'Sullivan, demure seventeen-year-old [sic] Dublin, Ireland beauty, who was introduced to the American screen via John McCormack's first talking-singing picture, has made good in Hollywood in more ways than one. Not only has she superseded Janet Gaynor as Charlie Farrell's leading lady, she has stolen the heart of young Russell Gleason (who was a star in *All Quiet on the Western Front*)."[11]

She was already "a vastly grown-up young lady of eighteen [sic] with a house of her own and a Ford car that she drives at great speed here and there about the country side. And what about the men in her life. 'That would be telling,' said canny Maureen, as indeed it would. "I have just lots of boyfriends. I like them all. You know, I never know when I am in love or when it is just infatuation,' she sighed dreamily. And then she went right on to admit that she thought Frank Albertson was 'a darling,' that Lew Ayres is charming, and she admires Ronald Colman and Fredric March; and George O'Brien is handsome, and oh, so is John Garrick! And Frank Borzage is wonderful, and Will Rogers is a 'dear.' And if that isn't just about liking them all, I'd like to know whose feelings are hurt!"[12]

Soon enough, however, Farrow, Lee, and Maureen would play a sort of Russian roulette with their (at least in the gossip columns) romantic lives: "Lila Lee is seen everywhere nowadays in the company of Johnny Weaver, a Paramount writer, who has replaced John Farrow, also an author, in her affections. But Hollywood doubts if Farrow's heart has been too badly wrecked, for he seems to be taking a great interest in Dolores Del Río, who has been reported engaged to several film colony personages since the death of her husband two years ago."[13]

Maureen and Farrow began dating and became new grist for the tabloid mills: "Maureen O'Sullivan, that cute little Irish trick over at Fox, is stepping places with John Farrow, who might very well be called A Young Man About Town."[14] Many nights saw them together at the Ambassador Hotel's Cocoanut Grove: "Maureen O'Sullivan and John Farrow—Maureen in brown satin with ornaments of amber-costume jewelry."[15]

Still, when Lila Lee took "ill" in late 1930, Farrow was by her side: According to the *Los Angeles Times,* "Lila Lee went to a sanitarium in Prescott, Arizona, with 'shattered nerves.' She's eagerly awaiting her discharge, after which she will take a long ocean voyage, after which she hopes to be married, again, this time to John Farrow, screen writer. Farrow often flies to Prescott from Phoenix to spend an hour with Miss Lee. Virtually no other visitors were allowed to disturb her long hours of rest."[16]

After recuperating, Lee announced that she was going to tie the knot with Farrow: "Lila Lee, from her desert retreat, writes that she is quite recovered from the serious illness that threatened her . . . The desert's a great healer all right, but folks are willing to bet that it's old Doc Happiness who has fixed Lila up. She is engaged to be married to John Farrow, the scenarist. The romance looked shaky for a while, but John won his way back by thoughtful attention while Lila was ill and alone. Shortly, Lila expects to go to Europe to visit John's mother, after which the marriage will probably take place."[17]

With Farrow temporarily out of the picture, Maureen "picked Lew Schreiber, former associate of Al Jolson, to run around with." (Schreiber later became a casting director on a couple of films in 1935–1936).[18]

Farrow, as previously mentioned, had overstayed his time in the United States and, after being "asked" by the US immigration service to leave, in 1931 he took off for Tahiti and then England. At about the same time, Lila Lee traveled to Tahiti for a vacation, and subsequently John joined her there—but something happened:

> Lila Lee and John Farrow are no longer engaged. There is no secret that John's attention made Lila's long illness more endurable than it could otherwise have been. Lila was equally in love, and the "understanding" still existed when she was able to return to Hollywood from the remote Arizona sanitorium. Both of them were guests on a house party in Tahiti last fall. Something happened there. They ended the engagement. Lila returned home, and John is on an extended trip around the world.[19]

Here's the backstory behind that item. Farrow and Lila came *this close* to marrying when they visited Tahiti, one of Farrow's favorite islands. Also at hand was Lila's close friend, actress Patsy Ruth Miller, who wrote about the incident in her memoir.

Johnny Farrow actually loved two women, Lila Lee and Maureen O'Sullivan. He had known Lila, a studio contract player, longer than he knew Maureen. He adored Lila, but the two could never go very long without fighting and deciding to separate. Their separations, however, didn't last long. During one of the times he and Lila quarreled, Johnny met Maureen; they were instantly attracted to each other. And, as the attraction grew, he became torn. Did he love Lila or Maureen? Maureen or Lila?

In 1931, Lila invited Miller to join her on a trip to Tahiti for a long and much-deserved vacation. Johnny stayed back in Los Angeles writing film scenarios. He had yet to discover how much Lila and Patsy were enjoying their vacation—gallivanting around the islands, meeting new people and flirting with handsome, dashing young men from England, the United States, and Europe who were also enjoying a vacation in Tahiti.

According to Patsy, one night Johnny sent Lila a telegram telling her that he was on his way to join her in Tahiti; he had something important to talk over with her. She and Patsy tried guessing. It could be only one thing: Johnny wanted to marry Lila. What else would be that important to bring him to Tahiti?

When Johnny arrived the next week, he and Lila were gushing over each other for hours on end, as if they hadn't already known each other for years.

Patsy could no longer wait. She wanted Johnny to pop the question to Lila. It was all too much. As Patsy recounts, she asked Johnny straight out: Had he come to Tahiti to propose marriage to Lila? "Yes," he answered, he supposed he had. "That was a very good idea."

Lila rushed over to Johnny and held him to her, covering his face with kisses; then he returned the favor when he could get one planted on her cheek. Johnny thought the three of them should go have a drink to celebrate. But Patsy couldn't go with them, as she had an invitation to another party. But she would see them in a while.

According to Patsy, hours later she returned to their hotel. As she climbed the stairs to their floor, she was surprised not to hear giggling, laughing, and celebrating between the two lovers. Instead, when she opened Lila's door, she found the two of them sitting across the room from each other, staring at each other in silence.

They'd had a huge fight. Johnny was extremely angry to learn that Lila had been having so much fun during his absence. He was jealous to learn about all the men she'd met. After a few minutes, he then told Lila he didn't think he could marry her knowing how much she loved the company of other men. He then said good night. He was going to bed. Lila said to him, "well, go ahead."

Then, in the middle of the night, Patsy recounts, she awoke with the strange sensation that someone was in her room. She heard slight footsteps, a bump or two, then that was the end of it. But she became frightened when she realized the noises she had heard were from Johnny in the room next to hers; she heard more sounds as if someone were bumping into furniture; next she heard a moan and then complete silence.

Patsy hurried quickly and silently to Lila's room. "I think there might be something wrong with Johnny," she told Lila. Alarmed, Lila straightened up in her bed and said, "Oh no, perhaps we should go see."

Although Johnny's room was almost pitch black, a light from outside shone on his face, making it easy to see. According to Patsy, they looked down to notice that Johnny had pulled the covers up under his neck. Then they looked further and now could see one of his hands hanging down from inside the covers. They looked at his arm and saw blood dripping slowly from his hand onto the floor. They quickly picked up his other hand and found the same thing: Johnny has slashed his wrists.

In spite of their sheer panic, the girls remembered to call a doctor. Soon he arrived and as quickly as possible stitched up Johnny's wrists. He would be OK; he would survive.

Patsy could not remember the rest of the night. But when she awoke the next morning, she found Johnny downstairs at a table having breakfast and looking as if nothing had happened. Not really knowing what you say to someone who had just tried to commit suicide, she struggled to find the words.

"You're looking well," she said.

"Thank you, I'm feeling much better," Johnny replied. "I'm awfully sorry about what happened last night. I would never want to hurt you or put you through that again and I can promise you it will never happen a second time." Months later Lila returned to Hollywood alone and a few years later, after a rocky courtship, Johnny married actress Maureen.[20]

On the rebound, Lila quickly began spending time with director George Hill, who had just come off of a divorce with screenwriter Frances Marion. In June 1932, *Movie Classic* magazine reported: "If Lila Lee and director George Hill aren't altar-bound they certainly have succeeded in fooling old Hollywood. Never did two people appear more smitten with each other. They're dreamy-eyed. Gossip has it that Johnny Farrow, Lila's former flame, still cables her from London to come on over and make movies on the other side. The bets are that she won't accept—and George Hill is the best reason."[21]

In early January 1933, Farrow returned to the States and resumed his womanizing ways, dating Hollywood starlets. In fact, it was while dancing with Argentinean actress Mona Maris at the Cocoanut Grove on January 27 that he was arrested by Special US Assistant Secretary of Labor Murray W. Garsson, who was investigating illegal aliens in Hollywood. Sans Farrow in her love life, Maureen began to be seen around town with actor James Dunn. According to *Movie Classic*, "There's an Irish tilt to her chin, an Irish lilt to her eyes, and, as if her name isn't Irish enough now, they do say she's about to add another good old Gaelic tag to the end of it. She and James Dunn are even suspected of having Dunn it already—after a romance that has been as rocky as that well known road to Dublin. And if you don't think she has the luck of the Irish in her career, too, listen to the news that Johnny Weissmuller is to woo her a SECOND time *in Tarzan and His Mate.*"[22]

Despite the Lila Lee–Farrow breakup, their pairing still elicited gossip column rumors. In a March 1933 article titled "Lila Lee's Marriage to Director Will End Four-Cornered Romance," writer Joan Standish couldn't resist bringing up Farrow's name:

> The marriage will, for one thing, put a stop to all talk that George Hill is "making up" with his former wife, Frances Marion, the scenarist, and that they are planning to remarry. It will also silence all reports that the "romance" between Lila and George was merely a friendship and that her real heart-throb was her former ardent flame, writer John Farrow.
>
> It was to John Farrow that Lila, who was divorced from James Kirkwood in 1930, announced her engagement and approaching marriage when she first returned to Hollywood last year after two years of health recuperation in an Arizona sanitarium. Everyone knew that Lila and Johnny had been in love for a long time—for at least a year before Lila's health had forced her to leave the screen. Certainly, there was little doubt that Lila thought much of the popular and very British Mr. Farrow.
>
> But the romance between Lila and Johnny had always been stormy. And when Lila returned to Hollywood, it evidently picked up where it left off. It was during one of their numerous disagreements that Lila met George Hill, then just recently divorced from Frances Marion. The columnists dusted off their "that way" rumors, not failing, however, to drop casual hints about the possibility of a reconciliation between George Hill and Frances Marion or between Lila and Johnny. Right in the midst of the rumorings, Mr. Farrow went off to England for a vacation. However, Hollywood knows that he spent a great deal of

money, phoning Lila from London. And the reports about the progress of the Lee-Hill romance had just reached the persistent state when Mr. Farrow decided to return. Now, everyone is wondering if his return hastened Mr. Hill's decision to put that all-important sparkler on the correct finger of Lila's hand. In the meantime, John Farrow has been escorting Anna May Wong to various places of interest in Hollywood.[23]

John also had a fifteen-minute fling in the trades with Katharine Hepburn, a woman with a steely enough spine to make her verboten John Farrow material. But when Hepburn and costar Joel McCrea began shooting the film *They Came Unarmed*, the two were said to be carrying on a hot romance. RKO publicists quickly decided to scotch the story, redirecting the affair to John Farrow instead, an early contender to write the script for the upcoming *Little Women*. In a flash, gossiper Grace Kingsley hinted in her column that Farrow was now obviously two-timing Maureen O'Sullivan with Katharine Hepburn, briefly referred to as RKO's latest siren.[24]

Hepburn later swore she never indulged the gossip columnists, which may or may not have been true. Ironically, and more fascinating still, later on, Kate would find herself spending more time with Farrow than she'd ever have intended. Up until Farrow's death in 1963 he and Spencer Tracy were committed drinking buddies. No doubt Kate was dragged along to more than one of their sessions. Years down the line, her final summation of Farrow was direct and to the point. She called him "the most depraved human being I've ever met."[25]

By April 1933, "that very hot love affair that involved Maureen O'Sullivan and John Farrow two years ago has been resumed, much to the discomfort of James Dunn. Or is this a blind to hide a secret marriage?"[26]

Despite being paired with Charles Farrell and James Dunn, Maureen's true heart belonged to Farrow, and their romance was on and off for six years. Although Maureen was seen dancing and dining with Johnnie Weissmuller in August, "Maureen was being seen with Johnnie to try to counteract the unfortunate publicity he had at the time when the Weissmuller-Velez romance was hottest. Now Maureen is back with her old love, Johnnie Farrow, who was once Lila Lee's sweetheart."[27]

The hot-cold romance between Farrow and Maureen continued. Two months later, *Screenland* reported that Maureen said "she will not marry John Farrow."[28]

In December 1933, Maureen got an infection after her appendix was removed at Cedars of Lebanon Hospital. According to *the Los Angeles Times,* "Grave fears were at first felt for her recovery and a special serum from the University of California was used," but she won the fight and was sent home. "Her fiancé, John Farrow, screen writer, was constantly at her bedside during the crisis of her illness."[29]

A long profile that month in *Picture Play Magazine* titled "Maureen Laughs It Off" asked the burning question: "What does O'Sullivan mean to do about her boyfriends . . . Maureen smiles and goes her way," and summed up the pair's romance—in Hollywood terms, they were made for each other. According to *Picture Play's* writer, William H. McKegg, "For several years now, Hollywood's most baffling mystery has been the one woven around the friendship of Maureen O'Sullivan and John Farrow, scenario writer and reputed Casanova. Hollywood's objection to their acquaintance reared itself when no one knew the inside facts. To get the low-down has been Hollywood's pet aim this many a day. No one knew for sure whether their liking for each other was merely a pleasant neighborly friendship or a flaming passion. Hollywood is still guessing—wrong."[30]

When John was forced to leave Hollywood in 1931, "he wanted to remain in Hollywood with Maureen. Maureen was left alone, a state much to her liking."[31] And the Hollywood rumor mill worked overtime, wondering if Farrow had left for London because of Maureen's sudden interest in James Dunn, or whether she had "accepted Jimmy as her cavalier during Johnny's absence abroad. The pertinent thing is that Maureen did turn glowing eyes on Mr. Dunn."[32] In Farrow's absence, she gave up her Garden of Allah bungalow and rented a house near the Hollywood Bowl with her friend Kay English. The rustic retreat was a base camp for nightlife forays into the heart of Hollywood, a wild life that Maureen later denied.[33]

Shortly after Farrow's return, Maureen gave up her Hollywood Hills home and returned to the Garden of Allah.

"Johnny is the only one who really understands me," Maureen told McKegg at *Picture Play Magazine.* "He has such a wonderful humor. He is educated, traveled. It is a delight to be in his company. That he is too worldly for me is positively ridiculous. I like people for their real selves. I don't know anything about Johnny's 'wild' reputation. Maybe he is the bad man of the world Hollywood credits him with being, and does the many things he is accused of doing. I don't know. I do know I regard him in a very high light for what I know him to be, and I shall continue to."[34]

Now, as part of her devotion to Farrow, Maureen lobbied with the federal court in early 1934 to help get perjury charges (arising from his illegal immigration arrest in 1933) against him dropped. She also decided that after finishing *The Barretts of Wimpole* (during which she knitted a woolen muffler for Farrow), she would "take that combination rest-cure-vacation she's been promising herself for months. Her destination is to be the Emerald Isle, where she will visit her family and introduce her finance, John Farrow."[35] In April, the pair received reentry permits from the LA immigration director prior to leaving for Ireland.[36] In June, Maureen left for Ireland to visit her sick father while Farrow went off to Honolulu as a prelude to working on *Last of the Pagans* (1935).

Hollywood gossip had it that the pair's romance was in trouble, but Maureen was quick to dispel that rumor: "Miss O'Sullivan was asked yesterday at Metro-Goldwyn-Mayer if their engagement is over. 'This doesn't look like it, does it?' she asked as she held up her hand to show she is still wearing the ring. Incidentally, this is about the closest Miss O'Sullivan has ever come to admitting she is betrothed to Farrow."[37] Despite all the gloating in the press about the pair's forthcoming nuptials—and the verbal cues from Farrow and Maureen—their marriage was still a long way off.

Los Angeles Times writer Alma Whitaker took a crack at the situation in a July 1934 article titled "Maureen O'Sullivan's Long Betrothal Baffles Filmdom":

> Destiny moves for Maureen O'Sullivan this year. Both fame and romance are casting their benign rays upon her. This week she sails for home and Ireland. She will be accompanied by John Farrow, her fiancée, and if the family gives the union its blessing, they will be married in Ireland in the Catholic Church before she returns for *David Copperfield*. When it comes to romance, Maureen is a little peeved with Hollywood. "They simply don't understand a normal formal engagement. According to them, a couple is either married (or ought to be) or divorced. John and I have been accused of being secretly married. We are not. I am a Catholic. We take marriage seriously and do not believe in divorce. That is why we are engaged in the old-fashioned formal way. We shall visit my people in Ireland that they may meet John and give us their blessing. I owe it to them to be married there. It is all so simple, really, but Hollywood can make things so complicated."[38]

Despite her disdain of "complications," the forthcoming Farrow-O'Sullivan union was indeed complicated. Farrow had traveled to Liverpool and then Canterbury to assist in shooting scenes for *David Copperfield* (only one screen of the Canterbury Cathedral was used in the film, which was shot at the MGM back lot and Malibu). According to an article in the *Pittsburgh Post-Gazette*, Maureen, who was visiting her family in Ireland, said "'Our marriage will almost certainly take place in Dublin or London, but whether during my present month's visit to Ireland or on my return to this side, I cannot say.' She said she expected to remain in her native Ireland for from three weeks to a month. But there was a hitch to their marriage: A reliable source in Dublin said Miss O'Sullivan and Farrow have been denied permission to marry in the Procathedral there."[39] Apparently, before heading off to England and Ireland, Maureen had requested a special dispensation from Rome because of John's divorce from "Felice Lewin Farrow, daughter of the late Arthur Lewin, millionaire San Francisco mining man. They have an eight-year-old child in custody of [Felice] Farrow's mother."[40]

On September 19, the pair returned home, landing in Quebec City. The *Los Angeles Times* announced on its front page: "It's still single blessedness for Maureen O'Sullivan, Irish-born film star, who returned today aboard the Empress of Australia from a short visit to the 'Ould Sod.' Rumor had it she would marry John Farrow, young film director, who crossed in the same ship as she on the outbound voyage, but Miss O'Sullivan returned alone and from the deck waved a significantly ringless left hand."[41]

A week later the *Times* reported that Farrow and Maureen were hopeful of a Christmas Day wedding. The pair had just finished spending several days "in the wilds of Arizona hunting and fishing at a resort near Winslow." Although they were awaiting the church's dispensation, "Miss O'Sullivan announced that she and Farrow received the blessings of her parents during their visit with them. 'We are working ever so hard to get the necessary dispensation from the Pope and we are hopeful that it will come,' she said, as Farrow nodded assent."[42]

As the year wore on—and there was no marriage in sight— the gossip columns took to chronicling the pair's off-screen adventures:

> Maureen O'Sullivan and John Farrow don't believe the
> old adage that good things come in small packages. When

Maureen's birthday came along, Johnny surprised her with a wardrobe trunk to help take her home to Ireland on a visit. The trunk took up one corner of Maureen's living room. When Johnny's birthday rolled around, he found a package so large that it covered half of his living room. It was a compass for his new boat, complete even to the platform on which to stand. By this time they're in England happily married—if plans were carried out.[43]

According to *Photoplay* in early 1935, while Maureen was in Ireland the previous year, "so overcome were the natives with Maureen's visit, they refused to let her drive anywhere. Instead, they insisted on pushing her car from street to street. But the height of their enthusiasm was reached when Maureen was awakened every morning by a bagpipe serenade under her window!"[44]

In February, the *Los Angeles Times* reported that:

In about three weeks or maybe less time than that, a slick white new schooner will glide over the waters into one of the local yacht club mooring. John Farrow, the writer, is the owner of the craft. His fiancée, Maureen O'Sullivan, will officiate and crack a bottle of champagne over its prow when it is christened Mavoureen. The boat is coming down from the Vancouver B.C. shipyards. And there are those who say it will be the Farrow-O'Sullivan honeymoon yacht, as extension of papal dispensation for their marriage is expected by them any time soon.[45]

Without a marriage to report on, the press jumped at any opportunity to print news about the couple:

What might have ended in tragedy developed into a humorous situation when John Farrow decided on a swim while sailing at Santa Monica with his fiancée, Maureen

O'Sullivan, in her 12-foot sail boat. He was about a mile off shore when he decided to haul down the sails and take a dip. While he was swimming, a heavy wind hit the boat and carried it away from Farrow. He called for Maureen to hoist the sails and swing the boat around so he could get aboard. She became so excited, however, and the harder she worked the farther became the distance between Farrow and the boat. Miss O'Sullivan finally managed to get close enough to throw him a rope and a completely exhausted Farrow dragged himself to the deck. He couldn't help but chuckle after he was safe over Maureen's difficulty in rescuing him.[46]

Finally, the pair got a papal dispensation and, on September 5, 1936, they applied for a marriage license. The *Los Angeles Times* reported "Maureen Paula O'Sullivan, film actress, left her work long enough yesterday noon to appear at the marriage license bureau with John Villiers Farrow, writer and director, to obtain a license to wed. . . . The young couple said they had not as yet completed their plans for the wedding ceremony, but that it would be held possibly within the next week or ten days."[47]

They were married September 12 in St. Monica's Church in Santa Monica. Sally Blane was matron of honor and A. H. Tandy, British vice consul of Los Angeles, was best man.

Five

TWISTED BLISS:
AT HOME AND ABROAD

Maureen O'Sullivan believed fully in happy Hollywood endings, especially the one in which a naive woman from a small town chases her dream of romance or fame and is rewarded in the end. She suffers the requisite hard knocks, learns a thing or two about life and about herself, and, just before the lights go up, walks down the aisle with her Prince Charming, if not the head of production at a major movie studio. Later, the children will frolic in front of that beautiful vine-covered cottage. And come they will!

After all, this is the dream that brought Maureen to Tinseltown, and to the man, and now to the wedding, she secretly longed for all her lonely years.

Loving the movies—*truly* loving them—as Maureen and other dreamers always have, comes from the all-too-intimate knowledge of what lies on the flip side of that dreamy world European moguls invented: the ordinary, the miseries of everyday life, the hardships that the real world doled out. The Hollywood version of life offered the antidote, the temporary cure for all the wanting and all the not getting, all the deprivation, and all of the wishing to leave your wounded soul behind you. Hollywood movies offered hope in the face of despair, loneliness, and, especially, of being ordinary.

Maureen now lived the dream she had longed for, and she expected her marriage to John Farrow to ensure that the dream lasted a lifetime. Yes, she knew he had demons, and that she might have trouble fitting him into the contours of her dream. He could be moody, unpredictable, even cruel. But she was willing to try, even though she didn't yet know the depth of his tortured soul.

Maureen also knew that living the Hollywood dream meant spending much of her life in the public eye, under the pressure of public scrutiny. Although already in the public eye, she'd have to be ready for the unexpected X-ray treatment if she married a man with all of Farrow's rough edges. Maureen's first years in Hollywood had given her a first-class education in covering up in public. No matter what trouble or controversy might find her, no matter what probing questions the gossipmongers might throw at her, she would make certain she maintained her composure; she would respond with only a benign comment that said nothing.

Over the years of their marriage, as the number of John Farrow's not-so-secret indiscretions mounted, Maureen became the gatekeeper of silence. She was there to repress all of the chaos John served up to the public. Before, she'd been described as "perky." Now she was serious—and always clever. After she "made" John install a secret door leading to the outside from his private bedroom—so she wouldn't have to see him leaving in the middle of the night to meet Ava Gardner[1]—the press wanted more details. Maureen simply quipped about John's busy social life and never mentioned Ava.

After their wedding, Maureen and John expected a bright future; like most newlyweds, they never factored in the broken childhoods they brought to the marriage—John's being the most severely damaged. John's young life had a dark side impossible to ignore since it still ruled his often erratic behavior. Maureen had her own disturbing history, having been consistently belittled as a child by her own mother. Rather than rewrite herself,

68

Maureen chose silence about her childhood and said no more. When Farrow married Maureen in 1936 and the children came, they created a family of seven much like themselves. They were devout Catholics who lived by strict rules. In society they attended to the everyday business of running a home with seven children. They took care, writing polite letters to business associates and higher-ups in the Catholic Church, to which they were extremely active in their devotion. They wrote thank-yous to friends who donated time or money to the Church and responded promptly to thank-yous received for favors doled out to others. But beneath the ruled behavior lay an emptiness made of repression and the aversion to grief. Sooner or later the train would have to pull into the station. Unable to shake their traumatic histories, they had no choice but to bring them on their journey. Locked up but always in tow, these histories eventually revealed themselves, putting the Farrows' lives on the fast track until they collided head-on in the inevitable train wreck that awaited them.

Maureen spent enormous energy sweeping much of the Farrows' lives under the carpet. It seemed her nature to exhibit a quiet, balanced demeanor—and to deny to others that any demons flew at her. Living in the public eye heightened it. In interviews throughout the years, she'd make light of John Farrow's obsessive womanizing, verbally chipping away at it until it seemed merely one of Farrow's idiosyncrasies instead of the full-blown perversion that it was.

John may have wanted a large family to compensate for *his* family running off on him, as it were. How would that fit in with his sense of isolation that was by now a troublesome aspect of his personality? His kind of solitary also meant being self-absorbed and abrasive, liable to erupt at hearing any opinion different from his own. Almost without intending it, solitude was not only Farrow's best friend, but it was his sustenance— he'd spent the better part of his life seeking it out. Having to oblige a family would chip away at it and throw his life out of alignment. He'd already abandoned one family, Felice and their daughter. He was his father, Thomas, all over again.

Yet, he was more grounded when he and Maureen married. He had the makings of what could be a sterling career. He would easily catch up with Maureen's popularity with movie audiences and studio heads. He had little talent for or interest in winning popularity contests, however. He'd rather do the work because it fulfilled him. But he had little consciousness or awareness of himself in the world and the behavior it required. When his lack of self-awareness caused problems with others in his world, he was helpless. His needs superseded others' needs; that would never change. There was trouble ahead.

Maureen probably had, by now, torn up the long shopping list of John Farrow's negatives, the least of which was his insatiable need to have sex with every woman he could get his hands on. She ignored every part of him she abhorred: his rudeness, his self-absorption, his bad temper, his difficulty getting along with most everyone he knew (including himself). She especially disliked his habit of rubbing his genitals up against her when they were on the dance floor. And she would never forget how hurt she was when he ran off to Tahiti with a young starlet and stayed three months—all because she was on location out of town. Lining up these grievances in her mind got Maureen nowhere. She wanted "Bad Boy Johnny Farrow" and she would have him. For her husband, for keeps.

She seemed the type of woman who was made for motherhood. She appeared cool and calm while throwing off a negative thought or comment with a little laugh tossed over her shoulder. Did her interviews in women's magazines show merely her steadiness? Was there something else that helped her up? Was it her deep faith in God that not only steadied her but also helped her avert her eyes from the harsh realities of life? It was still too early to tell.

Hollywood would long remember the marriage of Maureen O'Sullivan and John Farrow. Far from Hollywood, Maureen's father had announced the upcoming nuptials, from the O'Sullivan home in Ireland.

The announcement had triggered a flurry of events, from Maureen's huge bridal shower to gossip columnists stepping over news reporters and photographers to get a word with the bride-to-be. Maureen was everywhere; she inspired the latest Hollywood frenzy; her picture graced the covers of women's and fan magazines from coast to coast. Averting her face from logic, Maureen married John in a large church ceremony. What else could she do? She loved him. They would live a charmed life, she decided, and for the first few years of their marriage, they lived out their plans for building a house in Beverly Hills, thereby stabilizing their life together. Soon enough they pined away for each other as the physical separations began: Johnny went to war; Maureen went on location.

Eventually, Maureen gave up her career to bear and raise seven children; as they came into the world, John Farrow adored each one. The couple could not wait for the day that each could stop traveling.

The birth of the Farrows' first child (on May 30) was big news in 1939 Hollywood. The *Los Angeles Times* featured a lengthy article on the arrival in its June 22, 1939 edition:

> "Now isn't it just like Hollywood," someone is bound to exclaim—"a star having a baby just at the same time that the character she plays in a picture has one." But MGM explains earnestly that *Tarzan Finds a Son* was written as a part of the Tarzan series long before Michael Damien O'Sullivan-Farrow was thought of, and furthermore the Tarzan son is adopted. Well, maybe so, maybe so!
>
> No, he isn't a "system baby." Why, Maureen doesn't even know what a system baby is! But he is having wonderful care, is taking his nourishment at nature's fount, and mama Maureen, being a bit old-fashioned, is going to rock him to sleep if she feels like it. So there![2]

Michael Damien Farrow led a privileged life as the firstborn of a pair of successful Hollywood celebrities. He was christened by Archbishop John J. Cantwell at the Chapel of the Immaculate Heart at St. Vincent's Hospital in Los Angeles.[3] And, after his birth, Louis B. Mayer's wife sent the Farrows a wire of congratulations, adding: "Give me first option on your son's services." Michael received so many gifts from Hollywood's elite that John and Maureen had to purchase only two items for their son, a bed and a clothes basket. Actor Lionel Barrymore supplied the silver porringer set.[4]

Hollywood also had other news on its hands: the war in Europe meant that the United States' involvement in World War II was inevitable. Despite the prospect of war, Maureen decided to travel to England to film *Busman's Honeymoon* for MGM, leaving John at home with Michael. Per the *New York Times*: "Maureen O'Sullivan, film actress, sailed on the Queen Mary of the Cunard White Star line yesterday with her 18-year-old sister, Sheila. The actress said she had made up her mind to carry out her plans yesterday morning after a telephone conversation with her husband, John Farrow. . . . Mr. Farrow had talked with friends in London and had told his wife that there was no reason to fear a visit abroad."[5]

But as soon as she arrived, MGM began hedging its bets and made plans to recall its American stars to Hollywood.

In the meantime, however, John wrote her constantly. Despite the ups and downs of their six-plus-year romance and John's reputation as a bad boy, the pair expressed their love for each other on an almost daily basis: John wrote:

> I am dashing off these few lines between "takes." Work is swinging along very nicely today, this is due to a happy and accomplished cast and crew. We are working at the studio today and the heat doesn't bother us so much on the stage but yesterday it was awful. We were working at the ranch and extras were falling to the right and left. The heat wave

hit Los Angeles about two days after you left and has continued since.

I am glad to report that everything is progressing serenely at the house. Your son could not be enjoying better health, gaining steadily seldom weeping and as far as I can see continually smiling and laughing. Although it didn't seem to distress him the new formula the doctor tried last week didn't seem to sit very well on his little tummy so this week the formula was changed from fresh milk to tinned milk. I believe this is a protection against the changing standards of the dairies. Anyway, whatever the reason, Mickey seems to be thriving on it.

This morning I played with him for almost an hour—from 6:30 to 7:30—with Olive's permission of course.

I had lunch with the Archbishop on Monday and a Chinese bishop. The latter is very young and one of the most striking prelates I ever met. In spite of his race he stands 6'4" and resembles the Pope. Like his Holiness he speaks nine languages fluently.[6]

And on the very next day:

Well, here's some news from home. Again I am dictating between "shots" on the set. I don't know how interesting it is to you but I will babble on anyhow. By the way, you don't have to answer these letters. I know how you feel about writing and this is very easy for me.

Today is Thursday. Yesterday was the nurse's day off and when I returned home from the studio about seven o'clock I discovered that Mickey had slept, fortunately for me, one full hour past his regular feeding time so I had the fun of supporting his bottle and then after playing with him for a while I took him to my bedroom and he slept with me until about midnight when his nurse returned. She took him from me but this morning I was awake bright and early listening to the war news so I carried him in and left him on my bed—gurgling and cooing—while I dressed, read the paper and had my breakfast.

Speaking about the war news it has been well covered—too well covered—by commentators in every European country. Every half hour or so the assistants turn the radio on and tune in on London, Paris, Rome and Warsaw and we hear the latest information and rumors in these countries. It is all very thrilling but by the time you get this letter I suppose, and sincerely hope, that the whole thing has been settled. I can't imagine why Hitler should really want to go to war—surely he must know that the moment the conflict starts the ex-corporal will be pushed into the background by the head staff in high command of the German Army, which even though it is no longer Imperial, still keeps its pre-war standards.[7]

And two days later:

Here it is Saturday and still we don't know whether there will be a war or not. I think I might as well acquaint you with my status as a combatant. It does not look like I will be a combatant at all for Aubrey received a letter from the Embassy yesterday which stated my services will not be needed for a while anyhow. He said that I am earmarked for some sort of position over here but in any event I shall be seeing you—perhaps even before this letter reaches you in Ireland—for Thau telephoned to assure me that MGM is definitely not going to make the picture in England and that you are to be sent home on a neutral vessel.

Dorothy Cooper was over last night to see the baby and Cooper stayed on to talk about the war. Both he and I would like to be in it very much except for two reasons—Dorothy and you. Hope Lighton, Anne Warner and several other people have telephoned to inquire about you.

So that the garden will be in order for your return I am having Harry put in a couple of men to weed and sow the winter plants next week.

I must say that sentiment is all pro-English and I have not heard one single word in favor of Hitler or his regime. The British Consuls in all cities have been besieged with applicants to join the British Army but so far they have not accepted anybody saying there is no need for any one as yet.

This must be rather a disjointed and dull letter but until twelve I have been on a stuffy process stage so I have a headache and feel rather stupid. I am ending this now for the time being.[8]

And five days later:

Darling:

This letter is arriving by the plane that is bringing you back. To use the local vernacular—am I glad. I never realized before how much of a part you play in my life. In fact you are my life and I am thoroughly miserable without you.

I am glad we got tickets for you on the Clipper. When the war news came I was alarmed at the thought of you coming back across the Atlantic. Not that there would be any great danger coming home on a neutral ship but because I thought a week on the ocean would be nerve-wracking at such a time. M.G.M. were willing to help in any way that they could but they seemed to be in their usual confused state so with the help of Merian Cooper, whose brother is Vice-president of Pan-American, we got tickets for you.

If you have a chance phone Admiral Drax and tell him that I should like to go into active service under him if possible. There has been some talk of using my services in some capacity at the Embassy in Washington but I would prefer to do the real thing. Tell him I can quality as a watch-keeper on a large ship and, I believe, can assume even greater responsibility on a smaller craft.

Mickey is flourishing. Today he weighs fourteen pounds five ounces. John Loder and his wife came over last night and she thinks—like everybody else who sees him—that he is superb.[9]

After war in Europe was declared, MGM recalled Maureen to Hollywood; her Boeing Clipper airship arrived in Los Angeles on September 16, 1939. John and four-month-old Michael met her at the terminal.[10]

Though as early as 1936 John had placed his name on the "Emergency List" of the Royal Canadian Navy (RCN) for "service in time of war," it wasn't until November 1939 that he joined the RCN in Vancouver, stating that he was "a fairly competent seaman As per the *(Adelaide) Advertiser*: "His wife, the actress, Maureen O'Sullivan, will settle in Vancouver with their baby 'to knit socks.'"[11]

She didn't; she stayed in Hollywood to make *Pride and Prejudice*.

John was appointed an acting lieutenant in the RCN Volunteer Reserve in Ottawa in March 1940, and was appointed the Controller of Naval Information in June of that year. Still, the messages from John to Maureen were incessant.

On April 2:

Mrs John Farrow, 630 North Alpine Drive, Beverly Hills [*sic*] Calif

You have no idea my sweetheart how much happier I am since I heard your voice thank you and thank you again your devoted John[12]

On May 12:

Michael Damien Farrow, 630 North Alpine Drive, Beverleyhills [sic] Calif

76

Dear Mickey I am sorry that such a pitiful thing as a war prevents me from helping you celebrate such a glorious occasion as Mothers Day stop celebration for you it is because your mama is the best mother in a world where almost any mother is braver and nicer than we men never forget that my son

Your daddy.[13]

On May 14:

My Sweetheart,

Today is your birthday. There is so much to say that I am not going to attempt to use words and paper and pencil. I think you know how I feel about our separation—and this war which caused it—and my prayers and hopes for our future.[14]

On May 24:

Well Darling,

Am exhausted—not really—husband is writing you. I've been on the run for nearly 48 hours. Things are happening and I've been in the midst of them. I can't tell—same old story—but I've just left the Admiral and am full of enthusiasm for him. He is one of those chaps—also, so scant these days—who is a real [illegible]; the sort of man you would like to go into action with.

I regret that I can't explain, but we nearly had all our plans changed. I volunteered for something but was turned down. This morning I was excited. I was lectured and told I had a job to do here.

Saw Bishop Nelligan for a few minutes (he is Chaplain-in-chief). I believe I told you he had bought several Demiens and today he brought them to be autographed. He had just returned from his diocese and was full of stories of the quintuplets. It was the first time they had seen him in uniform and Cecily asked if he had joined the mounties. They also wanted to know who the friend was driving his car. "My chauffeur" replied the Bishop. "Do you know what a chauffeur is?" "Oh yes," said one of the girls "A man who knows everything."

When I think of it the little tot was not far wrong. Most chauffeurs assume that attitude. The quintuplets only speak French but nevertheless the Bishop says he will arrange for them to give Mickey a picnic—just them—when he comes up. Can you imagine five little girls making a fuss over the little thing.

[illegible] sweetheart

John

P.S. I hope Mick's party is a huge success

[in margin]: I loved the picture of him. Thanks and more thanks[15]

In August 1940, Maureen traveled by car to Ottawa to spend time with John, where the pair entertained visiting dignitaries and refugees from Europe—but then MGM called her back to Hollywood to costar in *Maisie Was a Lady*.

Still, their separation played heavily on them, especially Maureen. The *Los Angeles Times* reported, "From Canada comes rumor that Maureen O'Sullivan, madly in love with her husband, John Farrow (director who quit the movies to join Britain's war), may volunteer as a Red Cross nurse in order to follow him over there."[16]

In February 1941, John finished an officer's course and shipped out to sea, where he served three weeks on anti-submarine vessels in convoys in the North and South Atlantic.[17]

In April 1941, he was loaned to the Royal Navy and appointed to HMS Goshawk naval base in Trinidad, where he was an assistant to the senior British naval officer, Curacao. Before shipping out, he had a two-week furlough and returned to Hollywood to be with Maureen and Michael—but was scheduled to return to the war May 20—ten days shy of his son's birthday.[18]

For Maureen, the tears and heartache, the attendant anxieties and personal adjustments of the separation, weighed heavily on her.

Protected all of her life—first by her family, then by her husband, no matter their abysmal behavior toward her at times, she was also extremely sentimental in her femininity. It was difficult for her to carry on alone now. At first she fell to pieces:

> I couldn't take it at the beginning. . . . I gave up the large house and moved into a small bungalow, to save money and to escape memories. I wouldn't see anyone. I shut myself up with my own misery and refused to go out. I wasn't making a picture just then and didn't care if I never did. I stayed home with the baby and we retired at the same early hour. The more I secluded myself, the more wretched I felt, but I didn't have the will to go out.
>
> Then I received a call to report for another Tarzan picture. [*Tarzan's Secret Treasure,* which began production in July 1941.] People have often asked me if I haven't ever regretted being in the Tarzan series because it typed me and might have cost me other roles. I never thought one way or the other about it, but now I have a definite feeling about Tarzan—a feeling of gratitude—because Tarzan saved me. I was listless, worried, uninterested in things up until the moment I walked on the set, and then suddenly my whole viewpoint changed. When I saw Johnny Weissmuller and the same director and crew, I felt their friendliness leap right out to me. There were the same jokes, the same teasing. It was the first time in months that I laughed, and I felt better immediately.[19]

In late 1941, John contracted typhoid fever and was dispatched back to Naval Headquarters in Ottawa. He was given a medical discharge in January 1942, and returned to Hollywood, where he directed *Wake Island*, earning him a Best Director nod from the New York Film Critics.

In July 1943, he was commissioned an Honorary Commander in the RCN, possibly because he and Maureen were Hollywood royalty and "the powers-that-be at Naval Service Headquarters enjoyed rubbing shoulders with them. Farrow's Hollywood connections also provided access to a powerful public relations machine."[20] After returning to Hollywood, he entertained men from RCN ships when they visited Los Angeles.

In 1953, he received a CBE (Commander of the British Empire), one of the highest awards given by Great Britain to noncombatants during wartime; it's not known what exactly he did to earn his CBE.[21]

During times of war, separation from loved ones, families disrupted, and husbands or wives or sweethearts parted by battles across the ocean, tends to create romantic longing for the absent one—even if they were at war themselves before parting. The absent ones become idealized simply because they're not around. Yet when the separations end and everyday life resumes, the letdown assumes its former place, bringing with it the same disappointment, anger, and possibly resentment. No one has changed. So it was with John and Maureen. They married, saw the birth of their first son, Michael, and fell into that pattern. When one of them had to leave home, hearts became heavy with sadness just as letters gushed with loving words. With John in the service or Maureen on location, love blossomed in letters, and the future looked bright, at least on paper. Then the inevitable: their everyday lives returned, bringing with it the John Farrow who eventually and inevitably pulled away from his family.

The family grew nonetheless. As much as Maureen loved giving birth, she was nonplussed afterward, wondering what she was supposed to do with those children. But these issues were quickly solved: the kids had nannies that took care of the children and the problem.

John Farrow would eventually forgo evenings with the family, holing up in his bedroom-office instead. He'd much rather keep company with a book, a manuscript, or a movie script; he particularly disliked *any* children around when he was trying to work. There he worked, free to write, or to concentrate on other subjects that engaged him, such the Catholic Church, and for sure, a woman he found attractive and wanted to bed down. There he might release himself from the reins of the world around him and perhaps ruminate on John Farrow, the titan of clashing and opposing desires, each vying for first place in his psyche. Surely he needed this time alone, solo and untethered, to attend to forces in himself so at odds that they might redesign the rest of his life.

Yet Farrow found innumerable paths to each of these. He was keen on providing for his family, even spending time with each of his children now and then. But his bourgeoning career as a director became a virtual pot of gold that offered him leaves of absence from the brood when he needed to travel to location shoots on his films. The shoots provided fulfillment for his other needs as well: his artistic expression on each film, and, of course, endless opportunities to sleep with women other than Maureen. Both his family and his career grew larger by the day.

Each was and still is integral to understanding John Farrow the man and John Farrow the father. His family came to reflect the man himself. There were traumas and tragedies that came visiting and then stayed. He shaped his family by his reactions to them. They became the legacy he left them. Before them, before the legacy, there was John Farrow, Hollywood director.

Six

THE LOST ONE

Mr. Farrow, it seems, departed hastily from Nice for Tahiti, where he is to make a South Sea film, not because of a broken romance (ostensibly) with Diana Churchill, but because he has quarreled with [actor] George Robey, whose notions of how Sancho Panza ought to die in the filming of "Don Quixote" differed from those of the assistant director.[1]

In Hollywood, an assistant director rarely received the press coverage a director earned—unless, you were John Farrow. In his early Hollywood days, from the moment he stood poised to take a leap off the diving board at The Garden of Allah, Johnny Farrow's bad-boy behavior ensured his frequent appearance in fan magazines and gossip columns. Later on, Farrow actually discouraged the press knowing too much about him; he backed away from publicity whenever he could. If only he hadn't told so many stories that weren't true, such as the one above. The press and the public loved nothing more. Not even a director yet, Farrow already demanded the crew do things his way. There would be much more of that to come.

Farrow's time in Hollywood lasted roughly thirty years, during which he worked in every genre, with every top star and wrote scripts as entertaining as his virtuosity with the camera was skilled. But after his death in 1963 his name eventually dropped out of sight. He never found his permanent seat in the annals of Hollywood film history.

John Farrow was and still is an unsolved mystery to his family and to those who worked with him; he lingers on as a talented director by means of a select group of films he made—such as *Alias Nick Beal, The Big Clock,* and *Where Danger Lives*—considered classic examples of film noir, not only by means of their stark black-and-white composition but by the dark, brooding, even psychotic sensibility of their characters. They continue to spark debate for their brilliant psychological and also technical achievements. *Five Came Back*, released in 1939, set the standard for the airplane disaster film; *Wake Island* (1942) is the prototypical modern war film.

Yet Farrow the man, and the life he led, remain a huge question mark that still haunts shuttered soundstages and movie houses. A serious consideration of John Farrow and his film aesthetics is all but missing in action in our continuing conversation about Hollywood film history.

Few film aficionados talk or write about Farrow. For the most part, Hollywood history has lost track of him. Even though some of his movies draw raves from film fans, inspiring deep discussion among aficionados and renewed surprise that the director is hardly talked about and as revered as he should be.

Farrow's characters often start out as realistically drawn human beings who, sooner than later, distort what is realistic or find a landscape that seems odd. A closer look reveals their eccentricities. They stand on shaky ground and operate with shaky mental equipment, ultimately taking radical psychological paths in order to survive. Their finely tuned psychologies cohere with Farrow's inventive cinematic techniques: especially his infamous long takes that traverse his sinister cities and shadowy streets where fog rushes in to obscure faces, even the entire frame itself.

Despite the praise Farrow's artistry usually inspires, it seems momentary at best, after which a Farrow film heads back into the corridors of lost memory. Only rarely does anyone remember John Farrow.

One of these rare moments is the recent documentary *John Farrow: Hollywood's Man in the Shadows* (2021). Two Australian documentary filmmakers, Frans Vandenburg and Claude Gonzalez, have been thinking quite a lot about John Farrow. For more than a decade, Vandenburg and Gonzalez have searched Hollywood and the globe looking for traces of John Farrow. If no one knows him, they most likely wondered, why not? What's back there in the shadows with him? Their finished documentary, which debuted at Il Cinema Ritrovato in Bologna in summer 2021 is intended to reinstate Hollywood's handsome mystery man to his rightful place in movie history.

The documentary confirms John Farrow's sizable filmmaking talents by scrutinizing a myriad of his almost fifty films. Yet, the filmmakers unintentionally drive home once again the difficulty of knowing John Farrow the man. He still doesn't step out from behind the curtain. Farrow the man, even the artist, proves elusive still. The documentary gets closer, making it clear that Farrow was an artist riddled with unsolvable psychological conflicts. But the documentary travels no further and doesn't venture into those conflicts, nor do the filmmakers question how those conflicts might have come to shape Farrow's aesthetic, something that can be distilled from looking closely at his work. If you want to understand that aesthetic, film critic Chris Fujiwara points out in his review of the documentary, then the film leaves more questions than it answers.

In this film, Farrow remains a mystery still, his life and his films escaping scrutiny. "For all his facility with the medium [of film], there is definitely something in Farrow's work that does not belong to just to cinema," Fujiwara couldn't help but wonder, and then conclude: Farrow's art must belong to something much bigger than just the cinema. But to what, then? This could be read as a suggestion that Farrow's cinema lies beyond anyone's understanding? Is it that confounding and unreachable?[2]

The fact is: Farrow's art, Farrow's films, are hardly obscure, his aesthetic hardly mysterious. But to many, his landscape, the psychological place where the action occurs, where the characters live, is that of the unconscious, a messy terrain where unwanted, painful, even overwhelming material and emotions live, laying low, as it were, because they are often unacceptable to our conscious, waking life. In assigning the action to this fearful place, Farrow's films ask the audience to travel there as well, a psychological place difficult to tolerate, often too uncomfortable to confront or to acknowledge.

Farrow's films seem worked over by the unconscious, where disjointed, off-kilter and often contradictory elements make the everyday world a bizarre dreamscape, just as Farrow himself lives in a contradictory place. For him, that landscape was a kind of self-creation, a psychic society of one that he was forced to invent when his parents, his context for himself in the world, failed to materialize, or, we might say, was ripped away. It would only make sense that this landscape is also the natural habitat for Farrow's stories and characters. Since it is the business of films to hook us by our natural gravitation to an identification with its characters, the chances we live in the same frightening landscape as do his characters, the chances look pretty good.

Farrow's films show us the deplorable, the sinister, and the malicious. They wrap tightly around unexpected, and often sadistic, thought and behavior. To take them in is to accept that evil and psychic chaos live within us—and that even while we don't see them, they live all around us. It is like being able to stand on an empty soundstage at the end of the day and believe that the sounds that linger are remnants of something we cannot see, a drama once vibrant with life but now gone.

Farrow worked during the salad days of classic Hollywood, in the decades just before and after World War II. Male screen heroes were simple to read: they could be tough like Humphrey "Bogie" Bogart, rough and hard-nosed like John Wayne, even smart and sensitive like Spencer Tracy. Whatever they happened to be, they were gentlemen somewhere in their souls. They displayed an adherence to social and cultural codes of behavior and usually stayed in character. Their identity is dependable, easily deciphered. Women are more or less soft, accepting, even obedient (there are exceptions, of course). But if their sexuality becomes overt, they cannot also remain passive. They can only be whores then. Only two cultural stereotypes are truly open to women in the cinema. They must inhabit the stereotype of a whore, prostitute, or any other woman who has gone astray. Their sexuality shows their downfall. Motherhood and domesticity do not go hand in hand with a woman who is also a sexual being. Mothers nurture; the woman who beckons her man is more likely to take him down.

In the grand scheme of things, American cinema reflects the cultural codes that have long been locked in place. But Farrow's work eventually corrupts these codes, conflicts with these stereotypes. It wasn't that he consciously sought to collide with them. Each of his major films disclose a director who simply possesses those codes in his vernacular. In a cinematic time of identifiable (and comforting) symbols, characters, and behaviors, Farrow could scramble them, turn them on their heads, and render them unpredictable and unruly.

In spite of his success as a talented screenwriter and director, John Farrow seemed out of place in Hollywood. Daughter Mia writes in her autobiography and repeats in countless interviews that in her mind, her father was a talented director who, at the same time, had little respect for filmmaking itself as a true art form. The self-deprecation might be understandable (as a maneuver to deflect attention away from himself). And, when Farrow earned praise and big box office for the 1939 psychological thriller *Five Came Back*, sending audiences into a state of worry over which passengers in the story might make it home after a plane crash in the Amazon jungle, some of the praise had to touch him deeply. Yet he kept silent.

His films are his psychic property alone, born of his strangely arranged imagination, one that looks different from anyone else's, out of whack, we could say, aligned with an intellect that used a different lexicon from the rest of us. Farrow's films seem out of sync with the work of his peers, because Farrow was persistently out of step with others and out of sorts with himself.

While Farrow's characters and stories appear to behave and live according to the conventions of the time, in truth, they collide with these conventions. They emerge from and live in Farrow's unconscious; and while they try to coexist with rules and delineations of conventional society, they can't. They are different. In Farrow's *Where Danger Lives*, for example, Faith Domergue's character, Margo, appears to be a woman whose unhappiness stems from her husband, Frederick's mistreatment of her: he manipulates her and demeans her in front of others. He's a sadistic older gent who so intimidates her that she's even afraid to leave him. In truth, however, she is a psychotic who soon kills her husband and tricks her doctor friend, Jeff, into believing he killed Frederick. Then she uses Jeff to help her make her escape to Mexico.

Farrow's characters don't really fall into place with others in their society; instead they are threatening to others and to the urban landscape, bringing about disorder and chaos. He will easily take the most rational, conventional character in a script and undermine his stability. As a mirror of Farrow himself, this character might become erratic, unreadable, and untrustworthy. Farrow's film art is indeed bigger than the cinema; it belongs to a landscape much bigger, much more disturbing and dangerous than merely cinema—the landscape of his unconscious.

Director Rouben Mamoulian intuitively said, "Every film is the autobiography of its maker." As with any art, its maker is everywhere present in it. But no art makes the point as much as a film or a theater piece where actual human beings replicate the artist's voice and behavior themselves. Should the filmmaker consciously intend to reproduce his life or himself on the screen, then he creates autobiography, which ultimately is fiction and even wish-fulfillment. But the most interesting kind of autobiography in the director's work is the kind he or she *didn't* intend, when the director's thoughts, feelings and opinions *unconsciously* slip into the film. Reading a film for a director's unconscious material is the truest way to understand that director as artist.

Early in his career, Farrow uncharacteristically stepped briefly into public view when he helped market his 1938 film, the Kay Francis vehicle *My Bill*, "revealing" how he uses various psychological approaches to coax good performances from different actors: "According to Farrow, the best work can be obtained from Miss Francis by polite but business-like suggestions. Anita Louise needs picturesque comments that will amuse her and arouse her imagination. Bonita Granville needs encouragement and praise, while Bobby Jordan requires occasional sarcasm."[3]

The blurb points to a certain irony in Farrow's words. With his reputation as the town's most notorious womanizer, Farrow would seem the last person to be doling out advice about directing actresses, let alone even finding one who didn't hate him. The word passed around by actresses who had worked with him was that Farrow was one of the most toxic directors any one of them had ever worked with. The sentiment that lingered day and night on soundstages was clear: Avoid working with Mr. Farrow at *any* cost. Of course, this wasn't always possible: sometimes an actress had to eat and pay bills. Then again, some actresses just didn't listen. Those who watched her ascend those particular steps could often be heard muttering under their breath, "There but for the Grace of God go I." And Mia Farrow always maintained that her father didn't want her to become an actress for one reason: he simply didn't like actresses, period. He also said he'd never met a happy one (certainly not the actresses he worked with, for obvious reasons).

Another brief mention in the *New York Times* around that time opened the issue even wider. Farrow disliked male actors as much as female actors. His was an equal playing field of derision: "Mr. Farrow made no strenuous effort to refute the allegation but he tempered it somewhat with the observation that 'most actors are spoiled, selfish children. Any director who gives the stars all the close-ups they want is automatically a wonderful fellow. I guess they think I'm tough because I don't work that way.'"[4]

For Farrow, directing films was personal, almost secret information between John Farrow and himself. He talked to his crew as necessary, but his overall objectives and aesthetic choices were pocketed, and unless a producer or an actor he trusted (say, Ray Milland or pal George Macready) had an objection or an idea to share, Farrow's choices were not open to discussion. He may not have considered film directing a serious or legitimate art form, but that didn't cool his passion for the (extremely) long take or the close tracking shot, each considered to be masterfully executed in his work. No matter what the issue, Farrow wasn't having a discussion with anyone but himself. To the extent that his name is mentioned at all, the conversation has more to do with the trouble John Farrow created on his sets than about the films he directed.

PART TWO

Seven
WHERE THE KISSING
NEVER STOPS

John Farrow would carve out a career from his bifurcated self: being half gifted filmmaker, half bull in the china shop, bumping up against his actors and crew, stirring up trouble, even without intending to do so. Farrow's sadistic streak, it was said, was a chronological streak of disdain that shadowed his entire career. The stories seem almost endless—as with the film *China*, which began production on October 27, 1942. As Hedda Hopper dished in her syndicated gossip column on December 11, 1942, "I wonder why [there are] so many battles between director John Farrow, actress Loretta Young and actor Alan Ladd on *China*. Could it be a bad story? Could be . . ."[1]

Actually, much of the trouble stemmed from star Loretta Young's objection to the moment in *China* (1943) when her character condones the suicide of one of the Chinese girls in the story. Young said she would not propagandize suicide as the answer to anything. She was a devout Catholic and claimed that John Farrow and Buddy DeSylva, Paramount's production chief, had agreed to cut the scene but hadn't. It reappeared in the script further on during production. Again, Young refused and threatened to leave the film. Ultimately, the scene was not shot.

While John was battling on film sets, Maureen was home arguing with no one. Instead, she was living out her decision to put her movie career on the back burner and take up motherhood full-time. She gave birth to the couple's second child, Patrick Villiers Farrow, on November 27, 1942, in Los Angeles. Miss Young and John Farrow must have made amends quickly after clashing on the set of *China*; at the time of Patrick's birth, she was named the child's godmother. Who would have imagined that some years later, Patrick would find himself before a television camera in "The Glass Cage," an episode of the Loretta Young drama anthology series that aired on TV on August 20, 1960? The Farrow-Young relationship may well have had something to do with Patrick's short-lived acting career at the age of eighteen (he had little interest in performing).[2]

One of Classic Hollywood's legendary battlefields was the ongoing conflict between film directors and the Production Code, which the studios heartily enforced. The Production Code swept into Hollywood in 1934, setting down rules to harness any offensive, insulting, and wayward sexual and moral conduct. In an age of gangster pictures and murder mysteries, the killer must do penance by the film's end. A woman can show only a certain amount of skin. A director tried any means possible to get around the code for the film he or she wanted to make. Raoul Walsh shot every scene he could with his signature bawdiness; no matter what the scissors cut out, there was still enough footage left to spell "Raoul Walsh."

Farrow found his own way of avoiding producers' and censors' cuts: he tried as much as possible to not do "protection shots," which are conservative, formalized shots that can be used to replace a more daring shot that doesn't quite work. In that way, his films couldn't be remade in the cutting room.[3] Many other directors enjoyed playing cat and mouse with the Production Code, getting as close to the edge of "decency" as they could by stretching what was acceptable as far over to the side as they could: for example, Marilyn Monroe's revealing dress in Billy Wilder's 1959 *Some Like It Hot*. A piece of netting decently covered her breasts while still revealing their entire contour, leaving little to the imagination. Farrow and the Code would soon meet up again, and with curious results.

The war had not yet ended, and Farrow, much like other Hollywood directors who'd seen combat overseas, had not yet settled back into the Hollywood wars waiting at home. But the family grew nonetheless: children would wait for no one. Maureen gave birth to their third child, Maria de Lourdes Villiers Farrow, on February 9, 1945. The first of four girls in the family, Maria could only say Mia for her first name, so Mia she became, and the family followed suit. John Farrow couldn't have known that the little girl would grow up to be a kind of doppelgänger of her father, mirroring his love of reading, intellectual pursuits, and, as an adult, his near double in her delight of pretending to be someone other than herself when the situation called for it. Nor could he have imagined that her fame in the film business would far outweigh his own.

Mia was an exception among her siblings in later seeking a film career. The others wanted to take different roads eventually. John Charles, the youngest Farrow son, born on September 6, 1946, a year after Mia, would have his choice of a career when the time came. But no Farrow child had a choice about schooling. John Charles, like Mia, like every other of their siblings, got in line and marched straight into the unforgiving strictness of a Catholic education. Parochial boarding school would eventually come looking for Charles (and, ironically, he would later look back at boarding school as being on vacation compared to living at home with his father).[4]

The month John Charles was born brought with it the birth of another child named John, and a bizarre and somewhat horrific backstory that may be truth or may be fiction. Farrow's skirt-chasing took a turn toward the bizarre because he came too close to the infamous Black Dahlia murder case. In 1945 he began an affair with dancer and actress Lillian Lenorak (whose stage name was Lillian Hamilton). He met Lenorak through his friendship with Los Angeles doctor George Hill Hodel Jr. and

Hodel's wife, Dorothy Harvey (John Huston's ex-wife); Hodel was one of the suspects in the murder of Elizabeth Short (the Black Dahlia) in January 1947. According to ex-LAPD homicide detective and Hodel's son, Steve Hodel—who believes his father was the Black Dahlia murderer as well as a possible serial killer—and documentary filmmakers Claude Gonzalez and Frans Vandenburg, Lenorak got pregnant by Farrow and gave birth to a son, John Lenorak, in 1946.[5] Later in life John Lenorak took "Farrow" as his last name.

Lillian Lenorak herself was brutally murdered on November 7, 1959, after a quarrel with her lover, Hollywood television and film lenses manufacturer Dr. Frank Back, who left her on a road near Palm Springs; she was beaten to death by a disturbed twenty-one-year-old man who lived nearby and randomly attacked and killed her.[6]

At this time in his career, John Farrow was successfully (albeit often unintentionally) convincing all his coworkers that the conflict he brought to any production was indigenous; it came with the territory, as it were; conflict was simply part of Farrow's makeup, part of the package. When Farrow helmed his next picture, the classic sea adventure, Richard Henry Dana's *Two Years Before the Mast* (1946), which had just landed at Paramount as an Alan Ladd vehicle, more cannons were fired behind the scenes than on the big screen itself.

Farrow was the logical choice to helm a sea tale and was brought on to direct the production. In little time, sexual harassment reared its familiar head on the set, a clear indication that Farrow was on the premises. This time her name was Esther Fernandez, a pretty young actress who enjoyed great popularity in her home country, Mexico. Producer DeSylva wanted her face on screen for *Two Years Before the Mast*. As it turned out, Esther's stay in Hollywood was tumultuous (code for on-again, off-again) yet mercifully short-lived.

Smarter than many before her, Esther knew who to consult when Farrow hit on her. She wrote a letter to Hedda Hopper,

Hollywood's town crier, for assistance and whatever else she could get from this (Louella Parsons, Hollywood's other gossip diva, was already taken, snapped up by the Farrow family as designated Godmother to the seven Farrow kids).

Esther's timing was impeccable. She expressed her unhappiness on the set, describing all of Farrow's "indiscretions" aimed at her. The missive reached Hedda just as Hedda began corresponding with *Life* magazine writer Francis Sill Wickware for a large spread in *Life* on Hedda's life as a "columnist." Wickware had recently asked Hedda to describe her "working habits and method." Hedda offered full coverage. She told Wickware she had been in the business so long, thirty years or so, that she'd probably changed the diapers of many of the day's stars, and she told Wickware of the gripes as well:

> When there's a choice bit of dirt or injustice going on [any day] during the making of a picture, I know it by nightfall. . . . For instance, one of the things that is pretty disturbing right now is Esther Fernandez, who is the biggest star in Mexico City. She was under contract to Paramount; they did nothing for her. She went back to Mexico City and made two outstanding films. Buddy DeSylva persuaded her to come back and be the leading lady in "Two Years Before the Mast." They started it and director Johnny Farrow started giving her the business, which she didn't care to accept. So now the fat's in the fire. I don't know how it's going to turn out because she doesn't want to go on with the picture under these circumstances. DeSylva—who is a hell of a nice guy and he brought her back the second time—he's trying to work it out because he knows if they bitch her up twice our friendly relations with Mexico will go crash. So, I got into the middle of it, and this is just one of those off the record stories you can't use until I find out how the hell it's going to come out.[7]

Esther eventually decided to stay on the picture, with DeSylva's mediation skills still working overtime, no doubt.

Another actor, Howard Da Silva, who portrayed evil Captain Thompson in the picture, recalled an anecdote that said much about another side of Farrow's psychology. The crew who were on hand to witness a scene of punishment had to be dumbstruck at the very least. The scene called for one of the sailors to be flogged by another, part of the punishment the first sailor had coming to him. As much as the one actor flogged the other, Farrow seemed unsatisfied with each take. He asked the flogger to repeat it again, then again, and even again. After a while the actor being flogged couldn't take anymore. The skin on his back was bleeding profusely from the whip, and he was in agonizing pain. At that very moment, Farrow seemed almost to be coming out of a trance. He rushed up to the actor who'd received the flogging and apologized profusely. "I'm so sorry," he repeatedly said. "It's just that I couldn't stop; I was enjoying it all so much!"[8]

Having lost himself in the throes of his own pleasure, Farrow, for the moment, at least, was at war with no one, not even himself. Two years later, however, he made a brilliant turn-about in his masterly *The Big Clock* (1948), the film that sealed his reputation, if there was to be one, as a first-rate director. He put on display (more than likely, unintentionally) a man at war with himself. Farrow showed some true colors, and also showed the extent to which a director's interiority displays itself to the audience. Ray Milland plays George Stroud, editor-in-chief at *Crimeways*, a popular true crime magazine out of Chicago. When the film opens, he is immediately thrown into chaos: a woman has been murdered (for real) and George is assigned by his unsavory and seriously sadistic boss, played by Charles Laughton, to find the murderer in the building—who happens to be him (Laughton). George seems to have important conversations with himself, which become more urgent as he moves closer to looking like the murderer he is seeking. The film displays a splintered main character who must come to grips with himself, pull himself into a whole, even when that seems an almost impossible task. Milland's character is a man broken into pieces, going this way and that, nervous about everything around him, seeming innocent in one scene and guilty in the next. But the truth is difficult to discern amid so much chaos. Is Laughton's sadism going to do him in? Who is truly innocent and who is not? Living a fragmented life is the norm here. This condition exists within the frame relentlessly, beautifully displayed by Farrow, who knows more than he should about living in fragments.

In looking at the majority of films Farrow directed and Farrow's body of work as a whole, there emerges a world that is cracked, disordered, out of whack. But, more so, it is his characters that are psychologically damaged. Some disturbance has taken hold of them, creating an interior battle they can't resolve until it is resolved *for* them.

This kind of involvement in your work had to seem more exciting than anything that could happen at home. Perhaps nothing could compare with the unadulterated joy of self-absorption and creativity a movie set had to offer. Not surprisingly, as the years passed, family ties slowly unraveled. It was not only his flirtatious eye, or his need to isolate himself in his bedroom-office in order to work. His fanaticism about the Catholic Church took up much of his time as well. He wrote books on the subject and entertained members of the Church regularly in the Farrow home. Mia's memoir describes the conversations between Farrow and church members that lasted until all hours of the night. It's been said also that, unbeknownst to his family, after the clergy left the Farrow home, Farrow would wait a few minutes or so and go out looking for prostitutes.[9]

Still, if there was one misery that each Farrow child could count on, it was mandatory enrollment in the unforgiving rigidity of a Catholic education. As a companion piece to this unfortunate aspect of his children's lives, Farrow often became the absolute incarnation of rigidity. He created strict boundaries—both arbitrary and unforgiving—so as to keep the kids in line. If not followed, there was hell to pay: whacks across their bottoms with his belt, verbal abuse, even the shock of an unexpected whack to the body from Farrow's walking stick, which was usually close at hand.[10]

Mia suffered one trauma her other siblings were spared; she contracted polio when she was nine years old, sending her to an isolation unit at Los Angeles General Hospital to lie flat on her back for three weeks. This was a crippling and tragic disease that still affected children in the 1950s—ironically, the same decade Jonas Salk's landmark vaccine to prevent the disease came along. Children lined up at schools around the country to receive the shot in the arm that literally changed the landscape.

Upon Mia's discharge from the hospital, John Farrow came alone to take her home. Maureen hadn't visited her daughter during the "last week" of her hospital stay, Mia recalls in her memoir, *What Falls Away*, "nor was she there when I came home. I was told she was in another hospital resting." This episode in her life would have an emotional charge. Mia would later say, "I was nine when . . . my childhood ended."[11]

Mia Farrow, in her memoir, offers a detailed portrait of day-to-day childhood with parents John and Maureen. She often cites their faults and shortcomings yet takes on the persona of a benevolent narrator, almost a childlike diarist who ultimately wants to forgive anyone she can so as to hold and gather together everyone in her family:

> When I was about ten, I got hopping mad and called the nanny a fat bastard and ran away to the Wonder Bread factory across the Santa Monica tracks. I hid out there for a while and when it got dark I came home. My father was waiting and he whacked me clear across the room. He had an almighty temper.

Another incident involved the siblings cooking up trouble.

> When I was six or seven my brothers and I put together the
> filthiest poem we could think of. We even got it to rhyme.
> Only somehow my mother got hold of it. She said you just
> wait till your father gets home, which was the scariest thing
> imaginable. After a long hellish wait he sent for me. I had
> to hang on to the big beige chair and I thought he'd break
> my back with his walking stick. Jesus he was something.[12]

Mia's terror in waiting for her father suggests that she'd faced
this kind of situation more than once before. Her younger
brother, John, no doubt another recipient of his father's physical
wrath, said years later, "All I can say is that being sent off to
boarding school was like being on vacation."[13]

Maureen O'Sullivan was most likely not a mother who could
always be counted on to protect her children and keep them
out of harm's way. As Maria Roach, Mia's close childhood
friend, noticed, Maureen seemed to have little involvement in
her children's lives. The warning, "Just wait until your father
gets home," might suggest that Maureen was not the one to discipline her children and that it was left to John to play bad cop.
But years later, youngest daughter Stephanie Farrow suggested
otherwise. In 1981, when The League of Woman Voters celebrated its Outstanding Mother Awards at the Sheraton Center
Hotel in New York, Stephanie accepted for her mother and rem-
inisced about O'Sullivan's style of keeping her kids in line. "I
remember her screaming only once or twice, because screaming
wasn't her way. The hairbrush was her thing."[14] One could sur-
mise, then, that it's the little things that matter: at least Steffi and
no doubt each of her siblings were spared the ordeal of having
to listen to their mother yelling at them all the time.

But the albatross in the Farrow home was something larger
than dissenting disciplinary styles. As John Farrow's career took
off, he took off with it—traveling to different film locations

around the globe and into the arms of his leading ladies or other available women. Maureen temporarily put her acting career on hold and stayed at home with their brood to take up motherhood. The result was inevitable. Their separate bedrooms led to separate lives, even separate planes. Living in the same house and looking the part, they were nevertheless oddly estranged from their children and from each other, no matter the energy spent to make it seem otherwise. Indeed, Maria Roach had a close-up, even intimate, view of the Farrows. Roach, the daughter of producer Hal Roach, lived in a kind of palatial residence right next door to the Farrows and spent much of her time inside their home, which she described as "bizarre, almost like two houses":

> There was an adult part we were never allowed to go in. Mr. Farrow read all night long. One of our jobs was to put his ice out in the bar for when he got up. He had his own bedroom with its own entrance. Mrs. Farrow's bedroom was dark green. It was like a sanctuary. If you went there, you had to say your prayers. They were a beautiful family cosmetically, not as perfect inside.[15]

Maureen loved having children, but after giving birth she had absolutely no idea what to do with them, Maria Roach said. It's not likely that she attempted to solve the problem as she spent much of her time in her bedroom: "When you walked into that room, a world apart and separate from John's, you couldn't help notice that it seemed otherworldly. The room was painted dark green, there was a huge crush hanging over Maureen's bed and if you walked in there if you came into the room, she insisted that, before anything else, you kneel down next to the bed and pray."[16]

Of the four Farrow sisters, Prudence Farrow, born on January 20, 1948, in Los Angeles, is closest in age and experience to Mia. In her memoir *Dear Prudence,* her earliest memories of childhood hinge on the unpleasantness of her strict Catholic upbringing. She recalls a time in school with Mia when Mia suffered visions of being visited by the devil, a possible side effect of their mandatory parochial school education.[17] It would seem likely that the strictness of a parochial school would agitate any child's natural curiosity and energy. If nothing else, its frightening aspects left plenty of residual effects.

But even the frightening aspects of the kids' Catholic schooling couldn't rule their lives or take up their thoughts every moment of the day. Now and then the children felt a certain kind of cohesiveness to their lives, as if the family were as united as others looked to be in small community of Beverly Hills. Their lives moved along, bumps and all. They were the children of celebrities; this, they knew even if they didn't give it much thought. It was the life they knew. The girls had the same toys other girls in Beverly Hills had. The three brothers had the family's big backyard, customized cars, innumerable toys, BB guns, even boxing lessons.[18]

It's doubtful that any conflicts at home were enough to halt John Farrow's creative output or his desire to revel in it. Conflict, itself, seemed the very thing that sustained him: for certain it defined, even nourished, much of his best work as a director. Conflict certainly flourishes in Farrow's masterful *The Big Clock* (1948), with Ray Milland fleshing out Farrow's alter ego, George Stroud, a man who lives in chaos.

As the film opens, there's a battle going on in Stroud's mind. He is either a bundle of different voices or manifestations of different psyches. He's having a conversation, or listening to various internal voices (but who are they?), and all this takes place on a screen full of commotion, fast moves, anything that complicates or obstructs our understanding of him. In the opening scene of *The Big Clock*, Milland either talks to himself or carries on an interior stream of consciousness monologue with himself, just as the audience hears it as well. Is he crazy? Is there another conversation going on? The scene leads in various directions at once.

Farrow's 1948 *Night Has a Thousand Eyes* has Edward G. Robinson playing a psychic of sorts who is looking to solve a mystery. We can't tell if he is on the up-and-up or not. But one thing is certain: he suffers terrible guilt because, if he sees a tragedy coming in the future, he can't prevent it from happening. The story expresses the anxiety, the craziness, and the debilitating confusion of someone living in conflict. To make matters more tense, Farrow also takes the film's protagonist to a dangerous psychological place, to the guilt and the despair of feeling helpless to act while in the midst of great chaos.

Farrow's slippery shadow of a tale, *Alias Nick Beal* (1949), is a brilliantly conceived and realized work of darkness, intrigue and pure, unmitigated Evil with a capital E. The story of a politician who sells his soul to the devil, the film paints a dark, noirish canvas that also metaphorically represents Hollywood's battle with censorship. Farrow, being one of Hollywood's most infamous bifurcated souls, ironically, shows once again his concerns about losing any of a film to the Production Code. The story of a man who sells his soul to the devil has far more important life-and-death questions to answer.

Only on screen would Farrow most likely approach the subject so huge in us all, the battle of battles: eradicating evil and replacing it with good. As John Farrow the Catholic and John Farrow, Hollywood's own Don Juan, this battle was, as it were, close to home. Only after a life-or-death struggle does one defeat the other. Wish fulfillment? Humor? Self-disclosure? Well, autobiographical at the least. After several jousts between good and evil in the story, the devil takes a beating at the end. Farrow points his camera to the ground just as a Bible falls heavily and obliterates the devil's contract for good. Evil is effectively wiped out once and for all, even if it took a heavy hand to make it happen.

In this film, Farrow wants the battle to take on cosmic dimensions. As the devil, Nick Beal (Ray Milland) literally (and repeatedly) enters the frame as if he came out of nowhere. Farrow amps up the devil's eerie creepiness and toys with the possibility that this devil escapes caricature. We should all be really, really afraid. He even writes the script itself near the film's ending, putting words into characters' mouths and serving up dread that is almost cosmic. If nothing else, Farrow has two choices: he is either godlike in controlling the script, or he is the devil himself in controlling the script.

We have to wonder how cognizant, if at all, Farrow might have been in disclosing so much of his personal life in the film. The snakelike image (literally an arm twisted into a leg) that decorates the living room wall in Beal's apartment replicates the long tattoo of a snake that ran from Farrow's ankle, up his leg, ending right at his genitals. To this day, few people in the audience, if any, would know that.

Meanwhile, moving back to the kind of film that often got him in trouble, Farrow directed the spirited singer and dancer (and comedic) Betty Hutton, but not without adding her name to his growing list of ladies who wouldn't be back for more. Directing her in in the musical *Red, Hot and Blue* (1949), he ignored one of Hutton's basic ground rules: she didn't want anyone else to rehearse her dance numbers. One morning when she was late to the set, Farrow knew better but let another dancer show him the steps. Sure enough, Betty found out and became livid, staying that way until the picture wrapped. Betty handed out gifts to all cast and crew at the wrap party, giving each gift out personally. But she threw Farrow's gift on the ground, and he was obligated to retrieve it. Opening the gift, he was taken aback; Betty gave him a rare edition of a book he'd wanted for some time. That little moment of kindness was the best revenge Betty ever had.[19]

Farrow meant to have his way on all aspects of his films, and if the opportunity presented itself, he'd take it. And if the studio made a decision he couldn't accept or reverse, he'd walk. He made good on that promise to himself. Set to direct an adaptation of the F. Scott Fitzgerald classic *The Great Gatsby* for Paramount in 1949, Farrow wanted Gene Tierney cast in the part of Daisy

Buchanan, but when producer Richard Maibaum rallied production chief Henry Ginsberg to cast Betty Field instead, and Ginsberg agreed, Farrow left the picture. Maibaum later said:

> We [Maibaum and Ginsberg] agreed that the character was a beautiful, glamorous and unstable girl. Farrow, however, placed more importance on the glamour and beauty than I did. Hollywood was full of beautiful girls. I wanted more an actress who could handle what has been called the "disharmonic chatter of the 20s, the authentic sound of the feckless disillusioned lost generation." What we needed was a fine actress who could make believable the obsessive love she evoked from him.[20]

Maibaum's comment here points to John Farrow's superficial view of women. He could look no further than their physical beauty, which obviously aroused him often enough that he needed to have sex with as many of them as he could. Had he been able to see a woman in a deeper, more complex way—as a human being, that is—his view of women would not have been limited to their sexual appeal.

As an actress, if you were about to work on a Farrow picture, you just went and hoped for the best. Trying to predict Farrow's mood ahead of time was a crapshoot. Crew members just had to enter the danger zone and see what happened. They could count on only one thing: more juicy stuff would happen on the set than on the big screen!

Joe Youngerman, longtime assistant director to Farrow, was one of the few who managed to stay on Farrow's good side for years.

> I went through an awful lot of things with Bill Wellman and an awful lot of things with John Farrow. Everybody knew that Farrow ran around and chased with this one and that one. Everybody knew that if Wellman drank too much he would chase around just like Farrow did.[21]

Youngerman first met Farrow in 1945 when Paramount assigned him to be Farrow's assistant director on *Two Years From the Mast*.

> I remember when I was assigned to my first picture with John Farrow. You would think the production office would take a first assistant director and introduce him, but no that's not the way it worked. I was just told I was going to work with John Farrow. I introduced myself and said, "John, I hear an awful lot of stories about you, but I don't believe any stories unless I know for a fact that they are true." We got along perfectly from then on; no problem at all. [Eventually] John Farrow wouldn't do a picture without me.[22]

Farrow's conflicts, whether fictional on screen or all too real on the set, very likely faded temporarily with the birth of Stephanie Margarita Villiers Farrow. Being a Farrow, Steffi, born on June 3, 1949, in Los Angeles, also began life being famous. At least her family thought so. With a bit of Pomp and Circumstance in attendance, Prince Otto Hapsburg, son of the last emperor of Austria, became Stephanie's godfather.

Still, by the 1950s, Farrow's reputation as a bad boy preceded him onto the set, even though some actors knew how to work around his temper. Several even called themselves friends, such as George Macready, and even Robert Mitchum if he needed a dedicated drinking buddy. But overall, the words that followed Farrow from set to set were "abusive," "a bully," and, more commonly, "a son of a bitch."

If two men ever seemed further apart physically and emotionally, it would be Robert Mitchum and John Farrow. Yet Mitchum nevertheless worked like a charm in the films he made with Farrow, albeit he often blew hot and cold on the subject of Farrow. Mitchum could take more bull than many other actors and still keep a lid on it, take it in stride. After they met in 1949,

Mitchum wanted to work with Farrow, so he spoke to Howard Hughes, and RKO took on *Where Danger Lives*, produced and directed by Farrow and starring Mitchum and Hughes's latest protégé Faith Domergue as the female lead.

Hanging on the whims of a very beautiful but mentally disturbed woman, *Where Danger Lives* (1950) is riskier business than usual for the male protagonists in noir's dark landscape. Domergue plays a suicidal schizophrenic who increasingly disengages from the world; Mitchum plays a doctor who shadows her, becoming increasingly unable to stay awake, slipping in and out of consciousness himself. Unconsciously, Farrow pushes both story and visuals to the very edge of even film noir's shady borders. In this film, the genre's conventions are either exaggerated or turned on their heads. The genre's usual antihero is, in fact, a true hero with only one flaw: he's a vulnerable do-gooder. Being nowhere near shady, he falls for a dame who doesn't just lead him to the dark side; she *is* darkness personified. She lives there.

Jeff Cameron (Mitchum) is a young doctor who takes to the Hippocratic Oath like it was a religion. One night he attends a beautiful young woman, Margo Lannington (Domergue), brought in to the hospital after attempting suicide. When she gains consciousness, he tells her she needs to stay overnight for observation. Before he even turns around she's out the door, back home. The next night she sends Jeff an invitation to dinner and introduces him to her "brother" (Claude Rains), who is, in fact, her husband.

Hubby is sexually ambiguous, to say the least, which is not a problem for his wife, who has married him for his money. After hubby warns Jeff about getting involved with Margo, he and Jeff quarrel and hubby strikes the young doctor on the head with a poker, a mighty blow that renders him unconscious. He later awakens, not knowing if he was responsible for the now lifeless husband and, worse, for the rest of the film has a problem staying awake and conscious. Debilitated and now running off to Mexico with a woman who might be a psychopath, Jeff and his life hang perilously in the balance.

Echoing Farrow's own crises throughout his tenure in Hollywood, Jeff is not so much a participant in the world around him as the odd man out trying his damnedest to conceal his difference. He is not so much in the world (and the danger around him) as he is trying fiercely to hang on to it. Losing consciousness every few hours does very little for staying safe.

The road to escape and freedom is filled with potholes and chaos for the two. They spend as much time not trusting each other as they do just staying clear of the law and petty villains who want to profit from their desperation to cross the border. Just as they hit the border, their world goes apocalyptic; the law, the petty criminals, and Jeff's habit of passing out all converge. Farrow's breathtaking camerawork that tracks Jeff's halting journey down a spiral staircase delivers this hero to the vortex awaiting him. Margo tries to shoot him and he shoots back; all the while the villains are looking on. There but for the grace of God, and the Production Code, the good guy wins. Jeff deals Margo the final blow. As she lies dying, she confesses to all who watch that she killed her husband. There is a God, and tenderness sometimes does outwit the craziness to reach Jeff. It's the chicken and the egg: she loves him but she is also a psychopath. In Farrow's sinister world, love and a psychopath might often go hand in hand.

Mitchum biographer Lee Server writes that Mitchum, never a teetotaler, once said that John was the only director he met who could outdrink him. And the actor had a difficult time correlating Farrow's image of a ruthless philanderer with his other image as a devout Catholic who spent his time with Roman Catholic priests discussing Church doctrine and ecumenical history. Mitchum, at one point, asked him "D'ya ever dare go to confession?" John replied that he went every week and confessed to a priest at one of the oldest Spanish churches in Los Angeles, near Alvarado Street. And every week the priest would give him absolution. "The poor bastard doesn't speak a word of English," John said.[23]

"He was a professional Catholic, Farrow," said Reva Frederick, Mitchum's personal secretary. "Always surrounded by nuns and priests. But his private life was entirely different. He cast the extras—the women—almost entirely with women he wanted for his amusement, girls he would make at his command."[24]

Server mentions that, although Mitchum and John were drinking buddies, at work he could be unbearable and, according to Mitchum, he pinched every ass (he caddishly gave Maureen a cameo as an "understanding" girlfriend) and revealed a sadistic streak to the actor. In the famous aforementioned stairwell scene from *Where Danger Lives*, Mitchum crawls out of his room and then falls down three flights of stairs in a sleazy border town hotel.[25]

According to Server:

> Farrow demanded they shoot it without a stuntman, with the camera on a descending crane following Mitchum's fall. The hastily constructed staircase set was open at the sides, and when Mitchum started tumbling, he nearly slipped over, just avoiding a thirty-foot drop to the wooden plank floor. [RKO production chief] Sid Rogell happened to come onto the set as the take began and ran screaming at Farrow. "You goddamn idiot! Are you trying to kill him?" said Rogell. Carpenters put in a railing, and Farrow restaged the shot to minimize the risk to the performer. Rogell wanted them to use a stuntman. Mitchum refused— he wasn't going to have Farrow calling him a fairy for the rest of the shoot. Down he tumbled. But when the director blithely called, "All right, let's try it again," Mitchum told him to go fuck himself.[26]

Farrow also directed Mitchum in *His Kind of Woman* ("What kind of woman would that be?" Mitchum inquired),[27] which was completed in May 1950 but sat on the shelf until September 1951—just one of many other shelved films at the studio that year, given Howard Hughes's penchant for indecision. The film fell flat at the box office, taking decades to find its rightful cult status. It was a happy set, however, thanks to Mitchum's generosity; he continually bought drinks and lunches for the cast and crew.[28]

Costar Jim Backus thought that Mitchum "never learned to distinguish what is innocent fun and joy on a soundstage from what appears to be an insulting remark on the street . . . People who like or love each other . . . often call each other by ethnic names [stereotypes] . . . it's done with affection. . . . He had a thing going with John Farrow, a Catholic. He called him the Count of Malta or the Knight of Malta or the Militant Catholic. Someone else could have been the Militant Jew. Or he might say, 'Get your slimy Irish ass over on the set.' Done with love, that's common show business exchange. But taken out of context, out of an atmosphere where everyone understands the situation, it can seem dangerous and not very nice."[29]

Jane Russell and Mitchum would become close friends over the years. As Mitchum knew, Jane wouldn't put up with any nastiness from anyone. Having grown up with five brothers in the San Fernando Valley, she could take care of herself; she was tough inside but her soft heart often betrayed her anyway. "I was much too tough for John Farrow and he kind of knew it," she later said. "I just looked the other way and went about my business getting the work done."[30]

The plot of *His Kind of Woman* has little to recommend it, moving haphazardly along without making much sense. The noir revolves around a deported gangster's plan to reenter the United States by involving a gambler (Mitchum) at a Mexican resort. No big idea holds it together; instead, the good moments come around when either Jane Russell hits Mitchum with a quip, when the nightclub scenes get comical and sexy, or when a breakout five minutes of action peek through. It doesn't seem to matter, though; the actors are lively and unpredictable, which gives the nonexistent storyline a push in the right direction.

Though the plot was convoluted and involved an almost-ensemble cast with interwoven subplots (in addition to Mitchum and Russell, the cast included Vincent Price, Tim Holt, Charles McGraw, Marjorie Reynolds, Raymond Burr, and Jim Backus), filming went smoothly. According to Mitchum biographer Lee Server,

> although John Farrow's tough, even cruel behavior toward the crew and supporting and extra players continued to rub Mitchum—and now his costar, too—the wrong way. "He was nice to us, but he would be nasty to some of the other kids," said Russell. "Needling all the time. If you needled him back, that was okay, but if you didn't think you could do that . . . other people were kind of terrified." Farrow had a bottle of rare scotch in his trailer adjoining the set and sampled it daily. A raiding party from the crew went into the trailer one evening, emptied out half the bottle, and then, ritualistically, three or four took turns pissing into it. After that, evil grins met Farrow whenever he poured himself a belt of the prized whiskey.[31]

Server adds that some film crews began calling their pranks the "Farrow treatment." On the set of *Macao*, one such "treatment" was given to director Josef von Sternberg, who was a strict disciplinarian and treated the crew as "assholes": "His belongings tampered with, a reeking limburger cheese smeared through the engine block of his car."[32]

After the shoot ended, the film sat on the shelf a year until Hughes brought in another director, Richard Fleischer, to rework the ending. For Hughes, Farrow didn't give the ending enough action. Hughes was eventually happy with Fleischer's work and wrapped it up. Yet, Farrow was still around, one way or another. Also, "his careful staging was left intact, with atmospheric long takes and sweeping tracking shots" until the gritty climax, Server said.[33]

But John Farrow now had to turn his attention elsewhere, this time closer to home. Theresa "Tisa" Magdalena Farrow, the youngest Farrow, was born on July 22, 1951, also in Los Angeles. Early on, she learned her other moniker: she's been "Baby" to the entire Farrow clan for most of her life.[34] And like her siblings, Tisa received a strict (and mainly) Catholic education. In a *New York Times* interview in 1970, she said her

> upbringing was "very, very strict." Like most of her brothers and sisters, she was educated mainly in Roman Catholic schools. She hated school so much that she left in the middle of her 11th year. "I've never regretted it," she said. "Every morning when I get up, I say to myself, 'I'm so happy I don't have to go back to school.' I think Catholic education warps you seriously. When I went to a public school for awhile, I was terrified of changing my clothes in front of the other girls in gym class because the nuns had taught me it was wrong to show your body."[35]

During the *New York Times* interview, she wore a rosary around her neck that once belonged to her father.

But sooner or later it had to happen: After working with almost every famous woman in Hollywood, Farrow would have to pair up with the hottest and forever smoldering Ava Gardner. And so he did. He began directing the western *Ride, Vaquero!* in 1953, cowriting the script with Frank Fenton. This is the film that jump-started the infamous affair between Farrow and leading lady Gardner and the reason Maureen insisted that Farrow have a door built leading from his private bedroom to the street.

The film's storyline involves a range war in which good bad guy Robert Taylor and bad guy Anthony Quinn oppose nice guy Howard Keel and his beautiful wife, played by Gardner. Filming took place in Utah. Gardner's initial impressions of Farrow were not flattering. According to Ava's biographer Lee Server, "She passed the time drinking with the stuntmen and hating director John Farrow, a man she found to be a mean and lecherous character, cruel in equal measure to the horses and to the whores he flew in from Los Angeles." He'd spend all weekend days in bed with them and report for work Monday morning with a hangover.[36]

However much she was put off by his promiscuity as well as his sadistic treatment of horses in the film, she subsequently changed her mind about this "bad boy." It seems that Gardner acquired the sáme amnesia that hit Maureen and so many other women who ignored his reputation and then coupled up with him.

But, disliking Farrow was not something limited just to women. Glenn Ford appeared in Farrow's 1953 *Plunder of the Sun* and found the experience odious enough to cause him to have a change of heart after later being cast in *Hondo* (1953), to be directed by Farrow for John Wayne's production company, Batjac. Producer Wayne took the part instead, playing opposite heralded Broadway actress Geraldine Page in her first starring film role.

Hondo was a hit at the box office, joining two other films, George Stevens's *Shane* and Fred Zinnemann's *High Noon*, to form what critics have termed the frontier "family romance," where strangers come together and form emotional ties, the bonds of family, as they work closely to stave off a mutual enemy. In an often barren landscape, the frontier reinforced a sense of isolation that could feel overwhelming. The antidote was the imaginary creation of a family unit, a concept romantic enough to offset the pain of loneliness from being isolated.

Oddly enough for Farrow, *Hondo* emphasizes the importance of personal integrity that matters more than "pretty people." On the set, however, Geraldine Page's physical appearance indeed challenged her director and Wayne, himself. He was used to kissing beautiful Hollywood actresses and this was not the case. Had the makeup department played down the beauty of, say,

Maureen O' Hara, Wayne's frequent co-star, her beauty would have shone through any weather-beating she received. But Page, while a handsome woman, was not a beauty for the big screen. Nor would she have tolerated attempts to change that. Had this been a different character she played, such as Princess Alexandra Delago in the 1964 screen adaptation of Tennessee Williams' play, *The Sweet Bird of Youth,* Page would have shown up in full make-up regalia—made beautiful even by Hollywood standards. Page committed to whatever her character required, this time a frontier woman.

"Then John Ford showed up on the set, took a look at Page and told Farrow that no one would buy Wayne wanting to kiss a woman as plain as she was. So Farrow wrote a new line for her: 'I know I'm a homely woman,' she tells Wayne's character." This line could hardly have boosted Page's ego while making her first Hollywood film.

After the dirt and grime of the frontier, Farrow couldn't have minded very much returning to an adventure on the high seas to direct *The Sea Chase* (1955). But what should have been a fortunate turn for Farrow, given the film's A-list cast members—including actors Lana Turner and John Wayne—ultimately was not. Wayne's production company Batjac hired Farrow to direct, just as they had with *Hondo.* But Wayne later remarked, "John Farrow didn't have a great deal to do with *Hondo*, because it was a Batjac production. Everything was set up before he came on. But he did direct *Sea Chase* and prove to me that he should not be put in a producer-director position. He failed to tell the good story that was in the book."[37]

John Farrow proved to be a different kind of pain in the neck for Lana Turner. In her memoirs she wrote that she had never worked with Farrow before *Sea Chase* but knew him only by reputation—as a womanizer. On location in Hawaii, she found that her hotel room was directly next to Farrow's, connected by a sliding door. Lana became suspicious but wouldn't talk to him about it. She let it be known, though, that she would leave the production unless her room was changed. Farrow wasn't thrilled to hear this, claiming he put her next to him in order to go over the script together. Now done with her as a potential sexual mate, he was abrupt with Lana and hardly gave her any direction at all.[38]

Popular 1950s actor and "heartthrob," Tab Hunter, on board, no doubt, to help boost the film's box office numbers, was no fan of Farrow either. He thought most of what Farrow said during production on *Sea Chase* was "so much lip service . . . Like the lip service he paid to his religion":

> John Farrow had years earlier made a showy conversion to Catholicism and was now a big muckety-muck in the Roman Catholic Church. But despite all his holier-than-thou piety—not to mention his marriage to actress Maureen O'Sullivan—he seemed like a garden variety lecher. His only real interest in that production was his leading lady, on whom he doted lavishly—until Les Barker, Lana's husband at the time, arrived.
>
> It may seem odd for me—considering my sexual orientation—to lambaste a prince of the Catholic Church. But I can't stand hypocrites, and that's how Farrow came off. Plus he was just generally creepy, with beady eyes like a pair of piss holes in the snow. I couldn't work up any respect for him, professionally or personally.[39]

Tab Hunter's animus for Farrow was beside the point in light of the bigger picture affecting the director. Farrow's career began winding down after the mid-1950s. He found it more difficult to get work directing films. Had his reputation as a sadist, or even an unpleasant martinet, finally caught up with him? Yet prestige still beckoned for the moment. Producer Mike Todd (married to Elizabeth Taylor at the time) tapped Farrow to direct one of the most anticipated films of that year, and in August 1955 Farrow began work on Jules Verne's classic *Around the World in 80 Days*. Farrow would not only direct; he would write the screenplay along with S. J. Perelman and James Poe.

Farrow lasted one day—maybe two, depending on who did the talking. Mike Todd, a Broadway producer who'd recently set his sights on Hollywood, was a man who liked to call all the shots all the time. After hiring Farrow he subsequently decided that no one else, including Mr. Farrow, would call them on this film. Farrow was fired—although not to the chagrin of all others. S. J. Perelman considered writing partner Farrow's quick departure to be one of the best things to befall the picture (and, most likely, himself). But Farrow did get a little something for his trouble: an Oscar. The picture took top honors for adapted screenplay. Farrow, Perelman, and writer Poe shared the gold. The statuette would be the only Oscar he'd ever win.

The big bite television took out of the moviegoing public might have been one reason that audiences weren't going to movie theaters the way they used to; hardly any film director didn't feel the sting, and good scripts were harder to come by than in past decades. Whether or not Farrow's unpopularity had finally caught up with him is difficult to know, but conjecture that it had might certainly be in order. And Farrow's health began to deteriorate around this time, owing in some part, to the typhus he'd gotten at the end of the war.

Directing a picture takes great physical stamina, and if Farrow's energy level wasn't now waning, it was in serious question. If he felt any trepidation at being asked to direct what would be his last major Hollywood production, *John Paul Jones* (1959), surely he waved it on. This picture would be big, brassy, and bathed in glorious color. And a production it was, with four of the Farrow kids performing. Three of them—Mia, Tisa, and Patrick—were uncredited, and John, playing a young John Paul Jones, had his name appear in the credits (He had one other acting role, as a "young man" in a 1968 episode of *N.Y.P.D.*).

But to the legendary Bette Davis, it was a lot just getting through a cameo she'd agreed to do as Catherine the Great in the picture. Fantasies of murdering director John Farrow might have even crossed her mind. In his biography of the actress, Charles Higham writes that shooting even a brief sequence from *John Paul Jones* was unpleasant. Farrow was ill-tempered and directed Bette with a heavy hand. Also, producer Samuel Bronstein was having serious financial problems and all corners had to be trimmed in the production. Farrow asked Bette to play her part on a single note of "voracious sexual intensity." The suggestion irritated her, but not as much as it kick-started the movie queen in her. Although Farrow also tried to get her goat by calling her the queen of the rushes, Bette kept her feathers down. Letting out a huge sigh of relief when she finished the cameo, Bette grabbed her daughter and her sister and headed out for a vacation in Italy.[40]

In 1958, when Paramount commissioned Farrow to direct the adventure yarn, perhaps he had a premonition of things to come, endings of some sort looming on his horizon. He wanted his entire family with him when he ventured to Spain to shoot the film and then on to England to edit it. Although his children had visited their father now and then on a film set, this would be a first—the family together on foreign ground. Farrow most likely never expected that the trip might upset the lives of his children; and for certain, no one in the family could have imagined the darkness about to touch down on their lives, leaving them changed inimitably. As Prudence writes in her memoir:

> After the house was put up for sale, we continued living in it until we moved. It had become almost completely emptied of all but the barest necessities. . . . But as much as the emptiness symbolized an ending, it was also an omen to the beginning of an era of relentless upheaval, a harbinger of perceived loss and tumult yet to come. . . . Living those last

weeks in the backdrop of our empty house was like being on a movie set that had once been full and vibrant with life and was now devoid of all paraphernalia, props and role players. It was a "wrap."[41]

In Spain, oldest son Michael had just turned eighteen and wanted his independence. He went with the family only to turn around and return to Los Angeles. He enrolled in Occidental College. Michael was a member of the Pasadena USMCR, which pleased his father. But, not surprisingly, Michael had a wild side to him, and John Farrow had a growing sense—and with it a growing unease—that Michael's wilder side might take over if he were left alone.

In May 1959, fearing that his oldest son might get into trouble in Los Angeles with the rest of the family in Spain, Farrow wrote Reverend Edward Whelan at the Our Lady of Sorrows Rectory in Santa Barbara: "I have one worry in California. Michael is living, without supervision, at the house . . . I would appreciate it deeply if you could call him. Perhaps he might come up and visit you. He has, as you know, a great respect and devotion for you."[42]

But John Farrow couldn't have protected his son forever no matter how hard he tried. Five months later, on October 28, while taking student flying lessons, Michael's plane collided with another small aircraft over the city of Pacoima in the San Fernando Valley. Michael was dead. Police identified him by papers he had with him and by a former roommate, Ron Walrod, who was familiar with the tattoos on Michael's right arm that the police described. Michael was in one plane with David H. Johnson, twenty-one, a flying instructor; the single-engine planes collided at about six hundred feet in clear, sunny weather and fell two hundred yards apart. The Farrows again were front-page news in Hollywood.[43]

Maureen and John returned to Beverly Hills from Spain and planned the funeral, held at the Church of the Good Shepherd near the family home. Newspaper stories noted that Maureen, weeping heavily, was consoled by two hundred friends, including Loretta Young, Mrs. Bob Hope, Bob Stack, and friends of her son.[44]

Michael's death essentially destroyed what was left of John and Maureen's marriage, a union that had been disintegrating, slowly and secretly, over the years. As Catholics, however, they never actually divorced. But both began drinking more heavily than in the past, each hurting deeply yet unable to find solace in each other or their children.

Not a prayer in the stratosphere, not a prayer in sight, could alleviate the utter horror and anguish the family suffered the day Michael died. His death amplified the pain and emotional turmoil the Farrows already suffered in their daily lives.

Mia recalls a night shortly after Michael's death:

> Tension between my parents had escalated. Their demons were driving them apart and in their grief they found no solace in each other. My father was drinking heavy [as was Maureen]. One evening in an awful rage he began shouting and he charged my mother with a long knife through the ground floor rooms. I froze at the foot of the stairs until, knife in hand, he careened out into the night. My mother and I watched the door and after a time we made hot chocolate.[45]

Maureen was no slouch either when it came to taking care of herself, even if it meant putting herself first or even putting one of her children in danger. Still recounting her father John's exit from the house after chasing Maureen with that knife, Mia writes:

> But still I was shaking, so she put me in her long big bed saying when dad returns he'd find me there instead and he won't hurt me because he loves me. So then she climbed the stairs to the safety of my little attic room while I propped

myself up in bed with my face right under the lights and waited. . . . Oh dear God please take care of my mother. . . . make him put down his knife or throw it into the dark river but please don't let him come back here to plunge it into his sleeping child. . . . God one last thing I want to ask more. . . . If I should fall asleep please don't let my face turn away from this light.[46]

Prudence, in her autobiography *Dear Prudence*, reiterates the Farrow children's fear of their father. In the book, Prudence regrets her participation in the way the children shut out John Farrow in his last days. It was not done on purpose, she convinces, but was a teenager's response to a parent who seemingly got in the way of her mindset at that age. This is typical teenage behavior. But more striking is Prudence's conflict about feeling sad for her father after their oldest brother Michael's death. Prudence feels sadness for her father, but then, perhaps not so much:

The image of my father alone in unbearable pain emblazoned a hole in my heart that physically hurt leaving me with a sense of emptiness and desolation I have never before encountered. I remembered my friends' words to me after my brother's death . . . expressing that I did not feel the pain adults did but that I would someday know it. I was certain now I knew it. I watched frozen for sometime absorbing the situation . . . that my father was a broken man perhaps irreparably. I wanted to reach out to him and hold him in my arms but . . . I also recognized I still had one foot lingering in childhood. One annoyed look or a word from him could cut me to my core. I was too fragile. I instead I vowed to never again blame him for being incapable of taking care of us and sending us to boarding school. I swore also to always be thoughtful, kind, generous and sensitive toward him for the rest of his days. I hated seeing him [that way].

At the same time I was grateful because I would never resent parting from him again. I would always know he loved me.[47]

There was little extended family for the kids to turn to, but friends were on hand—even neighbors. Mia was especially close to actor Charles Boyer, a friendship that blossomed in the midst of Mia's mad crush on Boyer's son, Michael, but who didn't seem to cooperate and return the affection. Charles Boyer offered her the fatherly affection she may have missed in her own father, John. And whereas young Michael Boyer showed little interest in Mia, Charles was "an entirely different story . . . [she] liked him a lot." Boyer "always noticed" her:

> Not only did he remember which of the seven I was but he even asked me how things were going and seemed interested while I told him. It was amazing; what was more, he paid almost no attention to my brothers and sisters. I wish he didn't travel so much. I'd be happy about seeing more of Mr. Boyer . . . what he didn't know, what nobody knew, was that, after Eileen and my parents, Mr. Boyer [was] my favorite grown up.[48]

One afternoon, while out walking, they found a baby bird lying on the sidewalk that had fallen out of its nest. Boyer took great care, gently putting the bird back in its nest. Mia was taken aback at this display; never before had she seen such gentleness and tenderness from a grown man: "Boyer and I had shared an important thing." Then he placed his hand on Mia's shoulder. She writes that:

> the intimacy and tenderness and enormity of it all . . . was more than I could understand or bear . . . he turned toward me . . . he had a grip on both of my shoulders. . . . I felt I had to look right into his face and I did that even though it wasn't easy. Then in his beautiful French accent Charles

Boyer said, "Your life will be a wonderful one but a difficult one I think." Probably I said thank you or something
so I would not hurt his feelings, and I hoped with all my
might he understood that this was just too much for me to
begin to know how to respond.[49]

It played almost like a love scene and in one way or another—
perhaps feeding into that complex dynamic that little girls experience where her father is also her romantic figure—feeling for
each become entangled and inseparable. No matter what happened, Mia would never forget it.

Boyer had shown Mia great tenderness, something difficult
to experience in a family with John Farrow exerting so much
energy running around town having sex with so many women
other than his wife. Even if the children didn't actually see
Farrow with other women, they knew that what he brought
home with him was not always tenderness. Maureen and the
family probably knew details about some of the women John
slept with—more important, they knew there were many. Here
were the Farrow children caught in a collision between not being
a family and then suddenly being one. John and Maureen's separate bedrooms set this up long ago.[50]

Farrow may have been cognizant of the fearful atmosphere
he created at home so as to satisfy his own needs, to fill that
blank page, that empty screen. Until the final few days of his life,
as his heart was giving out and he demanded his children see he
was dying,[51] he sought ways to be alone, as if he were running
for cover. Within the silence lay that fertile space where he created and repaired—for the page, for his survival. That solitary
space lay as much inside him as around him. Since childhood, he
knew that landscape best.

The more that chaos and conflict played in Farrow's mind,
the more he needed complete control, eventually creating lines
of division in the family home. Literally and figuratively: the
children lived on one side and he on the other. On the occasions

Farrow actually spent time with his family, the emotional climate in the room could be chilly. Not only did this man seem more and more a stranger to his children, but interacting with his own family could foul his mood, lead to an altercation with one of his children and conclude with the inevitable emotional or physical assault.[52]

The Farrow children told no one outside their family about the physical and mental abuse their father handed out. It was their secret. But no one could miss Farrow's autocratic behavior (often leading to mistreatment) of others on his film sets.

For John Farrow, on the set or in his family life, there appeared to be no middle ground. There was only "extremely this way" or "extremely that way." Overreaching defined his everyday reach. On the set, "extremely" meant his way or no way, just as it did when it came to disciplinary tactics he placed on his children.

Always threatening, that uncontrollable need for sex, that confounding part of his psyche where two extremes, going in opposite directions, simply collided, as if two opposing yet symbiotic parts of himself couldn't exist without the other each at the very same time.

He had seen battle in World War II; he had seen war up close and re-created war on movie sets. But his life held a different war, a personal battle, which never resolved itself. In his life, there was no middle ground; there was always overreaching, the extreme, the too much, the too needy, too compulsive, too obsessive.

So, for John Farrow, getting a sexual jolt was on his mind most of the time, but he kept this a secret. No one, not even his wife or his family, knew, and certainly no one outside his family had an inkling. Had they known, he was certain, they would see something wrong, something twisted and distorted and not at all tolerated at the time. It was enough that people around him tolerated what they saw as aberrant behavior,

The Farrow kids were probably somewhat aware of their father's serial affairs outside of his marriage. It was no secret that Farrow slept in a different bedroom from Maureen with its own private entrance. Maureen had that put in during his affair with Ava Gardner in 1953 while they were filming *Ride, Vaquero*. "I thought I'd be annoyed if I heard him coming in the middle of the night," Maureen once said. This is, at the very least, a curious reaction from a wife listening to her husband creeping back into the house and into his bed after a typical night of sex with another woman.[53]

Yet, it's doubtful that any of the children, or even Maureen, knew about Farrow's bizarre request made to Julie Barton back during production on *Red, Hot and Blue*. At the time, Barton was Hutton's singing coach on the production. Farrow found her attractive and, not surprisingly, asked her out to dinner more than once—and she obliged. After one of their dinner dates, Farrow drove Barton home and she asked him up to her apartment for coffee. He said yes and then made a request she could have never expected. "Would you mind, very much, Julie, if I made just a few small cuts on your arm with this little knife? Just a few small ones. It couldn't matter to you much." He showed her the knife he'd taken out of his jacket pocket. He was very polite, Barton recalled. He didn't push himself on her or make any demands: just a simple little question.

As calmly as she could, Barton said, yes, she would mind. Then she got out of his car, looked straight ahead, and walked as quickly as she could up the steps and into her apartment building without looking back.[54]

Farrow's unsated sexual appetite and his obsession with the teaching of the Catholic Church made for an odd duplicity: Farrow's ability to move in two extreme directions at one time: the movement toward devout Catholicism (and obeisance to what makes a good Catholic father, headed by the vow to avoid all sex outside of marriage), the move in the opposite direction, having sex with every woman he could and hardly trying to hide this fact.

At the time of his marriage to Maureen, Farrow converted to Roman Catholicism, and for the rest of his years grew ever more devout, to the point where logic failed and where his religious faith turned to fervor, even obsession. He grew increasingly rigid in his behavior toward his children and intolerant of others' opinions, in his home and out in the world around him. His unbending willfulness of course attracted public attention no less than sparking frequent conflicts on his film sets and with most anyone he met who didn't share his views. This would not include those whose company he enjoyed immensely: the groups of Jesuits who visited the Farrow home and stayed for dinner and on into the night discussing religious matters with much fervor. Of course, it has also been said that, after the Jesuits departed late in the evening, that would give Farrow time to leave the house searching for prostitutes he might bring home for what was left of the wee hours.[55]

Actor Tab Hunter (not a friend of Farrow by a long shot, despite working with him) called Farrow's Catholicism a fakery, something he needed as a token of his importance, of his being grounded when in truth there was no ground.[56] This might have been true; the way sex and Catholicism went hand in hand, both being so extreme, makes it quite clear that he needed that extreme behavior, that extreme opposition, anything extreme, to compensate for the extreme loss he suffered as a child, the extreme need he had for a family and that he could never experience.

The seven Farrow children lived in a war zone in the middle of Beverly Hills and no one outside its walls and lush foliage knew what was contained within. No lush foliage could soften the emotional blows that came at the children. "My childhood was half fairy tale, half nightmare," Mia would write in her memoir years later. She and her siblings could see their home as little other than a battlefield with two parents fighting, each drinking to dull the pain of their incompatibility—drinking that became heavier after Michael's tragic death, from which neither parent ever truly recovered. The fact that more than one or two of the children moved their lives to the East Coast after leaving home is testimony enough to understand the wish to escape their childhoods. They practically willed themselves into adulthood by a sheer drive to escape the scene of the crime. Their childhoods were shaped by the sharp edges of their father's unruly physical and mental outbursts, coupled with both parents' emotional stinginess.

Mia inadvertently became the family's historian and arbiter. Living as loudly as her family lived silently, she fell into the role of mediator by accident, yet she eventually took on the task with gusto. Her 1997 memoir, *What Falls Away*, described some revealing details about the childhood she experienced as both fairy tale and nightmare. She sets the sad and dark tone of her childhood in the memoir's early pages, remembering a visit back to the family's second home in Beverly Hills, the house on Roxbury Drive, that "nobody loved anymore" and where her father had died.

She said, "The suffering and disarray of my family had stuck to the walls, crouched in the shadows; I entered each gloomy room slowly to allow ample time for ghostly withdrawals. With each passing day my father's presence became more vivid: memories and illusion became so intertwined that I could barely distinguish them."[57]

These walls embraced the scene of her father's crimes against his family. But there must have been brief episodes of love and happy affection as well. Perhaps those moments were too rare and too brief. In her book, Mia ruminates about the aftermath two years after Michael's death: ". . . the feeling of failure slowly settled around me . . . we had been through too much . . . and now in the isolation our grief had imposed on us we could not reach one another . . . in the face of these incomprehensible things and the unutterable pain of being here on this earth."[58] In her own memoir, Prudence writes about her father's last days:

> We all knew our father was dying for he spoke of his death
> constantly. . . . I was very aware of how frail and fragile

his lingering existence was yet to my own astonishment my behavior towards him became increasingly out of control . . . we grew tired of hearing about how sick he was . . . every complaint was more intolerably boring than the last until we got up and walked out heartlessly in the middle of his monologues refusing to let him finish . . . how could we do such things, and yet we did.[59]

As Farrow's employment in film began to wind down (although there was work in television now and again.) Maureen left Los Angeles for New York to star on Broadway in the play *Never Too Late*. Farrow was now the terribly lonely figure of a man who shuffled across the house with his bathrobe hanging on him.[60] He demanded the kids in the house pay attention and realize how sick he was. He received little in return from them. The irony could not have escaped him. After all, Farrow must have recalled all the glory from the past. This was the same man who did the honorable thing in 1950 at the DGA when Cecil B. DeMille attempted to oust then-Guild President Joseph L. Mankiewicz and wreak havoc for any Guild member who would not sign a Loyalty Oath. For someone thought to be "just to the right of Franco," Farrow must have recalled, "I surprised everyone and did the right thing."

"We were all quite surprised at this," George Stevens Jr. said years later. "All the others who voted not to sign were liberal! Who is this man who surprised everyone and became an instant liberal, refusing to sign a loyalty. There he was doing the right thing and turning left."[61]

But Farrow's death came soon enough, while he was still living with some of his children. As Prudence recalled:

. . . he frequently had to shout to us several times to come down and kiss him . . . he always waited at the foot of the stairs . . . he complained that no one loved him . . . one Friday, the night before he died, he waited at the bottom

Lucy Savage Farrow, John's mother, age nineteen. Lucy suffered from postpartum depression and was institutionalized shortly after John's birth; she died in 1907, never knowing her son.

John Farrow claimed that he met David O. Selznick in San Francisco in the late 1920s; he claimed that Selznick told him to take his movie star face to Hollywood. Farrow went but his face stayed behind the camera.

Frank Borzage, noted Fox Pictures movie director, always kept an eye out for local talent when shooting on location. After seeing Maureen O'Sullivan at a dance in her home-town in Ireland, he took her back with him to Hollywood.

Sincerely yours
Lila Lee

Lila Lee, the silent film star that Farrow was romantically involved with when he met O'Sullivan. Lee ended their turbulent affair in 1932.

MAUREEN O'SULLIVAN.

Maureen O'Sullivan in an early 1930s slinky pose, when the studio promoted her sexuality.

Maureen O'Sullivan as the "girl next door."

Maureen O'Sullivan with Johnny Weissmuller in 1932's *Tarzan the Ape Man*. Her skimpy outfit titillated audiences and raised the ire of would-be censors.

Maureen O'Sullivan stepped out of the jungle to cement her standing as a rising MGM star in 1934's *The Thin Man*, starring Myrna Loy and William Powell.

Jane meets her mate: John Farrow and Maureen O'Sullivan on the set of *Tarzan Escapes* in 1936.

Maureen O'Sullivan and John Farrow made their wedding vows on September 12, 1936, at St. Monica Catholic Church in Santa Monica.

Ray Milland and Charles Laughton headlined *The Big Clock* (1948), the grand moment in John Farrow's oeuvre, a dizzying film noir display of murder mystery mayhem.

John Farrow took on the Faust legend in *Alias Nick Beal* (1949), transforming it into a shadowy film noir starring Ray Milland and Audrey Totter.

Faith Domergue and Robert Mitchum starred in *Where Danger Lives* (1950), a delirious film noir in which a kind-hearted doctor gives in to lust and falls prey to a disturbed woman.

Even the magic of Jane Russell and Robert Mitchum couldn't save the mixed up scenario of *His Kind of Woman* (1951). Producer Howard Hughes was so unhappy that he called in Richard Fleischer to rework the ending.

When Lana Turner joined John Farrow and John Wayne in Hawaii to shoot *The Sea Chase* (1955), she was upset to find that Farrow had booked her room next to his . . . with a connecting door. Knowing that Farrow was a notorious womanizer, she demanded that her room be changed.

Mia Farrow made her acting breakthrough when she was cast as Allison MacKenzie in ABC-TV's primetime soap opera *Peyton Place* in 1964.

Frank Sinatra and Mia Farrow cut their wedding cake after they tied the knot on July 19, 1966. The marriage lasted a little over a year: Sinatra served her with divorce papers in November 1967 and their divorce was finalized in August 1968.

Roman Polanski directs Mia Farrow in a scene from the landmark horror film *Rosemary's Baby* (1968).

Mia and Andre Previn, early in their marriage (the early 1970s). Mia had become pregnant with their twins while Previn was still married to his second wife, Dory Previn.

Woody Allen and Mia Farrow in a scene from his smash hit *Broadway Danny Rose* (1984).

of the staircase for the entire hour of the television show, *Route 66*, calling out every 5 to 10 minutes . . . we forgot about him . . . that night after I went to bed and he was falling asleep I suddenly remembered my father . . . we had forgotten him entirely, as he said we would . . . I raced through the dark . . . I went to his room . . . he died the next night.[62]

Prudence then added, "In the morning I saw him for the last time . . . I left after kissing him briefly on the cheek. . . . I rushed off. . . . Tisa found our father Sunday afternoon . . . the phone receiver was in his hand as if he is if he were about to make a call . . . he had a calm peaceful look on his face [that said] he was asleep, but . . . he was not."[63]

John Farrow died on January 27, 1963. He was two weeks shy of his fifty-ninth birthday. The night before, Farrow had tried to reach Maureen, then in New York to star in the play *Never Too Late*.[64] Mia was with her mother. When Farrow asked her to put Maureen on the phone, Mia lied to him by omission, afraid to hurt him She didn't tell him that Maureen was on a date with the play's director, George Axelrod, with whom she was having an affair. When John called a second time, Mia just let the phone ring, never answering. By morning, he was dead. Police arrived at Maureen's apartment door to deliver the news. Maureen later confided to a friend, "I'll never know if he was trying to call for help or calling one of his women."[65]

For Mia, though, losing her father set her off on a conflicted road of love and ambivalence, the two tied hopelessly together in her memories and actively influencing her responses to future struggles in her life. John's death also left Prudence with unfinished business in her heart. She would describe in her memoir the difficult task of coming to terms with her conflicted feelings about her even more conflicted father. Other Farrow siblings haven't spoken much about their father; it's safer to live your life in order to take hold of it. Maureen O'Sullivan would go public about John Farrow whenever asked, applying the gauze of her dreamy Hollywood fantasy over the lens that peered into her life. Maureen provided the Hollywood that moviegoers will always want to see, even as the fantasy so important to so many believers chips away as the years pass.

After John Farrow's death, and much like before, Maureen was the sole breadwinner for her still young family. She sold the family home in Beverly Hills and moved to a New York City penthouse. For the present at least, she made her living on the Broadway stage. The East Coast was now home; none of the family ever migrated back to the West Coast. If one did, it was ultimately a temporary arrangement. Beverly Hills, as strange as it might seem for a family once so rooted in its natural, physical beauty, was now a city full of ghosts.

John was gone, but Maureen still had a family to raise. The apartment she found on Central Park West would be her home for the next twenty years, and also the place where the children could live or could visit when they chose. In the midst of her shock at losing John so suddenly, and despite the years of resentment that built up for her in light of his philandering (and drinking, she told her biographer, which she thought had warped his brain), she had to look back at the choice she made to marry a man she deeply loved but whose lifestyle and psychological demons she knew would make her unhappy. At least she would always have the loving, early years of their marriage to take with her. She never suffered for lack of work after John's death; she kept up a busy pace as the acting offers came in often. Later on, in the mid-1970s, Maureen even bought a cottage in Rutland, Vermont, kitty-corner to where son Patrick, who married in the mid-1960s, lived with his wife, Susan.

Now geographically dispersed and tilted toward the East Coast, the Farrow children seem light-years away from their early days in Beverly Hills. But no matter how much its narrative rearranges itself, childhood cannot be exorcised, outrun, or erased. After the present tense in a life, it simply transforms itself to become the future.

Eight
DEPARTURES

John Farrow left his children a legacy he could never have intended—a fairy-tale life that eventually cracked and splintered under the weight of conflict, traumatic events, and ultimately tragedy. It is only human nature that chaos of what happens to us in our lives lies buried, unknown, yet certain to reach up and grab us in one manner or another.

Farrow handed to his children only what he had to pass on. Bereft of the family ties that early on would have given John Farrow the ground beneath his feet, the emotional context within which to see himself, he grew to manhood condemned to freedom, taking on the life of a wanderer who could have landed anywhere—and did. Floating from one seascape to another, from the island of Tahiti to another and back, he became a master of self-invention who created any narrative he needed in order to support himself. Yet, having to answer to himself only, he lived by rules and codes of his own making. Sooner or later they would come to conflict with larger, collective codes of the social world around him.

After finding work in Hollywood, he thought to settle down, marry, and start a family. He no doubt wanted some kind of structure to ground him, a belief system large and solid enough to hold all of his conflicting selves together. He most likely found that very structure in the Catholic Church and committed himself to it fully. His decision to join the Roman Catholic Church had little to do with Maureen's being raised a Catholic. John was baptized a few years before he and Maureen married. Why he warmed up to the strictness and the often unforgiving nature of the Church was anyone's guess.

John Farrow's life-changing encounter with the story of Father Damien left him in awe of the way one single human being, himself suffering, nevertheless made serving others in need his life's work. Perhaps that early encounter appealed to the romanticism in him, and forever colored his view of Catholicism's work—displacing Father Damien's spirit onto the Church itself.

Then again, perhaps Farrow, who chased intellectual pursuits all his life, saw the Church's wide intellectual reach and wanted to be part of the ongoing thought, the persistent discovery and discussion of intellect and history that the Church represented—and, more so, contained within itself. Both Mia and Prudence noted the frequency with which their father entertained the Jesuits in their family home and held long discussions into the night. We have only to look at the histories of the Church Farrow himself published, as well as biographies of various Popes, in addition to a biography of Sir Thomas More.

Yet, for Farrow, belief in Church doctrine was not only conflicted but seriously compromised. As a devout Catholic, Farrow nevertheless refused one of its basic tenets: the belief that sexual relationship outside of marriage is forbidden. This refusal is the one great irony of Farrow's life. His legendary sexual encounters were not so much hypocrisy as the fulfillment of an unconscious wish, perhaps, to be in control of women—especially the woman who left and may have triggered the need: his own mother

The male who is in control (of a woman, a family, even a culture) feeds right into one of the Catholic Church's significant contribution to Western culture itself: the dominance of patriarchy. In subscribing to the Church's system of belief, Farrow also subscribed to the great partnership of patriarchy and Catholicism. Historically, the secrecy hidden in this partnership is legend. Farrow did all he could to add a chapter or two. And he did this with great fervor. Farrow's defining posture—in his behavior, his needs, his demand for control—was one of excessiveness, of the maximum *extreme* he could get from any encounter. It would always be too much, too far, too dangerous, or too hurtful.

Farrow seemed to live a life controlled by his own needs, at times obsessively so. Fulfilling them would also have to be obsessive, over the top, leading to compulsive behavior, abusive of others if need be. In his family life, his children suffered the psychological fallout of this dynamic; it became their inheritance—and for years a silent inheritance at that. It was secret, nonexistent outside the home. Only decades later did Mia and Prudence bring it up in their published memoirs.

Each talked about it (and Prudence more sparingly at that) as an issue in their childhoods. Both sisters bathe their narratives of John Farrow in pathos and reverie, looking back at him elegiacally, as if he were the victim of his demons as much as the true bully in the family. Sadness over the loss of a love object overcomes any rage still brewing for the man who could be a monster when he was angry.

While not intending to, John Farrow abandoned his family long before he died. It might be that he wanted nothing more than to have a family. But, looking forward from the time they were young children, or looking back after they became adults, the pattern that developed is clear as black type on a white page. Farrow was simply not often there for his children. He might have taken pride in showing them off during production of *John Paul Jones*. He may have shared intimate moments with them, each different. He read books with Mia. He taught the boys the best way to dive into the ocean or how to steer a ship. The fact that Prudence describes these moments as joyous, as celebrations, in her memoir tells us that they seemed special because they didn't happen very often.

Just as he had lost the ground under his feet as a child, John Farrow put no consistent time or piece of himself into a foundation to hold up his own children. He paid the bills (until he couldn't) and he built a beautiful castle, of which they could have one side. But they couldn't easily or comfortably find him on their own. He was not at "home" as much as he was everywhere else. And when he doled out physical or emotional blows, he was not at home either. A bridge connected John Farrow's absence from his boys to their tragic adult lives. Trauma lay waiting on the bridge. For whether trauma comes at you blow by blow or as one huge blast to the psyche, it's a story and a suit of clothes that waits forever and shape-shifts with each generation. What else could the boys have done? Just as Farrow did as a child, they would have to find their own way. But as they did that, they had to bring their anger and resentment along with them. As Mia noted, they'd have to do it on their own.

The emotional fallout from Farrow's behavior around his children, or from his frequent absence from their lives, did not always show on their faces or look to be influencing their lives later on. After returning from his schooling in Europe, middle son Patrick tried his hand at college (premed), then drifted around the Los Angeles area, trying his hand at welding in the Topanga Canyon artists' colony. In October 1962 he was arrested for narcotics possession but given a suspended sentence and a light fine that included five years of probation.[1] Self-taught, he had shows in Beverly Hills, New York, and Florida.

In 1966, he married artist Susan Hartwell-Erb, and they moved around the country, living in Oregon, New Mexico, Martha's Vineyard and finally settling in Rutland, Vermont; where they spent the next forty-three years living an easygoing life in a small community. Patrick worked as a sculptor for more than thirty-five of those years, which also included designing jewelry. He was a fellow in the National Sculpture Society as well as a board member of the Chaffee Art Center, where he volunteered endless hours. His most famous work, *The Leash*, was donated to nearby Rutland; it's a "slightly larger than life racing dog and a parking meter that, with the absence of the leash, incorporates Patrick's ironic style. The parking meter represented the restraints of time while the dog was the beast who longed for freedom."[2]

In the early 1960s, Prudence began to rebel against her strict upbringing and started experimenting with drugs and hanging out with "beatniks" and junkies. She was fascinated with the folk and peace movements, and began to explore her mental and emotional states, going deeper and deeper into her mind—generally with peyote and LSD. In early 1964, Maureen hired a psychiatrist for Prudence, and she was sent off to a boarding school in Vermont. By the time of her eighteenth birthday, in 1966, she had given up "bad acid trips" and was turning to Eastern religious thoughts. She spent the summer in Malibu with her brother Patrick, who was living with his wife in an abandoned restaurant, and there she was introduced—by a friend of Patrick's—to Transcendental Meditation (TM). At the end of the summer, Maureen arranged to have Prudence attend a finishing school in Florence, Italy; while there, she traveled to Lourdes, where she became so at peace "in the grotto of a Roman Catholic shrine" that she decided to return to the States and get more involved in TM. In October 1967, she opened a yoga institute in a rented room in a Unitarian Universalist church.[3]

In 1968, along with Mia and brother John, she traveled to Maharishi Mahesh Yogi's ashram in Rishikesh, India, where she took TM training courses. While the Farrows were there, the Beatles—also enthralled with the Maharishi's brand of TM—showed up and, though serious about mediation, did spend time playing and having fun. Prudence was dead serious about her studies and spent most of her time in her room. At one point, John Lennon was asked to "contact her and make sure she came out more often to socialize" and he wrote the song "Dear Prudence"—which, much to Prudence's chagrin, immortalized her in song lyrics.[4]

Then, in 1969, while attending a TM teachers' retreat, Prudence met Albert Morrill Bruns, also a student with plans to teach TM. They married in December 1969, committing to each other, and to an almost nomadic life, for decades to come. Teaching TM as they had planned, the two first lived in Canada before uprooting to Washington, DC, then on to Florida, out to California, and back to Florida again. No matter their traveling, they have remained committed to their teaching.

But, unlike Prudence and the other Farrow sisters, who seemed to display some kind of continuity to their lives in the midst of occasional chaos, John Charles, much like his older brother, Patrick, found it difficult to remain steady or grounded. In June of 1967, he was arrested by sheriff's deputies in Topanga, California on suspicion of marijuana possession;[5] in August he was acquitted of narcotics charges. Two years later in Malibu he was arrested for possession of marijuana and for growing peyote; the charges were later dismissed on a technicality.[6]

In 1969, one of Mia's friends, director Roman Polanski, introduced John Charles to twenty-one-year-old Polish fashion model and countess (by her first marriage) Ava (Eva) Fichtner. She and John married in July; one month later Ava was invited by friend Sharon Tate to join her for a get-together in Benedict Canyon; her car broke down, saving her from the Manson family.[7] After eighteen months John and Ava realized their incompatibility and divorced. Ava later rode to fame and fortune by marrying William Donner Roosevelt, FDR's grandson, in 1983.[8]

John Charles began describing himself as a "sometime screenwriter and boat salesman."[9] Then he became the co-owner of Chesapeake Catamaran Center in Annapolis. He lived in Edgewater, Maryland, with his second wife, Sandra Hall.

In her freshman year of high school, Tisa found herself enrolled at the progressive New Lincoln School in New York City. There she learned about surviving in the real world, waitressing at Schrafft's, and after that, at a Mexican restaurant in Greenwich Village and an Indian restaurant on the West Side.

But Tisa really wanted to make movies. She began knocking on the doors of New York City agencies and trying out for commercials—with no success: "I would always run into some career woman who disliked me right away because she didn't like my sister Mia."[10] She thought of it as her burden. During that time she had her own apartment in New York but, after getting robbed twice, she moved in with Maureen.

Tisa was eighteen in 1969 when she landed a role in the independent Canadian film *Homer*. She played the girlfriend of a Wisconsin farm boy alienated from his family. The film had little going for it, save for the nude scene Tisa was asked to do. She agreed, but asked that the scene be filmed on the last day of shooting, which it was.[11]

Tisa became romantically involved with one of *Homer's* producers, Terry Dene (who was twenty-nine) and, on July 25, 1970, she gave birth in Canada to their child, Jason Jeffrey. Tisa and Dene planned to marry "as soon as he gets a divorce from Evelyn Patrick, the former Mrs. Phil Silvers. They have a small cottage near Toronto where they've avoided the public eye."[12]

Tisa's film career lasted for a bit and she appeared in some thirteen films, including *Some Call It Loving* (1973), *The Initiation of Sarah* (1978), James Toback's *Fingers* (1978), *Manhattan* (1979), *Winter Kills* (1979), the TV movie *The Ordeal of Patty Hearst* (1979), and three Italian exploitation films: Lucio Fulci's *Zombie* (1979), Antonio Margheriti's *The Last Hunter* (1980), *and Anthropophagus: The Grim Reaper* (1980).

Early fame also took Tisa to *Playboy,* where she appeared seminude in a photo article in the July 1973 issue, photographed by Mario Casilli. But by 1977, she was living in a "rather seedy section of Hollywood and working as a waitress and a cab driver to support herself and seven-year-old son."[13] Tisa exited the film business in 1980 and moved across country to Castleton, Vermont, where she embarked on a nursing career, working at the Rutland Regional Medical Center.

Only decades later, in 1992, did Tisa go public again. After Woody Allen's affair with Mia Farrow's daughter Soon-Yi made headlines, Tisa referred to Soon-Yi as having "a double-digit IQ.

It's not like she's a drooling idiot, but she's very naive and very immature."[14]

While Tisa had an on-again-off-again relationship to her acting career, older sister Stephanie climbed steadily upward in the fashion world before virtually disappearing from public view. She became a top model in the late sixties and early seventies, was featured on the cover of *Harper's Bazaar* among others, was one of fashion designer Barbara Hulanicki's favorite models, and appeared in a "Rock & Roll Gypsy Lifestyle/Crash Route USA," a spread in *Look Magazine* in 1969, along with New York artist Jim Kronen. In 1970, she married the twenty-four-year-old Kronen in a ceremony that took place at St. Bartholomew's church at Leigh, a small village twenty miles south of London, on Sept. 13, 1970. Present were Maureen and Mia and her husband André Previn, who provided the wedding music on the church organ (Mia and André had just said their wedding vows a week earlier). The newly wedded couple took up residence in a house across the lane from the Previns in Leigh.[15] Son Joshua Kronen was born February 27, 1971, in London. He eventually settled on a career producing documentary films.

But sister Prudence, one year younger than Mia, has not skimped on living up to the Farrow family tradition, adding controversy, even danger, to the mix. In late 1978, she began a three-year affair with real-estate scion Robert Durst while he was married to Kathie McCormack. According to a 2015 article in the *New York Post,* in late 1981, Prudence called McCormack and demanded that "Kathie give Bob up," Eleanor Schwank, a college friend of Kathie's, told the newspaper in June 1982.[16] "She wanted him all to herself." Two months later McCormack went missing. After Durst was acquitted of murdering a neighbor in 2003, Farrow contacted law-enforcement authorities, concerned about her safety. She said Durst became enraged when she tried to break off their relationship back in 1982. In 2021, Durst was convicted of murdering his friend Susan Berman and sentenced to life in prison without parole.

He was charged with McCormack's disappearance shortly after his sentencing but died in 2022 before a trial could begin.[17]

In 1979, Stephanie was seen around town in New York on the arm of Previn: "Andre did show up at a New York opening night party with Stephanie Farrow, but when questioned, wouldn't discuss his choice of dates and muttered something about composing a piano concerto in London."[18]

In 1982, Woody Allen hired Stephanie to be sister Mia's stand-in for *A Midsummer Night's Sex Comedy*. According to Mia's nanny, Kristi Groteke, Stephanie and Mia had a falling-out because "Steffi didn't like Woody, and the strength of her dislike for him affected the sisters' relationship. Later on, Mia confided to me that she had found photos of Steffi in Woody's apartment." During the filming of *Sex Comedy*, Woody would "go to lunch with Steffi, guiding her elbow with his hand. Mia said she used to find them together *all* the time. She would walk into a room, and there they would be, just the two of them, talking intimately . . . she was really uneasy about it, which was why in recent years she hadn't had much contact with Steffi at all."[19]

In 1983, Stephanie took a role as a waitress in James Toback's *Exposed* and had a small part in Woody's *Zelig*; in 1985, she played Mia's sister in Woody's *The Purple Rose of Cairo*. It's also been suggested that she was the "model" for one of the sisters in Woody's 1986 *Hannah and Her Sisters*.[20] But since those years of appearing on screen, Stephanie has become a more mysterious figure. The press doesn't follow her anymore. Whether or not she designed it or willed that life to anonymity is anyone's guess. Perhaps being a Farrow was hard work when she was young; perhaps it took some time to realize that.

Yet Maureen, still enjoying an acting career as the years passed, found yet another happiness when, in 1980, at an art exhibit of son Patrick's metal sculptures, she met and later married New York businessman Jim Cushing, eventually moving with him to Phoenix, Arizona.

Prudence Farrow did not necessarily keep away from the public eye. While Maureen appeared in public either on the stage or screen, daughter Prudence found her own way. If her public appearances have been few, they haven't been without controversy. In producing an autobiography, Prudence has followed some of her family members in placing herself inside a narrative. She also has a bit of the entrepreneur in her. From 1980 to 1989, Prudence ran her own film and theater production company, which led to work as a production assistant on the film *The Muppets Take Manhattan* (1984) and coordinating the art department for her erstwhile brother-in-law Woody Allen's *The Purple Rose of Cairo* (1985). Prudence also developed the film *Widows' Peak* (1994), which featured Mia in a part originally written for their mother, Maureen.

Unlike his younger sister, Patrick Farrow chose a less public lifestyle. In 1995, Patrick and his wife, Susan, bought a 122-year-old church in Castleton and turned it into a combination workshop-art gallery-living quarters.[21] He was a lifelong peace and environmental activist, and was active in the city's political life, running two unsuccessful campaigns for a seat on the city's board of aldermen.[22] He spoke out against the war and occupation in Iraq.[23]

Tragedy struck younger sister Tisa on May 24, 2008, when her son, Army Sgt. 1st Class Jason F. Dene, thirty-seven, died just weeks away from finishing his second—extended—tour in Iraq. The Department of Defense reported that he died of injuries suffered in an incident in Baghdad unrelated to combat; an autopsy determined that Dene's death was due to an accidental overdose of an Army-prescribed antidepressant drug to treat post-traumatic stress disorder.[24] By then, Tisa was no longer living with Terry Dene.

No matter what came at Mia and her sisters, her two brothers, Patrick and John, seemed far more destined to turmoil and tragedy. Patrick was devastated when his nephew died. At the time, he told the Associated Press he felt as though he had been "kicked in the stomach." "I've been opposed to this war since the beginning," Farrow said. "This lying Bush administration has gotten into this thing that has now killed my nephew. It's up close and personal, and I am deeply angry."[25]

He told the *Huffington Post*, "If there's not going to be a private, outside-of-the-military investigation, I don't trust a word out of their mouths. They have lied to us all along, and I don't see why they wouldn't lie if they found out something that was embarrassing to them."[26]

On June 15, 2009, alone in his gallery, Patrick Farrow put a gun to his head and pulled the trigger.[27] He left behind his wife, Susan, three daughters, and five grandchildren. In a touching and rare anecdote accorded a member of the Farrow family, a local news item reported that, he was "predeceased by his beloved parakeet Clark, who sat on his head and went to work with him every day."[28]

According to the *National Enquirer*, of all sources, Mia Farrow maintained that her nephew's death pushed Patrick over the edge—and that he "killed himself from the grief of losing their nephew."[29]

As if Patrick's sad ending weren't enough to throw the family back into the arms of tragedy, what seemed like three short years after Patrick's suicide, John Farrow Jr. added unexpected, and very public, grief to the Farrow family legacy.

In August 2012, two men came forward claiming that John Charles sexually abused them as boys between 2000 and 2008. According to court documents, Farrow abused the boys in his own home—a few times he used a nearby camper. The victims told police that he would show them pornographic movies; the encounters then escalated to touching and then to oral sex, the documents said. Authorities said he abused one victim for seven years, beginning when the boy was nine, and abused another boy from the ages of eight to thirteen. He was arrested in November of that year following an investigation by Anne Arundel County, Maryland, police. His bail was set at a half-million dollars.[30]

John Charles's wife stood by her husband and called the victims "vipers." He asserted his innocence and claimed that the men were trying to get money from him.[31]

In July 2013, just before trial, John Charles, now sixty-seven, entered an Alford plea to two counts of child abuse. This would allow him to maintain his innocence while admitting prosecutors have enough evidence to convict. He had faced thirty-nine counts. On Monday, October 28, Anne Arundel County Circuit Court Judge Laura Kiessling sentenced John Charles Villiers Farrow to twenty-five years in prison, with all but ten of them suspended.[32] He served seven years of his sentence before his release on February 12, 2020. He then returned, on probation as a registered sex offender, to his home in Edgewater. He now lives there with his wife, Sandra.[33]

There is a certain irony here. In 1992, John Charles commented on the controversy surrounding Mia's custody battle with Woody Allen, and Allen's relationship with Farrow's adopted daughter Soon-Yi. He told *People* magazine that Allen "is going to be indicted, and he's going to be ruined. I think when all of it comes out, he's going to go to jail."[34] Yet Mia remained silent about her brother for years.

With the family now so identified with tragedy and tumult—much of it self-inflicted, as if the siblings' childhoods would not ever let go of them—there was still more trouble to come. Tisa managed her tragic loss as best she could. But on September 17, 2012, at 9:20 a.m., a Vermont State police officer on Vermont Route 22a in the town of Shoreham stopped Tisa, sixty-one, after observing that she was driving a car with an expired inspection sticker. When he approached the car, he saw signs that she was intoxicated and observed three empty six-to-eight-ounce wine bottles in the car. Tisa then told the trooper that she had consumed the contents of the bottles that morning; in the car was her twenty-two-month-old grandson. According to the police report, Tisa was driving with a criminally suspended license (for a prior DUI) and was under the influence of alcohol.

She was arrested and cited for endangering a child under two, a third driving-under-the-influence charge, and violation of conditions of release for her previous DUI. Later that year she was convicted on all three charges.

Prudence now lives in Florida and still teaches Transcendental Meditation with her husband Bruns. According to the *New York Post*, they live "off a dirt road in a mobile home hidden behind thick vegetation. The home doesn't even have a mailbox—seemingly the perfect place for a person who does not want to be found."[35] Prudence and Bruns have three children and four grandchildren.

Nine

FROM PRINCESS MIA
TO MAMA MIA

Mia Farrow's path from childhood to adulthood led her, ironically, right back to her father. The only child of John and Maureen to achieve lasting celebrity, Mia never moved far from her parents' orbit. While Tisa and Steffi flirted briefly with acting careers, they, along with Prudence and the two brothers, Patrick and John, scattered around the country, eventually settling on the East Coast. Patrick once commented that as an adult he wanted to separate himself from the entitlement and privilege the Farrow name provided. No doubt there was more to it than that.

Mia remembered John Farrow cautioning her not to become an actress. First off, he didn't like actresses much (one wonders if that included the actresses who bedded down with him), not that he truly liked more than a few of the actors he directed such as Robert Mitchum, Ray Milland, and his good friend, George Macready. Farrow also told Mia that actresses were not usually very happy with their lives.

But her father's words didn't stop her from seeking out an acting career soon after he died. The family needed money, of course, and Mia had already had a taste of independent celebrity, having been a teen model for several years. Now, after John's death Mia went straight for her target—a career as an actress.

It would make sense that Mia's conflicting feelings about her father would be lifelong. Losing the kind of father John had been had to create conflicting feelings in a seventeen-year-old, who still needed his presence to guide her forward. How could a girl her age not experience both love and resentment for this father, a conflict fed by longing for the man who left her (in so many ways and so many times)? This dynamic has defined Mia's actions over the years—from repeatedly partnering with men who were so much like her father until they became too much like him to surrounding herself with children who might give her and also allow her to give unconditional love she might have believed her parents never gave her. These were great desires, perhaps—bold dreams. But how often do they work in the real world?

Mia Farrow and her father not only share the same story; their imaginations live in the same kinds of stories, whether they be rooted in the real world of fact or in fiction, Mia is intrinsically linked to the man she claims she never truly knew. She's made guesses about him, imagined what he thought, and ultimately has found her father a conflicted soul, "both priest and lover," a man who wanted to be both "the Pope and Don Juan" at the same time.

Once again, Mia Farrow's memoir (in truth, an autobiography in that it covers a full life, instead of recalling an influential event in that life) conveys the portrait of her life she would like the public to know. For her, it contains the true facts. In her book she writes that John Farrow had little respect for his own profession, even when he excelled in it. He never considered moviemaking to be a legitimate art form. This nonchalance, even disdain, for one's career, seems to have run in the family, like carrying the gene for having blue eyes. Mia's desire to become an actress was no surprise to anyone; what else could you do if your godfather was George Cukor and your godmother was none other than Louella Parsons, the most powerful gossip columnist in Hollywood? Who would expect anything less from one of Hollywood's chosen few?

Mia Farrow has implied that her acting career was not born of deep desire or inspiration. She rarely saw acting as a way of reaching for the stars or stretching her talents. Instead, Mia made it clear early on her motivation was practical: "I discovered that only in drama class could I manipulate people and use them, even make them notice me through this marvelous game of pretending, where I didn't have to be me." It seems fitting that a Farrow would make this statement and mean it. Self-protection was key. Pretending made self-protection possible.

Mia Farrow began life as a public figure and had little choice about becoming one. It was no different for any of the Farrow children—Maureen and John were more concerned about giving their kids a good Catholic education than about teaching them celebrity etiquette, but celebrity was just in the air; they just couldn't help but breathe it in.

By the time Mia grew to adulthood, she knew celebrity like the back of her hand. The role seemed easy to fill. No matter what else you do, you cover up, protect, and preserve yourself from others. To do this you find a public persona behind which your true self, your genuine feelings, roam freely in safety. Being a Farrow, Mia had benefited from a first-class education in deception. She had been taught by the masters.

Mia's persona simply grew out of that countenance, the way she looked. With her enormous blue eyes and blonde hair cut like a pixie in the late 1960s, Mia Farrow was the waif, the innocent, almost otherworldly creature who might have stepped out of a fairy's den. She brought innocence back to public consciousness in an era that was brimming over the top with chaos, war, embattled and wounded psyches—a society and a culture devastated by divisiveness. Mia looked more wounded than anyone, but beautifully so, like a doe-eyed innocent. She looked like bliss: she was a physical embodiment of what every male wanted to hold on to, what every woman wanted to *be*. She looked into the camera and knew exactly what to do. You stand in front of it and become anyone you want to be—except yourself.

Mia's beauty may have worked against her in the 1960s when she and Prudence visited the Maharishi in India, whom she later said was no gentleman after she accused him of trying to grope and molest her. Mia's accusations showed up in newspapers around the globe, an eerie foreshadowing of her life to come.

John Farrow was always Mia's role model and inspiration. His contradictory nature only rendered him more fascinating (along with frustrating, no doubt) to her. As a director he was usually somewhere else on location. Even when he was actually in town or at home, he was still somewhere else. How much Mia knew about his philandering, especially as she grew older, is speculation. But to a daughter, the more he was absent, just always out of reach, the more he became the object of her love—the one she couldn't have to love, and the one she loved ambivalently given his physical abuse of her. As inspiring and as confounding as he had always been, now he was unavailable as well—and, held over for as long as he'd had a family, his unavailability had little to do with his being in the room.

John Farrow's availability for his children wavered instead of remaining constant. Whether intending to or not, he taught Mia, by his own example, how to be contrary, perhaps even how to be "two" people at the very same time. Cynthia S. Smith in *What Has She Got: Women Who Attract Famous Men—And How They Did It*, wrote that Mia "admired her father as the rare individual with an ability to be more than a single being and it became the theme of her life with the role model of a mother who transformed herself to gratify a husband with unflagging faithfulness despite his self-centered excursions and activities and powerful male figure of a father who spent his life pursuing a series of identities and succeeding in all, it is not surprising that Mia would become the champion male-pleasing chameleon of all time."[1]

Mia took acting lessons for a time. A big break came when she landed a part in a Broadway production of Oscar Wilde's *The Importance of Being Earnest*. But real fame, the kind that ensures your life as a cultural icon, came when Mia won a substantial role as Allison McKenzie in television's landmark series *Peyton Place*, based on the popular film, itself an adaptation of Grace Metalious's smut fest of a best-selling novel. Her meteoric rise to fame happened quickly and kept her a celestial Hollywood icon for the whole of her acting career. Young girls all around the globe wanted to look like Mia when she won the role in *Peyton Place*. And when she suddenly and arbitrarily cut off her long golden locks and made news with her pixie coif she left Alison McKenzie in the lurch and *Peyton Place's* producers scrambling to account for it in the show's script. As bizarre and radical as it was, the instant haircut just added to her allure.

But more than a few people noticed when Mia did exactly what John Farrow warned her not to do: she met, fell in love with, and married John's worst nightmare, or competition, Frank Sinatra. Farrow had also warned Sinatra not to go near or touch his daughter. To the most jaded of spectators, it might have seemed as if Mia and Frank got together specifically as an act of revenge against Farrow.

(Farrow was in Mia's thoughts when she was choosing a role, even years later. In 1969, slated to portray the young girl in *True Grit* with John Wayne, Mia's friend, Robert Mitchum, warned her not to work with the film's director, Henry Hathaway, who, Mitchum implied, disliked actresses as much as John Farrow did. Mia tried to get Roman Polanski hired as director instead but couldn't. So she walked.)[2]

Married to the Mob: Frank Sinatra

First husband Frank Sinatra was about to hit the mid-century mark when he and Mia Farrow married; he had thirty years of hard knocks and rough edges on her. She must have seemed mesmerizing to his tired old blue eyes when he first saw her, this refreshingly waifish young girl named Mia. It wasn't only the lush young skin, the big blue eyes, and the fawn-like countenance that attracted him, but also the revenge factor, the

148

chance to one-up John Farrow, who had warned Sinatra years earlier never to lay a hand on his daughter. That was the day Sinatra stopped by the Farrows' table at Romanoff's restaurant in Beverly Hills to compliment Farrow on his beautiful young daughter. No one that day mentioned the elephant in the dining room: John Farrow's very public sexual affair with Ava Gardner, Sinatra's beautiful wife, while directing her in *Ride, Vaquero*.

In countless articles written about Mia, published in magazines such as *Vanity Fair* as well as online sources such as *Huffington Post*, Mia stayed with Sinatra despite his penchant for humiliating her in public as well as his arbitrary decision regarding when she could or could not join him in public or at frequent Sinatra family events. Who didn't see the obvious? Sinatra was a dictator just as John Farrow had been. Soon enough, Mia would marry a surrogate for her father. And she would come to regret that move.

Sinatra enjoyed enough show business clout and a Mafia connection here and there to make him look tough.[3] But this little "waif" was tougher than she looked. He tried to control Mia to make sure she stayed subservient. If she didn't, he might even throw her a one-two punch in the kisser. She didn't, and he did.

Although Sinatra's abusive behavior toward Mia was obvious to their friends, for Mia it was a nonsubject, warranting the same silence that hovered around the name of John Farrow. Only with the appearance of Mia's *What Falls Away*, in 1997, did she publicly discuss Farrow's dark side. Years after the Woody Allen fiasco began, neither did she speak publicly about John Farrow's dark side, or the physical abuse she suffered at his hands. It appears almost as if Mia Farrow expects abuse to be part of the deal.

Before Mia and Sinatra wed, weekends were frequently spent at Sinatra's Palm Springs home. On one of these weekends, Jack Warner and his mistress, Jackie Park, also spent the weekend there. Park had begun her acting career in the 1940s and appeared in two films directed by John Farrow, *Red, Hot and*

Blue and later, *Copper Canyon*. She now told Mia that she had known her father, John. Mia responded by saying, "Oh, Daddy was so pure and holy, he should have been the pope." Jackie later told Sinatra biographer Kitty Kelley, "I was kind of taken aback by that one because I'd had a rollicking sexual relationship with John Farrow and I certainly didn't remember him as pure and holy! I asked her if she was happy with Frank, and she said, 'Yes, we're going to get married. I just know we are. This is my destiny, and there's nothing I can do about it.' I thought at the time that she was seeking a replacement for her dad, whom she adored."[4] When they married, in November 1966, the union could have been described in various ways: as an unconscious act on both their parts to retaliate against John Farrow's affair with Ava Gardner in the 1950s when they worked together on the film *Vaquero*; as an act of rebellion for both Frank and Mia when Farrow warned Frank to stay away from his daughter— permanently (she was only eleven years old at the time of the warning); and the most obvious, Mia's attempt to regain the father she lost by marrying another "father" who physically abused her, had the same wandering eye, and even wore the same cologne (the name of which is, unfortunately, lost to history).

When Mia lobbied hard and won the lead in David Susskind's television production of *Johnny Belinda*, Frank was anything but pleased. It was no coincidence that after a long stretch of rehearsals Mia landed in the hospital just before the live drama was set to air. Worried that he might have to replace his leading lady, Susskind flew from the East Coast to California to visit her. When he saw Mia he realized immediately that someone had worked her over but good. He saw "black welts all over her body . . . with mean red gashes and marks all over her arms and shoulders and throat, as if she'd been badly beaten."[5] She had also shown up for work with enough bruises to require makeup to hide them from the camera.

If Mia wasn't a replica of her mother Maureen, no one was. The years of living with her emotionally abusive mother, possibly coupled with her upbringing in the Catholic church, had some-how convinced Maureen that she deserved any pain she suffered. In a like manner, Mia liked the pain of praying with her arms held out as long as *she* could hold out. The more pain, the better; it was the same ecstasy, like mother like daughter.

Mia also put up with Sinatra's repeated physical and emotional abuse just as Maureen had tolerated John Farrow's abusive "love bites" on her face and body.

While physically abusing Mia in private, Sinatra saved the verbal abuse and humiliation he threw at her for public display Four months after they married, in November 1966, Mia sat ringside at one of her husband's Vegas acts as he joked with the audience, "Yeah, I sure got married . . . Well, you see, I had to . . . I finally found a broad I can cheat on."[6] Only Sinatra laughed at his own joke. Mia couldn't laugh.

Nor could she leave him. Just as her mother Maureen tolerated John Farrow's abusive behavior for years, Mia still stayed by Sinatra's side. But she fanned her husband's fiery temper to the breaking point when she refused to buckle down and play housewife. She took the star-making role of Rosemary in Roman Polanski's landmark "horror" film *Rosemary's Baby*, most likely knowing that her decision could be mean the demise of her marriage to Sinatra.

Right she was. Her marriage to Sinatra ended quickly but not painlessly. Sinatra finally realized that Mia meant business: she would never surrender her acting career to his insistence that a wife also meant being a cook and maid. His reaction was immediate. As Roman Polanski noted, Sinatra sent his attorney to find Mia on the set of *Rosemary's Baby*:

> We were just ready to roll when Sinatra's lawyer, Mickey Rudin, turned up. He said he had some important papers for Mia. . . . After a few minutes alone with her, Ruden emerged and left without saying a word. . . . I just went in. . . . There she was, sobbing her heart out like a two-year-old.

Rudin had come to inform her that Sinatra was starting divorce proceedings. What hurt her most was that Sinatra hadn't deigned to tell her himself, simply sent one of his flunkies—a callous move that didn't endear him to me . . . sending Rudin was like firing a servant. She simply couldn't understand her husband's contemptuous, calculated act of cruelty, and it shattered her.[7]

Even if Mia tried to puzzle out Sinatra's abusive behavior toward her, it wasn't as if she were a stranger to it. If you marry a man who replicates your father, it's easy for anyone to say, "you married him for it." Your father's double brings his behavior with him. Abandonment came to Mia every time John Farrow physically and verbally abused her. But Sinatra gave her both kinds of abandonment at the same time.

Who would have guessed what the future actually held for Mia and Frank, who ended their marriage on a bitter note? However, when Mia and Woody Allen fought their public battles years later, Mia repeatedly noted in many media outlets that she and Sinatra remained friends for the rest of his life. Then she tossed out the bombshell: after Sinatra died in 1998, Mia suggested that her son, Ronan (with Woody Allen), might very well be Frank Sinatra's son, not Woody's. But Sinatra's daughter Tina Sinatra, refuted the suggestion; she disliked Mia enough to break her own rule of not divulging personal information about her father. She stated that he'd had a vasectomy before Ronan was even born.

Nevertheless, both Mia and Ronan attended Sinatra's funeral, making a public show of her suggestion that Frank was Ronan's father. Then Mia tossed two items into Sinatra's coffin, her wedding ring from Sinatra and "a handwritten note, which she slid into the breast pocket of his suit."[8]

After Mia and Sinatra split up, she was a free agent to take advantage of the "swinging sixties" before they became the even crazier 1970s, when sexual freedom reigned supreme. As Mia's longtime friend, Rose Styron (widow of writer William Styron), recalled one episode during Mia's status as a single woman. Rose invited Mia to meet two of her friends during a dinner she was hosting: novelist (and Rose's neighbor) Philip Roth and a Czech politician she happened to know, Václav Havel, who was the guest of honor. Mia came to dinner dressed all in white leather, "looking gorgeous," and the two men fell for her. She had affairs with both."[9]

Eventually, though, Mia caught the attention of famed music conductor André Previn. Not as free as Roth or Havel, Previn was, in fact, married—to Mia's friend, the songwriter (and apparently not too emotionally stable) Dory Previn. Legend has it that Mia pretty much snatched Mr. Previn from the arms of his wife. Sooner than expected after Mia and André met, Mia became pregnant with twins, which turned out to be a quick road to pirating him away from his marriage to Dory Previn. Dory's reaction to the heist was a mental breakdown, followed by a suicide attempt. When she recovered, Dory got a bit of revenge; she wrote a hit song, "Beware of Girls with Blonde Hair," which hit the pop charts and stayed for a while.

After Mia and André wed, life seemed even-keeled enough—until Mia discovered André's bad habit of sleeping with other women. Another dance for Mia in the valley of indecision. She of course stayed, this time handling the situation by flinging herself into, at least for her, the calming arms of motherhood. After giving birth to three children with André, Mia began her adventures in adoption, gathering close to her every child she could find who lived in a third world country. Already made vulnerable by finding themselves in a strange new culture, the children shared another handicap: each was physically damaged in some fundamental way.

Surrounding herself with children seemingly more damaged than her, serial adoption didn't soften the nightmare that was Mia's childhood; it merely sent it in another direction that would reveal itself down the line. The nightmare not only clung to her,

153

but it also shaped every move she made, and later, every word she uttered. John Farrow had inducted his daughter, Mia, along with her siblings, into a haunted hall of mirrors that reflected back to them a traumatized child who could never escape, even in adulthood.

The love Mia has always claimed she wanted to give these children, according to several of them, turned into something else, suggesting, quite chillingly that Mia was indeed her father's (and to a small extent, her mother's) daughter. Staying calm, remaining steady, has always been the province of superhuman action figures, not of mere mortals, who are after all nothing more than perennially flawed human beings

Mia became a serial adopter—eventually taking to her heart and home a group totaling fourteen children. They came from around the globe, they came one at a time, like guests dropping in at a cocktail party. Like the woman who adopted them, each was damaged, emotionally or physically, in some essential way. But then, who was not?

Ten

CONEY ISLAND WOODY
AND HIS CINEMAMIA

What happens when a deli pastrami nebbish meets a beautiful shiksa sucking on a Catholic wafer?

Plenty.

The night Woody Allen of Brooklyn, New York, met Princess Mia of Tinseltown, the mere anticipation of the movies their coming partnership might create was in the stars, big enough to make all Hollywood take up again with its own roots, enough to inspire the long-buried studio moguls in Jewish cemeteries around Los Angeles, from Boyle Heights to Malibu to rise up from their graves, dust off their lapels, raise their glasses and, in unison, cheer, "mazel tov!" No doubt there was good reason: as Jack Warner (as always, the first one to pipe up) offered a few cheerful words, "I can see it now, ladies and gents. They're coming down the pike: great movies are heading our way!"

A decade (give or take) of (mostly) movie magic was about to go into production. All Woody had to do was pull Mia toward him under the perennial mistletoe that hangs in doorways and kiss her. For better or worse, soon he did, thereby greenlighting, for one thing, a decade of celluloid storytelling that invigorated the 1980s film industry and made Woody one of the darlings of film critics— such as Pauline Kael of the *New Yorker* and Stanley Kauffmann of *The New Republic*—from one end of the globe to the other.

It only takes one, Orson Welles once famously said, referring to Francis Ford Coppola's 1972 megahit *The Godfather*, which made the director and his film a household name.[1] If he hadn't reached American icon status beforehand, then between 1980 and 1992, Woody's films put him squarely and permanently cemented there—household name membership included. The films he and Mia made together ranged from enjoyable to meaningful to remarkable in their sophistication, off-kilter humor, and keen psychological insight into human nature, no matter how ugly or how flawed, or how well-intentioned it is.

In their twelve years together, Woody showed Mia a part of herself that she and movie audiences had suspected but never really saw: a gifted character actress of almost limitless range. In return, Mia gave Woody a treasure map to a prize he never knew he wanted: a loaded gun called fatherhood. The films looked delicious enough to mask the growing bitter taste Woody and Mia had to swallow off the set.

By the time Mia met Woody, she had perfected the art of marrying the wrong man, the one who replicated John Farrow all the way (the same whack across the face, the same bad temper, even the same cologne) and who liked other women too much to stop looking and touching. This kind of talent was likely enough to ensure her a place on the list of celebrities who made for good conversation.

But Woody himself was hardly unscathed when he met Mia (a fact that would of course qualify him as a human). He suffered his own kind of childhood traumas that he still carried with him. His wound stemmed in large part from his mother's inability to get close and nurture him. In fact, she seemed to have little time for him at all, leaving Woody with a huge psychic gash from which he could never heal. He believed that his mother never wanted him in the first place; no wonder she didn't want to get close to him. This was the one thing that defined him, and, as one biographer, Marion Meade, noted, "for the rest of his life, nothing could convince Woody otherwise."[2] If his mother didn't want or love him, who would? And why? The classic pattern took root: he would then steer clear of any future pain. Woody could go through the moves that intimacy with another person required. He could look involved, but he couldn't go inside the door.

Why would he? Mia's world was a nest of children, always bustling, always growing larger, always reminding him of what he might have hated most: himself as a child. He couldn't escape this with Mia. If some of her offspring grew old enough to fly away, there were always more to arrive and take their place.

Mia Farrow's partnership with Woody Allen, however ironic, also shaped the most prolific period she would know as an actress. Woody's CinemaMia produced charming, clever, at times enchanting films, as if they'd swallowed some magic formula.

A Midsummer Night's Sex Comedy (1982)

The plot is loosely based on Ingmar Bergman's 1955 Swedish comedy film *Smiles of a Summer Night*. It follows Andrew, an eccentric inventor (Allen) and his wife, Adrian (Mary Steenburgen), for a weekend at the New England country estate of her cousin, Leopold (José Ferrer), a wealthy charmer, and Leopold's young fiancée, Ariel (Mia Farrow), as well as another couple (Tony Roberts and Julie Hagerty). During the course of the long summer weekend, couples begin to mix and mingle, and sparks begin to fly between Andrew and Ariel. Farrow's role was originally written for Diane Keaton, but she was busy promoting *Reds* and getting ready for *Shoot the Moon*. The film garnered Allen's first and only Razzie, for Worst Actress for Farrow.

Zelig (1983)

This fictional documentary, set in the 1920s and 1930s, is about a man (Leonard Zelig), who wants to be liked so much that he mimics every strong or famous person he meets. He becomes their exact replica. With this unique talent, Zelig ingratiates himself with people from every sector of society. When his chameleonlike skill catches the eye of Eudora Fletcher (Mia Farrow), a doctor who thinks Zelig is in need of serious cognitive analysis, they fall into a relationship together. The story for *Zelig* originated in Jewish folklore

Zelig, a technical tour de force, was photographed and narrated in the style of 1920s black-and-white newsreels, which are interwoven with archival footage from the era and reenactments of real historical events. Because of the amount of postproduction work needed, *Zelig*, which was shot and finished before *A Midsummer Night's Sex Comedy*, actually opened after that film.

Since the film's release, *Zelig* has become so entrenched in our popular culture that it has inspired an actual psychological condition, "environmental dependency disorder," now recognized by the mental health community. People with this disorder become dependent on actual cues (physical features) from their environment to give them a sense of wholeness of self.

As a side of irony, Mia Farrow herself has called acting a way to manipulate others around her and to make them believe she is someone else. At times, she has added, when she looks in the mirror she hardly recognizes herself.

Broadway Danny Rose (1984)

Allen plays a hardworking, uphill-climbing Broadway talent agent named Danny Rose who goes the extra mile for his clients, so much so that when his latest, married lounge lizard Lou Canova (Nick Apollo Forte), won't perform at a big gig without his new girlfriend, Tina (Farrow), Danny Rose agrees to act as a beard and escort her to the gigs. Unfortunately, Tina's ex-boyfriend is a jealous gangster, and he sends his brother after the couple, who go on the run. The story is told in flashback by a group of comedians at New York's Carnegie Deli.

The Purple Rose of Cairo (1985)

This romantic fantasy comedy stars Mia Farrow as a Depression-era New Jersey waitress named Cecilia who loses herself in the movies to escape the drudgery of her life and the abuse of her husband (Danny Aiello). After Cecilia watches the adventure film *The Purple Rose of Cairo* several times, the main character in the movie, a dashing archaeologist named Tom Baxter (Jeff Daniels), leaves the fictitious black-and-white world on the screen and enters the real world to woo her. The pair fall in love, but complications arise when other Toms in other prints of the film attempt to leave the screen. The film's producer and Gil Shepherd, the actor playing Tom Baxter (also Daniels), fly to New Jersey to put an end to the weird romance. Gil begins to romance Cecilia, and when Cecilia leaves her husband and is asked to choose between staying with Gil in the real world or going with Tom to the film world, she chooses Gil—who then unceremoniously dumps her and flies back to Hollywood. Alone, Cecilia immerses herself again in the make-believe world of the cinema. The response from audiences and critics alike were extremely positive, and the film became a box office success—as well as gathering several BAFTA awards and a best screenplay nod from the Golden Globes.

Hannah and Her Sisters (1986)

Allen's tale of entangled family romances takes place over two years, at three Thanksgiving dinners, and follows three sisters—Hannah (Mia Farrow) and younger siblings Lee (Barbara Hershey) and Holly (Dianne Wiest)—and the men in their lives. Lee is the busiest sister: trying to end her relationship with a live-in partner, the elitist and ill-tempered Frederick (Max von Sydow), at the same time she begins a love affair with sister Hannah's husband, Elliot (Michael Caine). Third sister, Holly, an emotional wreck much of the time, eventually begins a solid relationship with Hannah's ex-husband, the dedicated hypochondriac Mickey (Woody Allen). Filmed in Mia's New

York apartment (which mom Maureen purchased after John Farrow's death), and most obviously featuring on-camera shots of Mia and Woody's adopted son, Moses, and one or two of his other siblings in the background, the film gets its most colorful moments when veteran actor Lloyd Nolan, along with Maureen O'Sullivan, steal scenes as Hannah's parents. Allen gives Maureen the most baggage: her character is an alcoholic and indulges in extramarital affairs.

Yet the material as Woody conceived it struck a little too close to home for Maureen O'Sullivan, and even Mia felt hurt, as if Woody had betrayed her. Later, in her autobiography, Mia said: "It was my mother's stunned, chill reaction to the script that enabled me to see how he had taken many of the personal circumstances and themes of our lives, and, it seemed, had distorted them into cartoonish characterizations. At the same time he was my partner. I loved him. I could trust him with my life. And he was a writer: this is what writers do. All grist for the mill. Relatives have always grumbled. He had taken the ordinary stuff of our lives and lifted it into art. We were honored and outraged."[3] Allen has claimed that much of his inspiration for the film came from the great Ingmar Bergman's *Fanny and Alexander*, a lengthy yet deeply layered saga of family life as seen through the eyes of its title characters, the family's two children, as they take in all the drama. As for Hannah, the film became a a critical and box office hit and one of Woody Allen's most admired works.

But the one issue no one mentions (how could they, we might think) is the uncanny, almost psychically chilling way that *Hannah*'s script foretells Mia and Woody's future. Incestuous affairs within the family, cheating, lying, and creating sexual cover-ups as everyday occurrences: only accusations of child molestation are missing. Most uncanny is Hannah's emotional stability among all the incestuous goings-on. Hannah is understanding and concerned about her siblings and her husband's well-being. Innocent and stable as a rock, Hannah is the exact nurturing soul Mia will want the public to see her as when 1992 rolls around. To say that *Hannah* contains an astounding resemblance (or re-enactment) coming our way is an understatement at the very least. Reincarnation lives in this film—either that or scripts are human psyches that can create the present *and* write and predict the future.

In all of this, Maureen O'Sullivan's performance is especially moving, artfully combining her off-camera life as Mia's mother and her on-camera role as Hannah's mother. She is elegant, realistic, and even eloquent as a woman who looks back longingly and somewhat remorsefully at her life. If moviegoers remember Maureen as this touching woman late in her life, it would be fitting. Maureen passed away in 1998; she could have easily looked back at the sadness as well as the later happiness she had in her life.

Radio Days (1987)

Allen intertwines the life of a working-class Jewish family in Rockaway Beach, New York, in the early 1940s with sentimental vignettes highlighting the Golden Age of Radio. Allen narrated the film, telling stories of growing up listening to radio shows and news while the ensemble cast—including Seth Green, Danny Aiello, Jeff Daniels, Larry David, Paul Herman, Julie Kavner, and Mia Farrow—visually fleshed out the radio vignettes and the family's homelife. The soundtrack featured music from the 1930s and 1940s.

September (1987)

The film is (perhaps unintentionally for Woody) a dreary drama focused on a love triangle among upper-middle-class professionals; Farrow claimed that Allen labored over the film, shooting and reshooting and going way over deadlines and budget—but to no avail as the critics and audiences hated it. Farrow plays Lane, who moves into her Vermont country house to recuperate after a suicide attempt. She's joined by her best friend, Stephanie (Dianne Wiest), her abrasive mother, Diane (Elaine Stritch), and her stepfather, Lloyd (Jack Warden). Complicating things are two neighbors: a struggling writer, Peter (Sam Waterston), and Howard (Denholm Elliott), a French teacher. Howard is in love with Lane, Lane is in love with Peter, and Peter is in love with Stephanie.

Another Woman (1988)

Allen's study of a woman going through a midlife crisis was an homage of sorts to Ingmar Bergman's *Wild Strawberries*. Gena Rowlands stars as philosophy professor Marion, who rents a furnished apartment downtown to work on her book. Next door is the office of a therapist, and Marion inadvertently over-hears the analysis of a stranger, Hope, played by Mia Farrow. Hope is in a state of despair and feels that her life is fake and empty, and these overheard feelings cause Marion to question her life, in particular her unhappy relationships with her second husband (Ian Holm), her brother (Harris Yulin) and his wife (Frances Conroy), and her best friend (Sandy Dennis). She also has deep regrets over missing a chance at true love with her best male friend, Larry, played by Gene Hackman. The film ends on an upbeat note as Marion takes the first steps to change her life for the better.

"Oedipus Wrecks" *(New York Stories)* (1989)

"Oedipus Wrecks" is the third segment of a three-part anthol-ogy of stories that take place in New York City (the other two are "Life Lessons" by Martin Scorsese and "Life Without Zoë" by Francis Ford Coppola). Allen wrote, directed, and stars in the segment about a New York lawyer who is harassed by his obsessively critical mother. He takes his latest girlfriend, Lisa (Mia Farrow), to meet his mother, and when they go to a magic show, his mother is called to come up on stage and disappears. After a while, she magically reappears in the sky over New York and begins to belittle him; Lisa then leaves him and he meets and falls for a Jewish psychic, bringing Mom back to earth.

Crimes and Misdemeanors (1989)

This two-pronged existential drama garnered rave reviews but flopped at the box office. It revolves around a wealthy ophthalmologist, Judah (Martin Landau), who turns to his gangster brother, Jack (Jerry Orbach), for help when his mistress, Delores (Anjelica Huston), not only threatens to tell his wife, Miriam (Claire Bloom), about their affair but also threatens to reveal some of his questionable financial deals. To solve the problem, Jack hires a hit man to murder Delores. Meanwhile, small-time documentary filmmaker Cliff (Woody Allen), unhappily married to Wendy (Joanna Gleason) is hired by Wendy's brother, Lester (Alan Alda), a successful TV executive, to make a documentary about his life. Cliff's heart is not in the project—he's working independently on a biography of famous philosopher Prof. Louis Levy—but he consoles himself by falling in love with Lester's associate producer, Halley Reed (Mia Farrow). One of the best lines in the film occurs after Prof. Levy has committed suicide and Allen learns that he left a suicide note saying only "I've gone out the window." In the end, Judah gets away with murder, Cliff loses Halley to Lester, and the universe is revealed to be "a pretty cold place."

Alice (1990)

Allen incorporated fantasy and Fellini in this romantic comedy about a spoiled Manhattan housewife of sixteen years (Farrow) who meets and becomes attracted to a jazz musician (Joe Mantegna). Because of Catholic guilt over even the thought of cheating on her husband, Doug (William Hurt), she develops backaches and is referred to Dr. Yang, an Asian herbalist whose treatment includes hypnosis and herbs. Alice has dreams about her upbringing, her mother, and her marriage, and comes to realize that she has lost sight of her youthful goals in exchange for material security. One of Dr. Yang's herbs gives her the ability to be invisible, and she discovers that Doug has been having affairs with other women. She leaves Doug, spends some time with Mother Teresa in Calcutta, and returns to Manhattan to raise her children on her own while doing volunteer work in her spare time. The film is a loose interpretation of Fellini's 1965 *Juliet of the Spirits*. The film lost money at the box office.

Shadows and Fog (1991)

This black-and-white homage to Franz Kafka and German Expressionism stars Allen as Kleinman (no first name), a bookkeeper who's awakened one night by vigilantes intent on capturing a serial killer. He gets involved with a coroner, the police, a pair of circus performers, and the serial killer himself in a rambling scenario filmed with stark black-and-white compositions. Mia plays Irmy, one of the circus performers, who runs off to become a prostitute, and John Malkovich plays Paul the Clown, in an ensemble that also includes Kathy Bates, Madonna, John Cusack, Jodie Foster, Julie Kavner, Kenneth Mars, and Wallace Shawn. The film received very mixed and lukewarm reviews; Allen himself, in his memoir *Apropos of Nothing*, said he "knew the film was destined for commercial doom."

Husbands and Wives (1992)

This was the last of the thirteen films that Allen and Mia worked on together. The storyline follows two couples, Jack (Sydney Pollack) and Sally (Judy Davis), and Gabe (Woody Allen) and Judy (Mia Farrow), and the undoing of their relationships. Jack and Sally separate first, which causes Gabe and Judy to reevaluate their relationship. Gabe begins a friendship with a twenty-one-year-old student and Judy begins an affair with a colleague. At the end of the film, Jack and Sally reunite, but Gabe and Judy go their separate ways. The film uses documentary-like interviews with the characters and ends in a fade to black with Allen saying "Can I go? Is this over?" Film critics loved *Husbands and Wives*, but it faltered at the box office.

At that point in time and in his own way, Woody might have also been asking if he could leave his relationship with Mia. And in his own way, he did—by beginning his affair with Soon-Yi.

To paraphrase John Milton, then, out of nowhere Mia was surprised by sin. She blinked once and paradise was gone. It ended in the worst way, exploding and sending shards of their personal grief to media outlets around the globe.

In 1992, Mia Farrow and Woody Allen, New York power couple, trendy, and glamorous, suddenly were no more. Their seemingly idyllic life together just exploded, and the sharp pieces of their once shimmering lives were now landing all around them.

Mia fought back as hard as she could. To Woody, especially, she might have seemed like a woman with a huge media army moving methodically and with purpose to bulldoze him.

Mia attempted to take the kids away. Then she accused Woody of molesting seven-year-old Dylan, the child who would do Mia's bidding, substantiate Mia's accusations. Mia had turned into an enormous freight train carrying dangerous explosives. She was headed right for Woody, traveling, yes, at the speed of light. Her aim was also perfect, her timing impeccable. The crash was heard around the world.

After the Princess Mia Express blew out of town, Woody's career left on the next train. There he stood, at the scene of the crime he didn't know he'd committed. He probably wondered: if he hadn't done anything he believed to be wrong, why was so much taken away from him? Why the huge, unending punishment? It had to be Mia who committed a crime against him. Perhaps he even knew for years that she had it in her. He caved in just a little as he scratched his head in a Stan Laurel posture of disbelief. That's right: he'd seen her throw out hints for years. The pins she'd stuck in the Valentine's Day card he's sent. The threats she had made that she'd hurt him. He saw all the red flags that popped up over the years; they were coming at him as a warning, waving him to the side of the road. Why he didn't pull over "and pay attention," he said, "I'll never know."

He wouldn't cease to wonder, publicly and privately: What happened? What could have caused the explosion?

Eleven

WOUNDED

The means by which Mia survived the shock of losing her daughter to her erstwhile husband—and the humiliation of such a public loss—could be governed by no rules, no socially acceptable behavior or codes.

There were available to Mia Farrow only her will and the part of ourselves we know the least about but which determines so much of what we do in our lives: the unconscious. It might be said that Mia's response to her shocking discovery was, perhaps, not entirely within her control. It might also be said of any one of us that our unconscious mind controls more of ourselves than we'd ever want to believe.

Sigmund Freud, the much maligned, much respected "father" of the unconscious as most of us know it in Western culture, reminds us that the impulse to project one idea onto another is an everyday human activity.

> Projection: A defense mechanism in which intolerable feelings, impulses, thoughts and traits are ascribed to other people in order to deny that they are part of one's self . . . characterized by: externalization, turning of tables, inability to [accept] one's own demons.[1]

Cognitive psychology tells us how projection actually works:

> that when one projects, or displaces, one thing onto
> another, we can only think of things we have already seen
> or experienced. We see ourselves everywhere we look.[2]

Mark Twain, in *Adventures of Huckleberry Finn*, offers a "cautionary," a plea to the reader to understand that the novel uses various dialects, each with its own distinctive agenda. Each is a shading, and has not been done "in haphazard fashion," but with the author's "personal familiarity with these several forms of speech." He's trying to avoid the very dreaded situation in the text when each person's words and stories bump into each other, agitate, then get messed up with everyone else's and come out backward, mutilated and misinterpreted. "I make this explanation for the reason that without it many readers would suppose that all these characters were trying to talk alike and not succeeding."[3] And just imagine the consequences if various dialects and various narratives all came from one person.

Somewhere between projection, displacement, and *Huckleberry Finn*, Mia Farrow told a story that seemed as if it were splintered: it could have been several stories all pushed together to seem like one story. The facts were clearly stated and the protagonists set in place. Yet the story never had an ending and never will. It won't end because somewhere at the beginning it got muddled, and the narrator got confused. It might not be possible to know the origin story and events because for Mia Farrow, given her background and her family, fact and fiction are forever entangled, stuck to each other, hopelessly inseparable. It's not the story but the teller we should examine, starting with the facts so as to understand what happened to them.

In February 1992, Mia found photographs in Woody's bedroom that shocked her. They showed her twenty-one-year-old adopted daughter Soon-Yi posing in the nude for the camera. Shock . . . disbelief . . . then outrage . . . then quickly back to disbelief. How would Mia get beyond the absolute disbelief of what she was now seeing? Soon-Yi posing nude? Or Woody, of course. Not only had Woody betrayed Mia in his intimate relationship with a woman outside of his partnership with her but worse, the young woman was her very own daughter. Mia and Woody had been a couple for twelve years! Although Woody refused marriage or any other such family entanglement with Mia, the two were nevertheless a couple. Or, were they? They could have a shingle in one of their apartments. It was a sign: two arrows simultaneously pointing in opposite directions. Go this way, no, go that way. It was *Alice in Wonderland,* but for keeps.

It followed also that Soon-Yi, Mia's adopted daughter, was neither adopted nor biologically connected to Woody. How, then, could she be considered his daughter in any sense of the word?

But Soon-Yi *was* Woody's daughter, and in a much larger sense—in the sense that as members of society we internalize its belief system, we subscribe and condone that shared system of social meanings. There is a certain order and set of codes that we inherently believe. They aren't values or rules; they merely create order. In the eyes of many, crossing them, stepping outside of them, or collapsing them lies somewhere between courage and pathology.

But as Woody had demonstrated time and again in his relationship with Mia, he subscribed only to Woody's belief system, not society's belief system. Whether or not Mia consciously realized it, Woody was another version of her father, John Farrow. Both Woody and her father lived by their own beliefs, not entirely by society's order. Here was Woody, having sex with a young woman who society, but not Woody, saw as his daughter. Once more, in an odd way, Mia had found in Woody another father replacement.

Suddenly coming face-to-face with nude, provocative photos of Soon-Yi was traumatic in the classic, Freudian sense of the word, throwing Mia into the crosshairs of one of the most commonplace human experiences of daily life: she became traumatized, hit by a psychic bolt of lightning. suffering a trauma that, in addition to this blow, triggers a past trauma and all the overwhelming feelings that it brought but that were too much to bear and so pushed into the unconscious mind to lay in wait.

In his explanation of a traumatic event, Sigmund Freud uses the story told by Tasso in his romantic epic *Gerusalemme Liberata*:

> Its hero, Tancred, unwittingly kills his beloved Clorinda in a duel while she is disguised in the armor of an enemy knight. After her burial he makes his way into a strange magic forest which strikes the Crusaders' army with terror. He slashes with his sword at a tall tree but blood streams from the cut and the voice of Clorinda, whose soul is imprisoned in the tree, is heard complaining that he has wounded his beloved once again.[4]

The actions of Tancred, wounding his beloved in a battle and then, unknowingly and seemingly by chance, wounding her again, evocatively represent in Freud's text the way that the experience of a trauma repeats itself, exactly and unremittingly through the unknowing acts of the survivor and against his very will. As Tasso's story dramatizes it, the repetition at the heart of catastrophe—the experience that Freud will call "traumatic neuroses"—emerges as the unwitting reenactment of an event that one cannot simply leave behind.[5]

What one cannot leave behind is ironically the very thing one cannot remember ever happening—until, that is, the voice that comes from the wound tells its story to the victim.

For Mia, this second psychic wound, the trauma of seeing pictures of Soon-Yi (and what they represent) posing in the nude for Woody Allen carries with it (through the voice in this repeated wound) the past story/trauma suddenly remembered:

John Farrow's physical abuse of Mia's body when he inflicted physical punishment using his hands to spank her, using his cane (as she recalls, that threw her to the other side of the room).

There are other such stories/traumas in Mia's childhood (and in that of the other siblings, we can only believe) that were experienced as catastrophic and therefore pushed aside to lay unclaimed at the time.

They were too large, carrying too much information, to experience. Instead the trauma and its overwhelming experience lay buried in her unconscious mind until now. It might have been one; it might have been more than one.

Now, here was a new trauma, looking right at Mia, and likely to bring up to the light any of these past events and feelings. It might have been any of the betrayals Mia experienced as a child: the beatings by her father (which, in being physical blows, are also molestations upon the body), that terrorized her but that didn't end, especially when he literally threw her across the room with that whack from his walking stick. It might have been the moment of her overwhelming feelings for Charles Boyer (Mia uses the same phrase, "Of all us kids, he noticed only me" as she and her friends use to describe Woody Allen's behavior with young Dylan: "Of all the children around, Woody noticed only Dylan and sought her out.") Mia clearly experienced Mr. Boyer as a lover in that episode, the object of her romantic longing, whether or not Boyer encouraged these feelings, they were overwhelming for Mia. It could also have been her mother's betrayal of her, putting young Mia in her own bed in case John Farrow should begin hunting Maureen down again with that kitchen knife in his hands. Equally shocking was brother Michael's death when Mia was thirteen. Her parents never truly recovered from that traumatic event; neither did the family. Did Mia now believe that Woody was having sex with his own daughter? If this were so, what web of thoughts could this have created for her? Was Woody now another man who betrayed Mia? Betrayal on that large order is its own kind of molestation, no less than

John Farrow's physical abuse of Mia as a child. Disrespect for another's body is its own kind of abuse.

Mia's struggle would always be with or between herself and those she felt betrayed her as a child. The present has meaning only insofar as it triggers the past, the real. But with trauma's story, the real and the imaginary—that is, the past and the present—cannot clearly be distinguished from each other. One is easily confused with the other, displaced onto the other and back again. Only Mia's trauma can be known. And as the child again, the victim, Mia would now be the one least likely to know . . . the one not to know. Was this real, or wasn't it?

This father, Woody, had made a serious mistake, taken a wrong turn in obliterating social codes and recasting the world according to his needs. Yet he claimed, time and again, that he had no idea of what he'd done wrong. In a small way, this denial replicates that of John Farrow, whose sexual desire outside marriage, his trespasses on women's hearts and minds, his perverse sexual needs: none seemed wrong to him. He didn't always understand the codes of the social world around him because it was so difficult for him to see past his own world, his own needs. one that, by necessity, he was forced to create as a child. The facts she faced at that moment might have seemed unfathomable, but here Mia was having to face them. Soon-Yi had replaced her in Woody's bed. Was this not incest? This was her daughter occupying a place where Mia should have been. Worse still, this was happening in her family. Again, no? A father cheating on a mother, for all intents and purposes. *Again? Was this real, or wasn't it?*

Mia struck back at Woody by attempting to take the kids away from him. In August 1992, she went one better, giving him the gift that never stops giving by nature of its odious connotations in our culture. She accused Woody of molesting their seven-year-old daughter Dylan. Mia's animus had no end. As she no doubt knew, first hand or not, nothing calls you E-V-I-L better or faster than being accused of hurting a child. To

Woody, Mia might now have changed permanently. Mia might have seemed like an enormous freight train carrying dangerous explosives headed right for him, and she hit her mark.

Mia's discovery of Woody and Soon-Yi's affair had to be a staggering blow, a betrayal of the first order—nothing less than a catastrophe. In other words, this was a trauma for Mia. It was, as Cathy Caruth points out, a second huge psychic wound that releases knowledge of an original trauma. The original trauma was too huge to be taken in at once, so much of it was stored in the unconscious until a second trauma triggers release of information about the original catastrophe consciously to the victim. Lying deeply buried as it did in her unconscious, the original trauma, a horrible conglomeration for Mia that could easily have begun with physical punishment (abuse) at the hands of her father, then made worse by anxiety about punishment in the church, and the great fear associated with Mia's bout with polio—all of this had been repressed, pushed down to a certain degree. Because all of it is too much information to hit at once, to process, the victim, Mia, could not claim this original information. But now, with a trauma of like proportions, the original trauma comes to consciousness. I can only imagine what came at Mia at this time. Consciously reminiscent of an earlier trauma introducing Mia to remembrances she had pushed down when she was a child.

Mia's original childhood trauma may have had far deeper roots than the mere physical beatings her father doled out. In 2018, Mia's adopted son, Moses Farrow (born January 27, 1978), said that Mia once confided in him that someone in her family had attempted to molest her.[6] In his autobiography, *Apropos of Nothing*, Woody Allen reiterates the same information:

> Another rumor that I heard early on was that Mia's brothers had been sexually aggressive with the beautiful Farrow sisters growing up. The Farrow brother who is now serving

173

years in prison for child molestation has said that their father had molested him and quite possibly his siblings. Moses says that Mia had told him she had been the victim of attempted molestation within her own family.[7]

Woody steers clear of direct accusation; he assumes nothing. With the Farrows, especially, even fact may prove to be fiction. Mia would likely not know of this until the shock of seeing Soon-Yi's photos brought on memories of her childhood traumas. Still, they are double-edged words from someone deeply hurt and unable to heal.

The lines of support formed quickly: Mia supporters on the right, and Woody supporters on the left—then back again. In defending Woody, Moses damaged Mia's image as a nurturing mother. He spilled the beans, so to speak, about her ongoing physical and emotional abuse of her own children. Moses understands that the Farrow family was dysfunctional long before Woody Allen came along. The abuse simply continued.

Moses said he saw some of his siblings—some partially blind or partially disabled—dragged down a flight of stairs and thrown into a bedroom or closet and locked in. Thaddeus, a paraplegic from having battled polio, had been locked in a shed, overnight, by Mia.

Soon-Yi seems to have taken most of the punches from Mia—they had ugly arguments, and Mia once threw a porcelain centerpiece at her head; luckily it missed. Years later, Mia beat her with a telephone receiver.[8] According to an interview in *Rolling Stone,* Soon-Yi claimed she and Farrow were "like oil and water," and Farrow "wasn't maternal to me from the get-go." She also said that Farrow would slap her and once screamed, "I should send you to an insane asylum!"[9]

Soon-Yi made it clear that her desire was simply to be left alone, which increasingly became the case. Even if her relationship with Woody was unconventional, it allowed her to escape. Others weren't so lucky.

Living as a Farrow didn't necessarily translate to having a happy life. Lark, the first child Mia and André Previn had adopted in 1973, ended up in poverty, struggled with addiction, and died of AIDS-related causes in 2008. Though most media sources said that Tam, born in 1979 and adopted in 1992, died of "heart failure" at the age of twenty-one, Moses says that she struggled with depression most of her life—and that Mia refused to get her help, insisting that Tam was just "moody." Moses believes that Tam committed suicide by overdosing on pills. Thaddeus, born in 1989 and adopted by Mia in 1994 at age five, eventually shot himself in his car near the family home. In short, "it was not a happy home—or a healthy one," Moses writes. Moses's words more than imply that the children Mia adopted were put in harm's way.[10]

The other children have been either near or under the radar of social media. Mia's biological twins, Mathew and Sascha Previn, born in 1970, have been completely supportive of Mia's claims against Woody Allen. Mia's third biological child with André Previn, Fletcher, born in 1974, has turned against Woody as well. Daisy Farrow, born in 1974 and adopted two years later, renamed herself from Summer to Daisy, the character Mia played in the film *The Great Gatsby*. She has supported Mia and her sister, Dylan, since this story began circulating. Mia's three other adopted children, Isaiah (born and adopted in 1992), Kaeli-Shea (born in 1993 and adopted in 1994), and Frankie Minh (born in 1989 and adopted in 1995), have for the most part remained out of the spotlight.

Mia would have had good reason to feel vulnerable after the deaths of three of her adopted children. It would be understandable that she would be verbal about that if given the opportunity.

But, her reputation as a mother on the ropes, damned by just some of her children, was not a place to be. Now, Mia faced the possibility of being seen as a toxic mother, the polar opposite of the image she wanted for herself.

To make matters worse, news surfaced that Mia may have discovered some good source material for the narrative she was giving everyone about Woody molesting Dylan. According to Woody, after Mia's accusations against him went public, he received a phone call from Dory Previn, whom he'd never met, who told him about a song she'd written in the 1970s called "In the Attic with Daddy," a song Mia knew very well and used to sing to herself. Here, perhaps, was the inspiration for Mia's retaliation against Woody for having betrayed her with Soon-Yi. Dory seemed convinced of this. As Woody tells it in his autobiography, *Apropos of Nothing,* "[Dory] was certain that's what gave Mia the idea to locate a fake molestation accusation in the attic."[11] Specific words used, such as the speaker being in the "attic" with her "Daddy," fall in line with Mia and Dylan's accusations. Also, the speaker says that this "Daddy" plays the clarinet, the instrument Woody Allen plays. But in Dory Previn's song, the speaker/daughter's voice is flat, and the song's tone is rather flat, suggesting a daughter who is sad, jaded, and weary, as if she has tolerated her father's abuse for a while now; this is not the voice of a child who recounts a single traumatic experience. Still, the similarities between the song and Mia's accusations are uncanny, to say the least.

There is never resolution, never evidence or factual proof that anything happened or didn't happen. Instead it remains a gathering storm, a larger and larger accumulation of stories each with a point to make. But the rain never falls. The resolution, the closure, never comes.

Dory Previn's accusation that Mia assembled a devastating fiction around a song written years earlier could be damning evidence given that the song's lyrics and Mia's story of Woody's alleged molestation of Dylan almost mirror each other—not throughout the entire song but enough to make them very close family.

We'd have to wonder, how could Mia have not seen the resemblance? Did she have a moment of memory loss? Was this a joke between Mia and Mia? Was she so deeply buried in her own unconscious that she momentarily lost sight of the outside world?

Could Mia find something golden, something or someone who might offer even a hint of redemption if her molestation narrative cracked open? Looking at the big picture again, such redemption, the break from the trauma, the tragedy, the bad luck, in the Farrow family might perhaps rest with Mia and Woody's only biological child, Ronan. Could he be the golden child who shines brightly through any messiness around him?

Ronan (originally named Satchel, after one of Woody's favorite baseball players, Satchel Paige), was born on December 19, 1987. Much like Mia in earlier times, he seemed to land in the media's eye almost as if he materialized, already famous, out of nowhere.

But Ronan had been busy all along, excelling at college, then easing his way into avenues of government (he was Secretary of State Hillary Clinton's assistant, then he worked in the Obama administration). Before he even made it as a Rhodes Scholar, he made himself famous as an investigative reporter, when, writing pieces for the *New Yorker*, he broke news stories about women being sexually harassed, even abused and raped, by movie mogul Harvey Weinstein.

Then he moved on Supreme Court Justice Brett Kavanaugh and men in government positions who had enough clout and money to keep their bad behavior with women out of the public eye. Taking down Harvey Weinstein was a major coup, as many other powerful company men came down with him, their dirty secrets now outed by the sweep of the #MeToo movement that hit. In that regard, no one was more golden than Ronan Farrow in the first two decades of the twenty-first century.

Yet no one can be golden forever. More recently, some journalists, such as Ben Smith of the *New York Times*, began to wonder if Ronan wasn't flying too close to the sun, and, like Icarus, thought too highly of himself and could fall. Smith implied that perhaps Ronan wasn't all he seemed—as a journalist, perhaps he should have done a little more legwork. Some of his claims couldn't be corroborated, it was found. Smith suggested, then, that perhaps Ronan is more interested in writing a narrative of his own creation than one that actually tells the truth.[12]

Smith was not alone in pointing his finger at Ronan Farrow. Former *Today* host Matt Lauer, accused by Farrow of raping a woman he worked with, thereby facing public shame and then losing his job, shot back by insisting that the young journalist didn't do his homework. Ronan's reporting in his 2019 book *Catch and Kill* was shoddy and he made false accusations against his victims, Lauer insisted.[13]

Could this be the Farrow family dichotomy handed down to a new generation and busy at work again? Fiction versus fact? Self-made narratives that celebrate the writer, now Ronan, rather than the truth? It's difficult not to see John Farrow here, handing his grandson a self-inflicted dilemma. What's more urgent and more satisfying—telling the truth or creating the artful narrative? For John Farrow, creating that narrative and sticking close to it might just be the one act that keeps you alive. For Ronan, it's too soon to tell.

If a golden child turned out to be only human, perhaps facing forward to tell the public all about yourself might be the best path to take. Both Mia and Woody did so, offering personal accounts of their public fiasco. Each published an autobiography, a text designed with self-preservation in mind. Mia's book came first. Her memoir, *What Falls Away*, appeared in 1997 and not only told her side of the story but just as crucially, gave Mia a platform to tell her readers who she really is and her way of thinking, to tell the story of Mia and Woody straight out.

The book might also help mend Mia's image as a benevolent, nurturing mother figure, which took a direct hit from the fiasco and now was tarnished by the accusations that flew at her: in some circles Mia was seen as erratic, abusive, explosive, manipulative, and a liar. Mia's life spilled out, an exposure that Mia, as a Farrow, abhorred. As Maureen had taught her, exposure was intolerable, unnatural, and unacceptable.

Mia as Autobiography

Would writing a memoir and making it very public help Mia's case? Would revealing her true self act as an antidote to this trauma? Would it win points with public opinion? Would it soothe, would it be cathartic? Would it also be revenge for the pain Woody had caused Mia? Including the court proceedings for the custody battle at the book's conclusion might be enough to convince the reader it is. Still, there is no overlooking the book's main agenda. In any type of life writing, the agenda is to let the reader know about oneself—in this case, the real Mia.

But is the "real you," the one who lived and experienced the past, ever available—ever truly and authentically reachable in the present? It's not likely, since there are stumbling blocks that get in the way. Writing a memoir and/or an autobiography is a frightening, often painful experience, Having to confront yourself truthfully (whatever that is) for a sustained period of time can be threatening, even terrifying, to say the least. You are required to disclose, reveal, and expose yourself to your reader, to the world—in addition to yourself. The autobiographer often doesn't realize this is necessary until the moment comes to start filling up the pages. Another issue arises. Autobiography, strangely enough, is a particular breed of fiction—the kind that poses as fact but is "remembered" and "reconstructed" at best. This kind of narrative always gets hijacked and compromised by being remembered in the present—the moment of writing. Trying to remember and explain the past gets sabotaged by and filtered through the present. This is simply the nature of the beast, the nature of writing autobiography, which can deliver only a version of one's life rather than the past as it actually occurred. That is gone forever. The minute pen hits paper, the autobiographer creates something new. Autobiography subverts the historical past, the actual life that occurred. The life that we see on the page is a life created in the present in the act of writing and re-creating; and what is more it is a life told by an autobiography that adds one more layer of fiction to the narrative at hand.

It is not uncommon for an autobiographer or memoirist to find a buffer between the self in the present and the past self that can stir up unwanted feelings. This would be a "safe" narrator, a persona who is neither you in the present nor you in the past, but a third kind of fictitious narrator who is telling the story, the events. This shield, this protective persona, can be as simple as an imaginary kind of self, just enough to shield the pain that is likely to rise.

The persona Mia takes on in her memoir is that of the innocent child (the same cloak she wears while talking in the 2021 HBO documentary, *Allen v. Farrow*). In the autobiography, for instance, she recalls that terrible night that her father chased her mother around the house with a kitchen knife. At last he runs out the front door, and Maureen and Mia breathe a sigh of relief. Then Maureen tells Mia her plan. She and Mia will switch beds. When John comes running back into the house he will go to Maureen's room, and, finding Mia instead in Maureen's bed, he will not hurt her because he loves his daughter. But what if John doesn't look before stabbing and hurts Mia instead? More so, why does Mia not resent that her mother would put her in harm's way like this? She never blames her mother in this episode. She still is not even aware of her mother's motive. Instead, she prays that everyone will be all right. As the adult writing about this moment where her mother betrays her, she's still the child, still the innocent.

Mia knows she might be facing public scrutiny, even judgment, indefinitely. If this is true, the memoir is essential in the way it combats negative public opinion with pure innocence. The posture of innocence is Mia's best defense against any negative public opinion. It's the surest way to repair any hint of being described as conniving, even as evil.

The innocence turns slightly into remorse in the memoir's pages where Mia heartbreakingly walks into her father's bedroom and bathroom years after his death. Opening the medicine chest on the wall, she finds her baby tooth that he obviously kept for years. It is tragic that Mia is so torn between hating a man who hurt her so badly physically and loving the man who died and missing him, and feeling her love for him to such an extent that in his death he has become idealized while still remembered as a tyrant. This is an impossible double-edged pain.

Mia's posture of innocence will become more prominent as the future unfolds. She will be the one who did not strike out but suffered the strikes of others—in many areas of her life. Mia calls her obeisance to the tenets of her strict Catholic upbringing and the persona she learned there a falsehood. The more innocent, childlike, and victimized she appears, and the more pain she can bear, the stronger, more convincing her martyrdom, the more convincing her enemy's villainy. The greatest revenge: transforming your enemy into a villain. Only a villain would harm the innocent.

Between the fiction inherent in autobiography, the displacement of past and present that trauma ensures, not to mention Mia's acting skills (and therefore skills at shape-shifting and manipulating her audience), Mia's book is a well-meaning, poignant work of fact-meeting-fiction.

In 2021, along came the HBO documentary, *Allen v. Farrow*, a work of art in the kind of seamless editing they teach in the best film schools. It is persuasive storytelling, propaganda, at its very best. The story is so inviting, so seductive, presenting an idyllic life interrupted. There have been few instances in the art of documentary filmmaking where a one-sided agenda is so brilliantly disguised as presenting balanced facts.

Mia seems even more innocent than she does in her autobiography. She now tells the viewer that she was as surprised as anyone by what happened between Woody and Dylan. The takeaway: Mia is the victim in this story, not Dylan.

181

One phrase that haunts this documentary is one heard before—by Mia, by her friends—that of all the children, Woody always seemed more interested in Dylan. He sought her out. This is the very same phrase Mia uses in her autobiography to describe Charles Boyer's feelings and actions concerning her, Mia, when she was a little girl.

Could it be possible that in a state of extended trauma Mia is displacing something from the past onto something in the present? Mia received abundant, unconditional affection from Boyer—the kind of affection and attention she wished she could have received more of from her father, John Farrow.

We can't discern the difference between fiction and Mia's narrative because, historically, this teller does not always distinguish between the two. Before assigning meaning to a story Mia has told, first we must discern a word's meaning for her. This is not always possible with any narrator, and for Mia, words may be pointing in a different direction than the one we expect.

We will never know the source of Mia's displacement of the past onto the present. We will never know if it is actual displacement itself. We should assume that Mia believes the stories she's been telling. Beyond that, all we know for certain is that Mia had a father named John Farrow who left his kids a childhood that still determines their lives. So it will for the next generation, and the one to come.

Conclusion
NO HOLLYWOOD ENDING

Mia Farrow carries the weight of the past as it transforms into the present. How the future will unfold might already be imprinted in her children. Her biological children have so far beaten the odds more successfully than many of her adopted children. Many years have passed since accusations flew from one side to the other in this uncivil war. That war, which began with John Farrow's childhood battles, has so far reached his look-alike grandson, Ronan Farrow, every bit the heir apparent to John's risk-taking genes. A writer and an intellectual in the same spirit as his grandfather, Ronan hit the media with a bang before being tagged by the public as having a bit of fiction to him.

The past is tricky territory. It can be erased and altered in name only. Fictionalizing it never erases or excises its demons— or the collateral damage these demons leave behind. Unfolding in Tinseltown, as the Farrows' story has, gives a sheen to trauma's story itself. Wrapping it in silence gives it even more mystery than trauma carries within itself. The Farrows' story belongs to fact and fiction simultaneously in a narrative that, silent or not, implicates all of us in trauma's narrative as it merges with the larger narrative that becomes history itself.

APPENDICES

Outtakes

When John Farrow and Maureen O'Sullivan came to Hollywood in the late 1920s, fan magazines, gossip mongers—and the ever-knowing public eye—tightly focused on the goings-on in Tinseltown. Some in the film colony—such as Maureen—basked in the attention. Others, such as Farrow, did not. But like it or not—as these outtakes show us—your life could become the latest hot news in Hollywood, in often surprising ways.

The short narratives collected here vary in source and subject. Together, they form a patchwork view of the lives John Farrow and Maureen O'Sullivan lived off the film set. Maureen gives advice to her female fans; John goes about his life, re-creating himself for others. Stories clash in their telling, yet there is always inspiration for more. There is humor, sadness, even tragedy, all of which would be passed on to the Farrow children, either as tales told to them or as experiences supposedly hidden that somehow escape into the atmosphere nonetheless. Theirs was a life of story-making and story-living.

Entitled

John Farrow loved titles—not just the titles of movies, of which he had plenty under his belt—but also the titles he could attach to his name, or use instead of his name, in order to impress others (and no less, himself) as being, well, entitled. He preferred titles that sounded historically significant, as they could ground him in history. After all, he did write histories, such as a book called *Damien the Leper*. Farrow never knew his parents and had no knowledge of his own family history. He needed grounding.

A title also offers pedigree, an add-on that gives you stature and the luster of which never dulls. And were it a title the origin of which suggested landownership, one could probably claim a family history of some wealth, not to mention power, at least over those who rent or work the land. Still, every little bit helps.

And for those title seekers with little aversion to risk-taking, why not adopt a title from the top of the food chain? John Farrow was a person of this ilk. Perhaps this is one of the reasons he told his children that he was born from the union of Lucy Savage and King Edward VII.[1]

As time marched on, Farrow perfected the art of "self-entitlement" or "self-titling." Landing in San Francisco at age twenty, he met a seventeen-year-old beauty, Felice Lewin, the daughter of a wealthy Jewish industrialist.

Nervous about his first meeting with Felice's parents, Farrow came prepared. Sporting what would come to be a permanent fixture/affectation upon his person, he carried with him a shiny silver-tipped black walking stick. Of course, his clothing was made of the finest fabric he could find. It was only fitting, then, that upon entering the Lewin home, he introduced himself as the Honorable John Neville Berg-Apton Villiers Farrow.

Felice's father was almost impressed but not quite. As Felice and John Neville carried on their affair, the climate went from hot to cold and back again. A separation was needed.

But, after some time away from Felice, Farrow reappeared sporting the name Lord Westmoreland and bearing the Westmoreland coat of arms, in which sign the Roving Sealord Conquered.

Stormy weather prevailed, and Farrow stepped away from the ruling family, mainly due to a difference of opinion between him and Felice's father. But no matter, Farrow returned once more, and this go-round he named himself Anthony Francis Saint Clair Lord Berghersh, Son of the Old Earl Farrow.[2]

He and Felice eventually walked down the aisle to matrimony—Farrow most likely taking a slice of each name he had concocted until he had yet another. The marriage was short-lived, although the couple had a daughter. Soon after, Farrow found himself repeating the actions of his father Thomas: he left his wife and daughter and lit out for new territory.

It was not until a decade or so later that John Farrow came upon a title not of his own making. In 1937, now directing movies in Hollywood, he happened upon a charming manor house while editing a movie he'd just shot in Surlington, England. The manor house had two bedrooms and lovely grounds, and it very much needed a landlord to take care of it. Now married to Maureen O'Sullivan for over a year, John decided to buy the manor. Both of them would now have a title. John was lord of the manor and Maureen was lady of the manor. They were soon to be called absent lord and lady of the manor, as they never actually occupied the house.[3] But, no matter; it's the title that counts, is it not?

Romance of the Little Red Devil and the Roving Lord

**Parents Snubbed Him, Police Arrested Him, His Captain Jailed Him,
His Own Consul Called Him Bogus—and Still She Loved Him Madly**

Felice Lewin, the San Francisco Society Lass Who Loved a Sailor and Swore She'd Wed Him Whether He Was Lord or Deck Scrubber

By Winifred Van Duzer, King Features, August 16, 1924

This is the story of the "Little Red Devil," the most courted girl in San Francisco society, who couldn't find a sweetheart to suit her until a mysterious, monocled youth came out of nowhere and claimed to be the heir to the imposing earldom of Westmoreland.

Of course the youth may prove to be what he says. And again he may turn out to be only the deck scrubber on the revenue cutter Shawnee lying off shore, with no more title than that of second class quartermaster.

At any rate he has won the heart of the "Little Red Devil," thereby pulling down upon the city's blue bloods what usually falls when beautiful young heiresses fall in love with unidentified gentlemen.

And now Miss Felice Lewin declares that she will marry the young man who calls himself the honorable John Neville Burg-Apton Villiers Farrow whether her friends and family or the whole English peerage like it or not.

"And she probably will," everybody says, "since she usually does as she likes!"

Miss Lewin is a fairly perfect example of the celebrated society flapper. Slenderly athletic, with chestnut hair trimmed to a boyish bob and level gray eyes looking straight into your own, she might have posed for almost any of the hundred and one portraits of sweatered young women behind steering wheels or tennis racquets on society pages.

Because of her vivacious charm, startling originality and artistic achievements, the daughter of Arthur Lewin, millionaire mining magnate, has been the petted darling of San Francisco exclusives—and the despair of her parents and friends!

For despite the dozens of eligible young men who have paid her court she turned a cold shoulder on Cupid. One after another she has nipped all hopes and gone her venturesome way undisturbed by marriage plans.

Perhaps Felice grew restless between Daddy Lewin's continual urge toward matrimony and her own determination to have nothing to do with it. For suddenly she surprised everybody by opening a studio on Russian Hill and coming out as a member of the crowd that lives in this Western Greenwich Village. Even here she quickly rose to leadership, since she painted rather well, danced a little, wrote verse occasionally and performed the other gestures that artistic souls recognize.

When this Bohemian set held its "Western Arts Ball" at the Palace Hotel, the feature of the evening was the "Little Red Devil" dance staged by Miss Lewin and three other girls from the colony.

The number was a miscellany of eccentric steps and figures that astonished the spectators. But what made everybody gasp were the costumes worn by the dancers: flame-colored silk tights from top to toe, with little red horns fastened upon either side of the head-piece!

The story of this dance went beyond the purlieus of Russian Hill and was the beginning of fame for Miss Lewin, who designed and led the number. She was described variously as a "Dangerous Sprite," a "Bohemian Vestal" and "The Little Red Devil."

It was this last sobriquet which clung when her portraits in the costume were being printed everywhere.

According to the story lately told by the dashing youth of the monocle, it was when one of these fell into his hands and he gazed long into the laughing pictured eyes of the San Francisco heiress that he felt his heart, long unwooed by women's wiles, breaking like thin ice.

He happened to be traveling the South Seas at the moment, expecting, he said, to return to England and Oxford. But when he saw that printed likeness—so he said—he wrote home that everything was off and rushed away to San Francisco to search for the lovely lady.

When next the "young and artistic English nobleman," as Russian Hill soon learned to call him, came to public view, he was being feted at teas, dances and studio parties by the Bohemians as the squire of Miss Lewis.

Then they remembered the American adventures of the present Lord Westmoreland when, as Vere Anthony Francis St. Claire Lord Burghersh, son of the old Earl and buddy of the Prince of Wales, he was brought to Washington by Admiral Beatty as his aide during the international disarmament conference.

Instead of confining himself to activities in the Capitol the young Lord spent much of his time on the Congressional Limited commuting between the British Embassy and Broadway, where Leonora Hughes was dancing.

Leonora taught him the toddle, together with many other things young Englishmen may learn from Yankee cuties. And just when everybody was watching the mails for wedding announcements, Burghersh was thrown into the Earldom by the death of his elderly relative, whereupon he promptly married the beautiful Mrs. Arthur Capel, daughter of Lord Ribbesdale, known as the "richest widow in England."

"But Felice has plenty of money—so Johnny needn't worry," their friends went on.

"We probably won't have to wait long now. Have you read the poem he wrote her?"

Somebody produced a copy of free verse:

> I am old
> Very old
> With much knowledge
> Of this world;
> Yet
> In her
> Seductive presence
> I am young
> Too young
> . . . . . . Soft clay
> In pale, Buddhistic hands.

It was about this time that the tale of Felice's romance got to Daddy Lewin and made him very angry indeed. San Francisco, it seems, is filled with unpractical, penniless, and romantic English boys both of good, and not so good, families who invade the Far West, relying on Providence or somebody to do right by them. California girls admire them while California parents fear them.

So it was little wonder that Daddy Lewin stamped and stormed and declared that there'd be no wedding.

Felice, however, sent word back that there'd be a gorgeous wedding just before she sailed for England.

"England!" sniffed Mr. Lewin. "We'll see about that!"

Someone was dispatched to interview the monocled and white-spatted youth, together with the British Consul-General and anyone else who might know young "Johnny."

The British Consul plunged into a fever of search through various directories of nobility. Afterward he stated with diplomatic care:

"The gentleman's connection may be legitimate but I fail to find the name 'Farrow' in the Westmoreland line. The family name is Fane."

And all the young man would say was that he actually was a Westmoreland, three times removed.

Then when Felice and her daddy stormed at each other, Farrow appeared one day as best man at the wedding of his friend, Captain Donell-Syker at fashionable Grace Cathedral. Immediately afterward he was arrested and charged with contributing to the delinquency of a minor.

Although her family and friends denied all responsibility for the arrest, and although the case was dismissed as soon as it reached court, Felice was furious.

She was so upset that she hurried to send out invitations to a big tea at the fashionable St. Francis Hotel. There, over the orange pekoe she formally announced her engagement to the Honorable John Neville Burg-Apton Villiers Farrow.

Meantime certain things had been happening on the Shawnee. The vessel that chases rum runners and rescues ships in distress was short one second class quartermaster. Captain C. F. Howell instigated a short hunt. A person who flourished a monocle and wore white spats was brought aboard.

"It's him," said the Captain. "Chuck him into the brig for breach of discipline!"

And when Felice's friends came round to tell the Captain that he was holding in durance vile a member of the English peerage he stated that, noble or not, the man obeyed the clarion voice of the boatswain piping "All hands to scrubbing the decks!"

Up on Russian Hill, however, the girl who had refused half the young men in San Francisco's gilded set clung fiercely to the deck scrubber—or possibly the Earl, as the future may prove.

"I'm going to marry him!" was her final word. "I'll marry him in spite of my family and Uncle Sam and everybody! Just wait!"

And that's what everybody is doing—waiting!

—*Winifred Van Duzer, King Features, "Romance of the 'Little Red Devil' and the Roving Lord: Parents Snubbed Him, Police Arrested Him, His Captain Jailed Him, His Own Consul Called Him Bogus—And Still She Loved Him Madly"*

The Immigration Setup

One serious thorn in John Farrow's side (when it wasn't himself) was the US Government, an unforgiving opponent in Farrow's battle to remain in Hollywood. Being an Australian in Tinseltown had its allure; women loved his accent, and he became nectar to the bees. But there were other sides to the fact of his alien status. One of them was a downside.

In late 1931, as the Great Depression showed no signs of abating, the US government mounted a campaign to deport hordes of foreign workers supposedly taking jobs away from American citizens. The project was mounted for publicity purposes to show Americans that the Department of Labor was protecting jobs and to justify payments to special immigration agents through large governmental expenditures to weed out communists and foreign gangsters. One facet of this "crackdown" was aimed at Hollywood immigrants, the most visible of these "aliens."

On October 6, 1932, the *Los Angeles Times* reported that special assistant to the Secretary of Labor, agent Murray W. Garsson, was in Hollywood investigating aliens. Labor Secretary William Doak explained that Garsson was doing "heavy investigation" on the West Coast. "According to Garsson, the United States government is in the fight against racketeers and aliens of the 'public enemy' type, and actors and actresses who have overstayed their visitor permits because of numerous complaints filed in Washington." Hollywood actors and directors were thus the most visible of these "aliens."[4]

Both Farrow and O'Sullivan got caught up in the crackdown. O'Sullivan, a legal resident, was questioned by Garsson; he asked her repeatedly about Farrow. At 1 a.m. on January 27, Garsson arrested Farrow while the "man about town" was dancing with Argentinian actress Mona Maris at the Cocoanut Grove; he was charged with overstaying his leave in the States. He wept as he was released on $2,500 cash bond the next morning.[5] Dozens of other actors, actresses, and filmmakers were

194

questioned about their immigration status; only some sixteen were marked for deportation but agreed to leave the country and come back legally. Among others targeted were Gilbert Roland, George Arliss, Chaplin, Dietrich, Paul Lukas, Boris Karloff, Greta Garbo, Bela Lugosi, and others.

Garsson gave O'Sullivan a "clean bill of health" on January 30, 1933, but asserted that Farrow misrepresented himself as a "Rumanian envoy" on his visitor's application, and moved for a grand jury proceeding on charges that he had violated the immigration act of 1929 in making asserted false statements for registry as an alien visitor.

On February 4, after a five-hour hearing with Garsson, Farrow faced new "charges of perjury and moral turpitude," the latter as a result of his "romantic interludes with film actresses."[6] On February 8, Farrow was indicted by a federal grand jury for making "false statements in his application for a registry to enter this country as an alien." "An arrest in San Francisco, his service in the United States Marine and Coast Guard services and the fact that he made two secret visits to Mexico, one to Australia, his native home, and one to Tahiti, are said to have been the bases for the charges."[7]

On February 10, Farrow surrendered himself to the US Marshals, pleaded no contest, and was released with instructions to appear later for sentencing. "'Out of all this furor of accusations,' said Attorney Roger Marchetti, counsel for Farrow, last night, 'all they find is that Farrow violated the Federal Penal Code Sec. 76, which deals with falsification of immigration documents. All Farrow did was to neglect to put certain information into one of the printed blanks pertaining to immigration. His act of omission was one of negligence, rather than premeditation, and we can prove it.'"[8]

Less than a month after his arrest, Farrow appeared before District Judge Harry A. Hollzer, reiterating his lawyer's claim that he was confused when he filed his papers for his visitor permit. The judge believed him and gave Farrow five years' probation with the proviso that "Farrow live up to the terms of his agreement with his divorced wife, Mrs. Felice Farrow, wherein he undertakes to provide support for their child. The agreement approved by the court stipulated that Farrow will pay to his divorced wife $100 monthly for the child and an additional 5 per cent of his gross income for the wife, the additional sum to be not less than $100 monthly."[9] Farrow was also instructed to report to Federal Probation Officers on a monthly basis. The judge also said that after five years, Farrow could enter a plea of not guilty (instead of no contest) and therefore clear his record.

But the judge then criticized Garsson, in particular in reaction because Farrow charged that, when first arrested, he was held for questioning without permission to retain an attorney. "We have here a branch of the government which set itself up as policeman, prosecutor, court and jury. Such a condition opens the door to abuse." Garsson soon quit his post, and his Hollywood alien deportation crusade was over.

Early in 1934, Farrow was granted permission to withdraw his nolo contendere pleading and enter a not guilty plea; this would force a rehearing on his perjury charge so he could be acquitted, end his probation, and become a US citizen. Judge Hollzer ruled that Farrow was not guilty, saying "The application which Farrow filled out without advice or assistance, and on which this charge is based, was plainly confusing, even to one of his intelligence."[10] This set the stage for Farrow to ask for permission to leave the country voluntarily, and to apply for legal entry under the Australian quota. Accompanying Farrow and his counsel to the hearing was Maureen O'Sullivan, and W. M. Gurney, British Counsel. Farrow traveled to Mexico and, on January 31, legally crossed the border back into California.

Why was Farrow the "poster child" for Garsson's Hollywood crusade? In March 1933, Judge Hollzer requested that the FBI investigate Garsson. According to J. Emmett Winn in his *Kinema* article "Targeting Alien Filmmakers in 1930s Hollywood," it turns out that Garsson had a prior relationship with some of the studio heads, including Fox's Winfield Sheehan, Louis B. Mayer, and Harry Warner, who loaned "him fifteen thousand dollars, supposedly on the promise that Garsson could do favors for Warner's interests." Garsson also tried to make money in Hollywood by "advising" the studios on visa applications for their stars. "Garsson's FBI file also includes references to Farrow's womanizing and suggests that because of his illicit relations, he was not liked by studio executives and that perhaps Garsson was attempting to 'assist some of the motion picture executives in getting rid of some alien actors under contract, which were not desired to be retained by the studios.' . . . In the end, there is no definitive answer for why Garsson targeted Farrow, but rather a series of reasons, including Farrow's prior immigration problems, his high-profile relationship with O'Sullivan, his personal life, and the probability that Garsson would benefit financially through some relationship or another with Hollywood studio executives."[11]

What became of Garsson? According to Winn, Garsson's FBI file indicates that, prior to his stint at the Department of Labor, he was accused of being a bootlegger during Prohibition, he furnished blondes to Louis B. Mayer, he smuggled arms and aliens, he was a gangster associate, and was involved in racketeering and extortion. During World War II Garsson and his brother set up a fake manufacturing company and bribed Kentucky congressman A. J. May to help get millions of dollars in government contracts. After the war, a federal court found all three guilty of conspiracy and bribery, and May and the Garsson brothers were sentenced to prison. After his release, Garsson died in poverty in 1957.

Maureen Tells All

But to go back—I'll never do anything desperate about anything else that may befall me because, when I have most reason to be desperate and depressed, I am the most do-and-darish. When I'm down, I'm up. I'm like my native Ireland in this respect. I parallel the history of my country—I'm at my best when I'm cornered and have to fight.

On the other hand, any little success I may have simply anesthetizes me. I just sit down and do nothing. I sink into the first comfy chair, with a book, and call it a day.

I've always been like this. When I was a tiny youngster, at home in Ireland, if I happened to be on the outs with my family and was being ignored and sent to Coventry, my back was up right away. I'd do drastic things to recall attention to myself. I'd work like a demon in school so that my report card would be better than the reports of my sisters and brothers. Or I'd give away all my clothes to the poor so that I could pose as a poor little martyr, stripped to the skin. Or I'd deliberately fall down stairs, injure myself in some carefully minor way so that I would be in the limelight, entitled to sympathy. It usually worked—and once I was reinstated I promptly lapsed again.

Not that this has anything to do with the subject we're talking about, but here's something about my coming to Hollywood I've never told anyone before. Dad, you see, didn't want me to come. Frank Borzage knew this and he said he would come and talk to Dad but that, if Dad to feel too strongly about it, I'd better abide by his wishes and remain at home. I was pretty certain Dad would say 'no.' And then, the night before Mr. Borzage was to call on us, my baby sister was saying her prayers, when Dad chanced to pass her door and heard her say, 'Dear God, please make Daddy let Maureen go to Hollywood, for thy Son's sake. Amen.'

It was on the wings of that dear little prayer that I really came to Hollywood . . .

After the McCormick picture, I was judged a 'success.' That was my undoing. Everyone was only too anxious to be nice to 'the little Irish girl.'

I just can't stand success. And this is what I did. the studio offered to give me singing lessons, drawing lessons, elocution lessons. But, I figured, if one could be successful without knowing these things, why bother to learn? I took one elocution lesson, two dancing lessons, no singing lessons, and then sat back quite pleased with myself!

Next they told me that I should see pictures and watch other actresses but I, in my ignorance, thought that the reason I was 'successful' was just because I didn't know how to act! (Must have been an acute case of swelled head which ballooned me up into that mirage!)

The final straw came when they compared me to Janet Gaynor who was my favorite star. From that point I just bent backwards doing nothing. Nothing has ever been as completely as I did nothing—if I make myself clear!

I didn't bother about my clothes, on the screen or off, I never studied. I stayed out late every night and arrived for work each morning in a state of total exhaustion.

Then—I woke up! I was down, alright, so I began to work. I thought, 'I'll show 'em!' It was a fight for fair. I hadn't saved any money, and I was broke. I was too proud to cable home for help, after my high hat attitude before. I was homesick, friendless, alone and depressed. So, the fight was on. I didn't sit down and 'take it.' I didn't mope.

I bought hats! I always buy hats when I am depressed. It has some strange psychological effect on me. I bought new dresses too, after the hat-buying orgy. When things are going well for me I'll go around, for months, in sweaters and slacks and think nothing of it. The moment things go wrong for me I invest in a wardrobe fit to knock your eyes out. Whenever you see me looking very toppy and all brand new, you can bet your life I've had a bad slump of some sort.

I made it a point to be nice to people—not insincerely—but for the first time I tried to be interested in others and to show it. I made myself do at least a few of the things I should do . . . such as publicity pictures, having my hair done smartly, wearing makeup before being photographed and trying to think of things to talk about before being interviewed.

This sounds very trivial. It isn't. For if you bring law and order to external things, you are very apt to bring it to external things, too. Which is just what it did for me. Into my thoughts, my way of living, came some kind of system—and until that comes you can do nothing. And so, with a kind of new strength and firmness of purpose, I asked producers for parts I felt I could do. I went to the mat and fought my own battles. Finally I got the part in 'The Barretts' and then one in 'David Copperfield,' and now in 'The Voice of Bugle Ann'—so I feel 'up' again!

Somehow I think that, with John's return and my consequent awareness of my own deficiencies, I reached—and passed—a turning-point in my life. Of course, I am about due for another relapse but this I'm going to—to keep on buying hats!

You see, I have a peculiar battle to fight with myself. One part of it is that success doesn't stimulate me as it does most people. It sort of lulls me to sleep instead. And when I'm unsuccessful and about as far down as I can get, I begin to gnash my teeth and thrash about. But you can't keep on being down, you know . . . for one of the times the count will be down and out!

I don't do anything to myself. I've never touched my hair. I don't use makeup, I don't dress in an unusual way. I don't swank about in opulent cars. I don't play the game at all—and what's worse, I don't want to. I don't go about to parties and meet the 'right people.' I don't entertain them.

I'll give it all up one day, if it doesn't give me up first. I'll say good-bye to Hollywood . . . a last good-bye. We'll travel, John and I, when we can be married. We'll do interesting things together and settle in England where we can have our home and children.

I may not be an actress, I'm sure I'm not. But I am an 'Irishman' and you can't keep a good Irishman down . . . not a fighting Irishman . . .

From *Modern Screen*, May 1936; accessed at The Media History Digital Library

Bad Company: The Black Dahlia

Farrow's womanizing catapulted him, indirectly, into the middle of the infamous "Black Dahlia" murder case. Twenty-two-year-old Elizabeth Short, a Hollywood party girl, was found murdered—her body mutilated and cut in half—in a vacant lot in the Leimert Park neighborhood of Los Angeles on January 15, 1947. The LAPD, sheriff's deputies, and California State Patrol officers (1,400 in all) began an extensive investigation that produced over 150 suspects, but no one was ever charged with the crime. Among the suspects was George Hill Hodel Jr., a well-connected LA doctor who was friends with many well-placed LA officials; his Hollywood connections included John Huston, whose ex-wife, Dorothy Harvey, a wannabe scriptwriter, Hodel married, and John Farrow (who was also Dorothy's friend).[12]

He was also a friend of artist Man Ray and writer Henry Miller, and regularly hosted wild parties at his Mayan-themed house, originally the Sowden House built by architect Lloyd Wright, the son of Frank Lloyd Wright, on Franklin Avenue in Los Feliz. Hodel ran LA's Social Hygiene Bureau, and one of the women who passed in and out of Hodel's clinic was Elizabeth Short.

According to George's son, Steve Hodel, an ex-LAPD homicide detective who believes that his father indeed was the "Black Dahlia" murderer, and has written several books about the subject, among the visitors at the Franklin House was Lillian Lenorak, a well-known dancer and actress (under the name Lillian Hamilton) who had an affair with Farrow in 1945.[13] According to Hodel and filmmakers Claude Gonzalez and Frans Vandenburg,[14] Lenorak got pregnant and bore Farrow a son, John Lenorak, in September 1946. This, however, has never been documented. Some twenty-five years later John Lenorak was told by a friend of his mother and former resident of the Franklin house that his biological father was Farrow. This too has not been documented, but John then changed his name to John Lenorak Farrow.[15]

Farrow's name also came up during a six-week LAPD wire-tapping of George Hodel's home in early 1950. Heard on the phone is Dorothy Hodel, speaking to an unidentified person: "Say Bob. I found a story of a black saint, a negro. Do you know John Farrow? I thought of him because of his Catholicism. I met him years ago."[16]

During the 1947 investigation into Elizabeth Short's murder, Lillian Lenorak met with DA Lt. Frank Jemison and made a positive identification of Elizabeth Short as being a sometime girlfriend of George Hodel. Lenorak herself was brutally murdered on November 7, 1959, near Palm Springs, after a lovers' quarrel with Dr. Frank Back, a wealthy physicist and businessman who developed and sold movie and television lenses. In Back's car on the way to dinner, the quarrel escalated, and Lenorak demanded to be let out on the highway. Her body was found the next day; her skull had been crushed and she had been bludgeoned to death with the butt of a rifle. Mirroring Robert Bloch's 1959 novel, *Psycho*, then adapted and anticipating the unleashing of killer Norman Bates on the movie screen in Alfred Hitchcock's film adaptation of *Psycho*, by a mere twelve months (give or take), the killer in this horror show turned out to be a disturbed twenty-one-year-old man who lived with his mother and who ran a motel a short distance from where Lenorak got out of the car.

Girl Talk

By November 1930, Maureen was already being touted as a Hollywood starlet: From an article titled "Dress Up Your Mind": "Advice to itinerant starlets: And ... and ... and unless you actually believe that you possess the sweetness and exquisite beauty of Maureen O'Sullivan ... Stay home and marry the banker's son."[17]

In an article about where Hollywood stars put their money, "Starry Money: How the film favorites spend and save: "Maureen O'Sullivan owns a big chicken ranch in Ireland."[18]

Maureen, despite remarks to the contrary, was, at times, a wild girl.

"At this writing, both Dorothy Mackaill and Maureen O'Sullivan are on probation for speeding. If they get one more tag, their driver's licenses will be revoked. No two more cautious drivers than these in all of Hollywood—at the moment."[19]

After the success of her first Tarzan film, Maureen became a darling of the gossip columns and fan magazines. She was described as perky, with a great Irish lilt to her face, and began being paired with Hollywood elites . . . and became the grist of rumor mills. In May 1933, *Screenland* magazine reported that "Despite all reports, Maureen O'Sullivan is not retiring from motion pictures, nor is she returning to Ireland to live—not for some time, at any rate. She has been signed to a new long term contract and will be a Hollywood citizen for at least a few more years, so rest easily, you O'Sullivan fans."[20]

Maureen became a favorite of Louella Parsons, who never failed to mention Maureen in her columns—especially when Maureen hobnobbed with the elite of society. One afternoon in July 1933, she was invited to the Hearst Ranch in Southern California, where she joined a circle of actors and writers hanging around with George Bernard Shaw, who was holding court in Tinseltown. According to Parsons, Shaw was so taken with Maureen's beauty and composure that he remarked to her,

"Why are you so commonplace as to ride a horse when you could ride a beautiful zebra?"[21]

"P. G. Wodehouse dedicated his latest novel to Maureen. Wodehouse and his wife and daughter visited Hollywood last year. Being friends of Mr. Farrow, they instantly became friends of Maureen, and instantly adored her—as every one must."[22]

"Although I have worked steadily ever since I came out for 'Song o My Heart' four years ago—I was only idle ten days in all that time—his is the first really worth-while part I have had [in *The Barretts*]. This new censorship business is going to help girls of my type, who have not been identified with sex stuff. It will mean better plays too—haven't you noticed what fine stories they are buying now? I am so grateful I was able to keep in the swim.

"I had been expelled from both my convents when I was 15," confesses Maureen. "That was for 'insubordination.' So I have not been to school since. I am afraid I was a bad example for my 13-year-old sister who is now being insubordinate at school— hoping this may lead her into pictures, too, perhaps. Perhaps I am growing up, for I see now that rules and regulations and discipline are necessary," dimples this wise little 23-year-old. "I am glad Fate brought me to Hollywood. How different life would have been for me otherwise! Although Mr. Borzage has taken no interest in me since, I shall always be grateful to him."[23]

A Fish Tale, Featuring John Farrow

John Farrow had a reputation for being arrogant and sadistic, causing more than one actress to rush to her dressing room in tears. During the 1940s, Farrow worked mainly at Paramount, where there was a fishpond in the courtyard between the administration building, the actors' dressing rooms, the producers' building, and the production offices. The pond was stocked with large goldfish. Repeatedly, Farrow was seen standing beside the pond, a silver-handled cane in his hand, hitting goldfish over the head. It seemed to be his favorite pastime.

—From an unreliable source

ACKNOWLEDGMENTS

This book began as a biography of John Villiers Farrow, the Australian-American director who gave Hollywood many memorable films in so many genres: his great sea chases and high seas adventures, the westerns with his quirky point of view and, most of all, some of Hollywood's greatest film noir classics of the 1940s and 1950s, including the masterful *The Big Clock*, the shadowy *Alias Nick Beal*, and the psychotically tinged *Where Danger Lives*.

Yet, the more I learned about the man, the clearer it became: if Farrow's films aren't edgy and conflicted enough, the man who directed them lived a life that was more conflicted and complicated, more tilted toward tragedy, than any dramatic and complex scenario he could create.

A troubled, problematic soul, John Farrow had demons he could neither acknowledge nor, at times, even recognize. More knowing than Farrow about these demons, the woman he married, Maureen O' Sullivan, could not turn away. As the two went on to have seven children, their lives would coalesce into psychological warfare, resentment, and the makings of a dystopia even Hollywood could ever know. This kind of turmoil, these chaotic lives, demanded a large canvas on which to tell their story. John Farrow's gifts as an artist—a filmmaker as well as a gifted novelist and historian—did not necessarily translate into a gift for fatherhood or member of the Hollywood community.

The Farrows' lives coalesce into a biography marked by turmoil, tragedy—and certainly, trauma. Given John Farrow's talents and demons, the Farrows are, if anything, Hollywood originals, steeped in the art of movies and storytelling—yet living lives well behind the protection of such artifice.

There were many publicity photos of the family taken over the years. Yet I have imagined yet another as I've written this book, one emerging after reading Mia and Prudence's words about their father. In it, John Farrow stands in his robe, surrounded by his children. He complains that they are ignoring him. He's peeved and he's hurt. But in this photo he is authentic. Looking at this scene, I wonder if this is a photo he'd have wanted but just couldn't achieve: John Farrow, family man.

Writing the story of the Farrows began and ended on an unruly path. Following lives—and ideas—that were often contradictory and at war with each other took vigilance and a huge crop of restarts and revisions. Many voices chimed in to help with this biography, and I thank every one of them for their insights and good advice.

To Bob Bookman, who shamelessly supported this book from the beginning and never wavered on moving forward with it.

To editor and researcher extraordinaire, Harley W. Lond, who helped me dig up information during the difficult time when COVID closed libraries and halted so much communication and research.

To Shane MacDonald, John Shepherd, and Brandi Marulli of the Catholic University of America, Washington, DC, for their great generosity in making The John Farrow Collection available to me. Their energy and enthusiasm left a lasting impression.

To Genevieve Maxwell and Kristine Krueger at The Margaret Herrick Library of The Academy of Motion Picture Arts and Sciences, Beverly Hills, California, whose help in getting information to me seemed like a lifeline.

And to those generous souls who helped make this biography richer: Paul Lynch, Frank Thompson, Tatiana Siegel, Ryan

Mazie, Mark Montgomery, Marsha Hunt, Jane Russell, Peter Bogdanovich, Roger C. Memos, George Stevens, Jr., C. Courtney Joyner, Shay Garner, Mia Farrow, Pat H. Broeske, Jane Allen, John Greenwald, Bob Weide, and Robert S. Bader.

And to my posse, the usual suspects: Pamela Edwards, Sandra K. Stanley, Virginia Crane, Frederic Lombardi, Wesley Kyles, Gayle Golden, Lynn C. Miller, Robert Pincus, Joan Cohen, Deloss McGraw, Sandra Jackson, and Linda Civitello.

And to two other essential humans who continue to hold up the foundation for us all: the great wit, Kevin Brownlow, and, who else but film history incarnate, Ned Comstock!

I am indebted to the late Lee Server, whose riveting and intimate biography of Robert Mitchum enriched my understanding of the seductive actor, an unlikely candidate to create cinematic magic with John Farrow. I wish I could have offered more here.

In addition, I would like to thank my agent, Elizabeth Kaplan, and my editors at Skyhorse Publishing, Caroline Russomanno and Susan Barnett.

FILMOGRAPHIES

John Farrow Filmography

Films

WRITER/TITLES

White Gold (1927)
Director: William K. Howard. Producer: Cecil B. De Mille. Based on the play by J. Palmer Parsons. Adaptation: Garrett Fort, Marion Orth, Tay Garnett. Titles: John Krafft, John Farrow. Art Director: Anton Grot. Cinematographer: Lucien Andriot. Editor: John Dennis.

Cast: Jetta Goudal (Dolores Carson), Kenneth Thomson (Alec Carson), George Bancroft (Sam Randall), George Nichols (Carson Sen.), Robert Perry (Bucky O'Neil).

DeMille Pictures. 7 reels. B&W, silent, 35mm.

The Wreck of the Hesperus (1927)
Director: Elmer Clifton. Screenplay: Harry Carr. Story: John Farrow. Based on Henry Wadsworth Longfellow's poem, "The Wreck of the Hesperus." Titles: John Krafft. Art Director: Stephen Goosson. Cinematographer: John Mescall. Editor: Eleanor Hall.

Cast: Sam De Grasse (Capt. Slocum), Virginia Bradford (Gale Slocum), Francis Ford (John Hazzard), Frank Marion (John Hazzard, Jr.), Alan Hale (SingaporeJack).

DeMille Pictures. 7 reels. B&W, silent, 35mm.

The Showdown (1928)
Director: Victor Schertzinger. Producer: Adolph Zukor, Jesse L. Lasky. Screenplay: Ethel Doherty. Based on the play, *Wildcat*, by Houston Branch. Adaptation: Hope Loring, Ethel Doherty. Titles: John Farrow. Cinematographer: Victor Milner. Editor: George Nicholes Jr.

Cast: George Bancroft (Cardan), Evelyn Brent (Sibyl Shelton), Neil Hamilton (Wilson Shelton), Fred Kohler (Winter), Helen Lynch (Goldie).

Paramount Famous Lasky Corp. 8 reels. B&W, silent, 35mm.

The Blue Danube (1928)
Director: Paul Sloane. Associate Producer: Ralph Block. Screenplay: Harry Carr, Paul Sloane. Story. John Farrow. Titles: Edwin Justus Mayer, John Krafft. Art Director: Anton Grot. Cinematographer: Arthur Miller. Editor: Margaret Darrell.

Cast: Leatrice Joy (Marguerite), Joseph Schildkraut (Ludwig), Nils Asther (Erich von Statzen), Seena Owen (Helena Boursch), Albert Gran (Herr Boursch).

DeMille Pictures. 7 reels. B&W, Silent, 35mm.

Ladies of the Mob (1928)
Director: William A. Wellman. Producer: William A. Wellman. Screenplay: John Farrow. Story: Ernest Booth. Adaptation: Oliver H. P. Garrett. Titles: George Marion. Art Director: Hans Dreier. Cinematographer: Henry Gerrard.

Cast: Clara Bow (Yvonne), Richard Arlen ("Red"), Helen Lynch (Marie), Mary Alden ("Soft Annie"), Carl Gerrard (Joe).

Paramount Famous Lasky Corp. 7 reels. B&W, Silent, 35mm.

The First Kiss (1928)
Director: Rowland V. Lee. Producer: Rowland V. Lee, B. P. Schulberg.

Based on the story "Four Brothers" by Tristram Tupper. Adaptation: John Farrow. Titles: Tom Reed. Cinematographer: Alfred Gilks. Editor: Lee Helen

Cast: Fay Wray (Anna Lee), Gary Cooper (Mulligan Talbot), Lane Chandler (William Talbot), Leslie Fenton (Carol Talbot), Paul Fix (Ezra Talbot).

Paramount Famous Lasky Corp. 6 reels. B&W, Silent, 35mm.

Three Week-Ends (1928)

Director: Clarence Badger. Screenplay: Louise Long, Percy Heath, Sam Mintz. Story: Elinor Glyn. Adaptation: John Farrow. Titles: Paul Perez, Herman Mankiewicz. Cinematography: Harold Rosson. Editor: Tay Malarkey

Cast: Clara Bow (Gladys O'Brien), Neil Hamilton (James Gordon), Harrison Ford (Turner), Lucille Powers (Miss Witherspoon), William Holden (Carter).

Paramount Famous Lasky Corp. 6 reels. B&W, Silent, 35mm.

The Woman from Moscow (1928)

Director: Ludwig Berger. Producer: Ludwig Berger, Jesse L. Lasky, Adolph Zukor. Screenplay: John Farrow. Based on the play *"Fedora, comedie en quatre acts"* by Victorien Sardou. Titles: John Farrow. Cinematographer: Victor Milner.

Cast: Pola Negri (Princess Fedora), Norman Kerry (Loris Ipanoff), Paul Lukas (Vladimir), Otto Matiesen (Gretch Milner), Lawrence Grant (The General).

Paramount Famous Lasky Corp. 77 minutes. B&W, 35mm.

Wolf Song (1929)

Director: Victor Fleming. Producer: B. P. Fineman, Lucien Hubbard. Screenplay: John Farrow, Keene Thompson. Story: Harvey Ferguson. Titles: Julian Johnson. Cinematography: Allen Siegler.

Cast: Gary Cooper (Sam Lash), Lupe Velez (Lola Salazar), Louis Wolheim (Gullion), Constantine Romanoff (Rube Thatcher), Michael Vavitch (Don Solomon Salazar).

Paramount Famous Lasky Corp. 93 minutes. B&W, 35mm.

A Dangerous Woman (1929)

Director: Rowland V. Lee. Assoc, producer: Louis D. Lighton. Screenplay: Edward E. Paramore Jr. Based on the story, "A Woman Who Needed Killing" by Margery Lawrence. Adaptation: John Farrow. Art Director: Hans Dreier. Cinematography: Harry Fischbeck.

Cast: Baclanova (Tania Gregory), Clive Brook (Frank Gregory), Neil Hamilton (Bobby Gregory), Clyde Cook (Tubbs), Leslie Fenton (Peter Allerton).

Paramount Famous Lasky Corp. 80 minutes. B&W, 35mm.

The Four Feathers (1929)

Directors: Merian C. Cooper, Ernest B. Schoedsack, Lothar Mendes. Associate Producer: David Selznick. Screenplay: Howard Estabrook. Story: A. E. W. Mason. Adaptation: Hope Loring. Titles: Julian Johnson, John Farrow. Cinematography: Robert Kurrle, Merian C. Cooper. Ernest B. Schoedsack. Editor: Ernest B. Schoedsack.

Cast: Richard Arlen (Harry Feversham), Fay Wray (Ethne Eustace), Clive Brook (Lieut. Durrance), William Powell (Capt. Trench), Noah Beery (Slave trader).

Paramount Famous Lasky Corp. 81 minutes. B&W, 35mm.

The Wheel of Life (1929)

Director: Victor Schertzinger. Screenplay: Julian Johnson. Based on the story by James Bernard Fagan. Adaptation: John Farrow. Titles: Julian Johnson. Cinematography: Edward Cronjager. Editor: Otto Lovering.

Cast: Richard Dix (Capt. Leslie Yeullat), Esther Ralston (Ruth Dangan), O.P. Heggie (Col. John Dangan), Arthur Hoyt (George Faraker), Myrtle Stedman (Mrs Faraker).

Paramount Famous Lasky Corp. 55 minutes. B&W, 35mm.

Seven Days Leave (1930)

Director: Richard Wallace. Producer: Louis D. Lighton, Richard Wallace. Screenplay: Dan Totheroh, John Farrow. Based on the play, *The Old Lady Shows Her Medals*, a play in one act, by Sir James M. Barrie. Titles: Richard H. Digges. Art Director: Bernard Herzbrun. Editor: Charles Lang.

Cast: Gary Cooper (Kenneth Dowey), Beryl Mercer (Sarah Ann Dowey), Daisy Belmore (Emma Mickelham), Nora Cecil (Amelia Twymley), Tempe Piggott (Mrs Haggerty)

Paramount Famous Lasky Corp. 80 minutes. B&W, 35mm.

The Shadow of the Law (1930)

Director: Louis Gasnier. Screenplay: John Farrow. Based on the novel, "*The Quarry,*" by John A. Moroso, and the play, "*The Quarry,*" by Max Marcin. Cinematographer: Charles Lang. Editor: Robert Bassler.

Cast: William Powell (John Nelson, Jim Montgomery), Marion Shilling (Edith Wentworth), Natalie Moorhead (Ethel Barry), Regis Toomey (Tom), Paul Hurst (Pete).

Paramount-Publix Corp. 69 minutes. B&W, 35mm.

Inside the Lines (1930)

Director: Roy J. Pomeroy. Producer: William Le Baron. Screenplay: Ewart Adamson, John Farrow. Based on the play, "*Behind the Lines,*" by Earl Derr Biggers. Art Director: Max Ree. Cinematographer: Nick Musuraca. Editor: George Marsh, Ann McKnight.

Cast: Betty Compson (Jane Gershon), Ralph Forbes (Eric Woodhouse), Montagu Love (Governor of Gibraltar), Mischa Auer (Amahdi), Ivan Simpson (Capper).

RKO Productions. 72 minutes. B&W, 35mm.

The Common Law (1931)

Director: Paul L. Stein. Producer: Charles R. Rogers. Screenplay: John Farrow, Horace Jackson. Based on the novel by Robert W. Chambers. Art Director: Carroll Clark. Cinematographer: Hal Mohr. Editor: Charles Craft.

Cast: Constance Bennett (Valerie), Joel McCrea (Neville), Lew Cody (Cardemon), Robert Williams (Sam), Hedda Hopper (Mrs Clare Collis).

RKO Pathe. 74 minutes. B&W, 35mm.

A Woman of Experience (1931)
Director: Harry Joe Brown. Producer: Charles R. Rogers. Screenplay: John Farrow, Ralph Murphy. Based on the play, *The Registered Woman,* by Farrow. Cinematographer: Hal Mohr.

Cast: Helen Twelvetrees (Elsa), William Bakewell (Karl), Lew Cody (Capt. Otto von Lichstein), ZaSu Pitts (Katie), H. B. Warner (Maj. Hugh Schmidt).

RKO Pathe. 74 minutes. B&W, 35mm.

Woman in Chains (1932)
Director: Basil Dean. Producer: Basil Dean. Screenplay: John Farrow, John Paddy Carstairs, Harold Dearden. Based on the play, *The Impassive Footman,* by "Sapper" (Herman C. McNeile). Art Director: Edward Carrick. Cinematographer: Robert Martin. Editor: Ernest Aldridge.

Cast: Owen Nares (Bryan Daventry), Betty Stockfeld (Grace Marwood), Allan Jeayes (John Marwood), George Curzon (Simpson), Aubrey Mather (Dr. Bartlett).

Associated Talking Pictures-RKO/ Harold Auten. 70 minutes. B&W, 35mm.

Don Quixote (1933)
Director: G. W. Pabst. Producer: Nelson Vandor. Screenplay: Georg Wilhelm Pabst. Story: Paul Morand. Based on the novel *"Don Quixote de la Mancha"* by Miguel de Cervantes. Collaborator for English version: John Farrow. Art Director: Andrej Andrejew. Cinematographer: Nicholas Farkas. Editor: Jean Oser.

Cast: Feodor Chaliapin (Don Quixote), George Robey (Sancho Panza), Sidney Fox (The niece), Miles Mander (The Duke), Oscar Asche (Police Capt.), Dannio (Carrasco).

Nelson Films-Van- dor Film. 73 minutes. B&W, 35mm.

Last of the Pagans (1936)

Director: Richard Thorpe. Producer: Philip Goldstone. Screenplay: John Villiers Farrow. Based on a story by Farrow, suggested by the novel *"Typee"* by Herman Melville. Art Director: Cedric Gibbons. Cinematographer: Clyde de Vinna. Editor: Martin G. Cohn.

Cast: Mala (Taro), Lotus Long (Lilleo), Telo A. Tematua (Native chief), Ae A. Faaturia (Boy hunter), RangapoA. Taipoo (Taro's mother).

MGM. 70 minutes. B&W, 35mm.

Tarzan Escapes (1936)

Director: Richard Thorpe. Producer: Sam Zimbalist. Screenplay: Cyril Hume, John Farrow, Karl Brown. Based on characters by Edgar Rice Burroughs. Art Director: Elmer Sheeley. Cinematographer: Leonard Smith. Editor: W. Donn Hayes.

Cast: Johnny Weissmuller (Tarzan), Maureen O'Sullivan (Jane Parker), John Buckler (Capt. Fry), Benita Hume (Rita Parker), William Henry (Eric Parker).

MGM. 89 minutes. B&W, 35mm.

Around the World in 80 Days (1956)

Director: Michael Anderson. Producer: Michael Todd. Screenplay: S. J. Perelman, John Farrow, James Poe. [Some books state Farrow and Poe uncredited, but both names appear on sighted print and all three won the Academy Award.] Based on the novel by Jules Verne. Art Director: James Sullivan. Cinematographer: Lionel Lindon. Editor: Howard Epstein, Gene Ruggiero.

Cast: David Niven (PhileasFogg), Cantinflas (Passepartout) , Shirley MacLaine (Princess Aouda), Robert Newton (Inspector Fix), Charles Boyer (Monsieur Casse).

Michael Todd-UA. 175 minutes. Color. 35mm. (Todd-AO).

DIRECTOR
The Spectacle Maker (1934) (Short)
Director: John Farrow. Screenplay: Farrow. Based on a story by Frank Harris. Cinematographer: Ray Rennahan.

Cast: Francis X. Bushman Jr. (Soldier), Nora Cecil, (Duchess), Harvey Clark (The Grand Duke), Cora Sue Collins (The Little Princess)

MGM. 21 minutes. Technicolor. 35mm.

Warlord (1934) (Short)
Director: John Farrow. Screenplay: Farrow.

Men in Exile (1937)
Director: John Farrow. Screenplay: Roy Chanslor. Based on a story by Marie Baumer, Houston Branch. Cinematographer: Arthur Todd. Editor: Terry Morse.

Cast: Dick Purcell (James Carmody), June Travis (Sally Haines), Alan Baxter (Danny), Margaret Irving (Mother Haines), Victor Varconi (Col. Gomez)

First National. 58 minutes. B&W, 35mm.

West of Shanghai (1937)
Director: John Farrow. Producer: Bryan Foy. Screenplay: Crane Wilbur. Based on the play, *"The Bad Man,"* by Porter Emerson Browne. Cinematographer: L. William O'Connell. Editor: Frank Dewar.

Cast: Boris Karloff (Gen. Wu Yen Fang), Beverley Roberts (Jane Creed), Ricardo Cortez (Gordon Creed), Gordon Oliver (James Hallett), Sheila Bromley (Lola Galt)

First National. 65 minutes. B&W, 35mm.

She Loved a Fireman (1938)

Director: John Farrow. Producer: Bryan Foy. Screenplay: Carlton C. Sand, Morton Grant. Based on the story, "Two Platoons," by Sand. Cinematographer: Lou O'Connell. Editor: Thomas Pratt.

Cast: Dick Foran (Red Tyler), Ann Sheridan (Margie Shannon), Robert Armstrong (Smokey Shannon), Eddie Acuff (Skillet), Veda Ann Borg (Betty).

First National. 57 minutes. B&W, 35mm.

The Invisible Menace (1938)

Director: John Farrow. Producer: Bryan Foy. Screenplay: Crane Wibur. Based on the play, "*Without Warning,*" by Ralph Spencer Zink. Cinematographer: L. William O'Connell. Editor: Harold McLemon.

Cast: Boris Karloff (Jewries), Marie Wilson (Sally), Eddie Craven (Eddie Pratt), Eddie Acuff (Cpl. Sanger), Regis Toomey (Lt. Matthews)

Warner Bros. 54 minutes. B&W, 35mm.

Little Miss Thoroughbred (1938)

Director: John Farrow. Producer: Bryan Foy. Screenplay: Albert DeMond, George Bricker. Based on the story, "Little Lady Luck," by DeMond. Cinematographer: L. William O'Connell. Editor: Everett Dodd.

Cast: John Litel ("Nails" Morgan), Ann Sheridan (Madge Perry), Frank McHugh (Todd Harrington), Janet Chapman (Mary Ann), Eric Stanley (Col. Whitcomb)

Warner Bros. 65 minutes. B&W, 35mm.

My Bill (1938)

Director: John Farrow. Producer: Bryan Foy. Screenplay: Vincent Sherman, Robertson White. Based on the play, "*Courage,*" by Tom Barry. Art Director: Max Parker. Cinematographer: Sid Hickox. Editor: Frank Magee.

Cast: Kay Francis (Mary Coibrook), Bonita Granville (Gwen Coibrook), Anita Louise (Muriel Coibrook), Bobby Kordan (Reginald Coibrook), John Litel (Mr. Rudlin)
First National, Warner Bros. 60 minutes. B&W, 35mm.

Broadway Musketeers (1938)
Director: John Farrow. Producer: Bryan Foy. Screenplay: Don Ryan, Kenneth Garnet. Cinematography: L. William O'Connell. Editor: Thomas Pratt.
Cast: Margaret Lindsay (Isabel Dowling), Ann Sheridan (Fay Reynolds), Marie Wilson (Connie Todd), John Litel (Stanley Dowling), Janet Chapman (Judy Dowling)
Warner Bros. 63 minutes. B&W, 35mm.

The Saint Strikes Back (1939)
Director: John Farrow. Producer: Robert Sisk. Screenplay: John Twist. Based on the novel, *"Angels of Doom,"* by Leslie Charteris. Cinematographer: Frank Redman. Editor: Jack Hively.
Cast: George Sanders (Simon Templar, the Saint), Wendy Barrie (Val Travers), Jonathan Hale (Inspector Henry Femack), Jerome Cowan (Cullis Criminologist), Neil Hamilton (Allan Breck)
RKO Radio Pictures. 67 minutes. B&W, 35mm.

Women in the Wind (1939)
Director: John Farrow. Producer: Mark Hellinger. Screenplay: Lee Katz, Albert DeMond. Based on the novel by Francis Walton. Art director: Carljules Weyl. Cinematographer: Sid Hickox. Editor: Thomas Pratt.
Cast: Kay Francis (Janet Steele), William Gargan (Ace Boreman), Victor Jory (Doc), Maxie Rosenbloom (Stuffy McInnes), Sheila Bromley (Frieda Boreman)
Warner Bros. 65 minutes. B&W, 35mm.

Sorority House (1939)

Director: John Farrow. Producer: Robert Sisk. Screenplay: Dalton Trumbo. Based on the three- act comedy, *"Chi House,"* by Mary Coyle Chase. Cinematographer: Nicholas Musuraca. Editor: Harry Marker.

Cast: Anne Shirley (Alice Fisher), James Ellison (Bill Loomis), Barbara Read (Dotty Spencer), Helen Wood (Madame President), J. M. Kerrigan (Lew Fisher)

RKO Radio Pictures. 64 minutes. B&W, 35mm.

Five Came Back (1939)

Director: John Farrow. Producer: Robert Sisk. Screenplay: Jerry Cady, Dalton Trumbo, Nathaniel West. Adapted from a story by Richard Carroll. Art director: Van Nest Polglase. Cinematographer: Nicholas Musuraca. Editor: Harry Marker.

Cast: Chester Morris (Bill), Lucille Ball (Peggy), Wendy Barrie (Alice Melhome), John Carradine (Crimp), Allen Jenkins (Peter)

RKO Radio Pictures. 75 minutes. B&W, 35mm.

Full Confession (1939)

Director: John Farrow. Producer: Robert Sisk. Screenplay: Jerry Cady. Based on a story by Leo Birinski. Cinematographer: J. Roy Hunt. Editor: Harry Marker.

Cast: Victor McLaglen (McGinnis), Sally Eilers (Molly), Joseph Calleia (Father Loma), Barry Fitzgerald (Michael O'Keefe), Elisabeth Risdon (Norah O'Keefe)

RKO Radio Pictures. 72 minutes. B&W, 35mm.

Reno (1939)

Director: John Farrow. Producer: Robert Sisk. Screenplay: John Twist. Based on the story by Ellis St. Joseph. Art director: Van Nest Polglase. Cinematographer: J. Roy Hunt. Editor: Harry Marker.

Cast: Richard Dix (Bill Shear), Gail Patrick (Jesse Gibbs), Anita Louise (Mrs. Ryder), Paul Cavanagh (John Banton), Laura Hope Crews (Mrs. Gardner)

RKO Radio Pictures. 73 minutes. B&W, 35mm.

Married and in Love (1940)

Director: John Farrow. Producer: Robert Sisk. Screenplay: S. K Lauren. Art director: Van Nest Polglase. Cinematographer: J. Roy Hunt. Editor: Harry Marker.

Cast: Alan Marshal (Leslie Yates), Barbara Read (Helen Yates), Patric Knowles (Paul Wilding), Helen Vinson (Doris Wilding), Hattie Noel (Hildegard)

RKO Radio Pictures. 58 minutes. B&W, 35mm.

A Bill of Divorcement (1940)

Director: John Farrow. Producer: Lee Marcus. Screenplay: Dalton Trumbo. Based on the play by Clemence Dane. Cinematographer: Nicholas Musuraca. Editor: Harry Marker.

Cast: Maureen O'Hara (Sidney Fairfield), Adolphe Menjou (Hilary Fairfield), Fay Bainter (Margaret Fairfield), Herbert Marshall (Gray Meredith), Dame May Whitty (Hester Fairfield)

RKO Radio Pictures. 70 minutes. B&W, 35mm.

Wake Island (1942)

Director: John Farrow. Producer: Joseph Sistrom. Screenplay: W. R. Burnett, Frank Butler. Art directors: Hans Dreier, Earl Hedrick. Cinematographer: Theodor Sparkuhl. Editor: LeRoy Stone.

Cast: Brian Donlevy (Maj. Caton), MacDonald Carey (Lt. Cameron), Robert Preston (Joe Doyle), William Bendix (Smacksie Randall), Albert Dekker (Shad McClosky)

Paramount. 78 minutes. B&W, 35mm.

The Commandos Strike at Dawn (1942)

Director: John Farrow. Producer: Lester Cowan. Screenplay: Irwin Shaw. Based on a story by C. S. Forester. Art director: Edward Jewell. Cinematographer: William C. Mellor. Editor: Anne Bauchens.

Cast: Paul Muni (Erik Toresen), Anna Lee (Judith Bowen), Lillian Gish (Mrs. Bergesen), Sir Cedric Hardwicke (Adm. Bowen), Robert Coote (Robert Bowen)

Columbia. 100 minutes. B&W, 35mm.

China (1943)

Director: John Farrow. Producer: Richard Blumenthal. Screenplay: Frank Butler. Based on the play by Archibald Forbes. Cinematographer: Leo Tover. Editor: Eda Warren.

Cast: Loretta Young (Carolyn Grant), Alan Ladd (Mr. Jones), William Bendix (Johnny Sparrow), Philip Ahn (First Brother-Lin Cho), Iris Wong (Kwan Su)

Paramount. 78 minutes. B&W, 35mm.

The Hitler Gang (1944)

Director: John Farrow. Producer: B.G. DeSylva. Screenplays: Francis Goodrich, Albert Hackett. Art Directors: Hans Dreier, Franz Bachelin. Cinematographer: Ernest Laszlo. Editor: Eda Warren.

Cast: Robert Watson (Adolf Hitler), Roman Bohnen (Capt. Ernst Roehm), Martin Kosleck (Joseph Goebbels), Victor Varconi (Rudolph Hess), Luis Van Rooten (Heinrich Himmler)

Paramount. 101 minutes. B&W, 35mm.

You Came Along (1945)

Director: John Farrow. Producer: Hal B. Wallis. Screenplays: Robert Smith, Ayn Rand. Based on the story by Smith. Art Directors: Hans Dreier, Hal Pereira. Cinematographer: Daniel L. Fapp. Editor: Eda Warren.

Cast: Robert Cummings (Maj. Bob Collins), Lizabeth Scott (Ivy Hotchkiss), Don DeFore (Capt. Shakespeare Anders), Charles Drake (Handsome Janoshek), Julie Bishop (Joyce Heath)

Paramount. 103 minutes. B&W, 35mm.

Two Years Before the Mast (1946)

Director: John Farrow. Producer: Seton I. Miller. Screenplays: Miller, George Bruce. Based on the novel by Richard Henry Dana, Jr. Art Directors: Hans Dreier, Franz Bachelin. Cinematographer: Ernest Laszlo. Editor: Eda Warren.

Cast: Alan Ladd (Charles Stewart), Brian Donlevy (Richard Henry Dana), William Bendix (Amazeen), Barry Fitzgerald (Dooley), Howard da Silva (Capt. Francis Thompson)

Paramount. 98 minutes. B&W, 35mm.

California (1946)

Director: John Farrow. Producer: Seton I. Miller. Screenplays: Frank Butler, Theodore Strauss. Based on a story by Boris Ingster. Art Directors: Hans Dreier, Roland Anderson. Cinematographer: Ray Rennahan. Editor: Eda Warren.

Cast: Ray Milland (Jonathan Trumbo), Barbara Stanwyck (Lily Bishop), Barry Fitzgerald (Michael Fabian), George Coulouris (Pharaoh Coffin), Albert Dekker (Mr Pike)

Paramount. 97 minutes. Color 35mm.

Easy Come, Easy Go (1947)

Director: John Farrow. Producer: Kenneth Macgowan. Screenplays: Francis Edwards Faragoh, John McNulty, Anne Froelick. Based on *"Third Avenue Stories"* by McNulty. Art Directors: Hans Dreier, Haldane Douglas. Cinematographer: Daniel L. Fapp. Editor: Thomas Scott.

Cast: Barry Fitzgerald (Martin L. Donovan), Diana Lynn (Connie Donovan), Sonny Tufts (Kevin O'Connor), Dick Foran (Dale Whipple), Frank McHugh (Carey)

Paramount. 77 minutes. B&W, 35mm.

Blaze of Noon (1947)

Director: John Farrow. Producer: Robert Fellows. Screenplay: Frank Wead, Arthur Sheekman. Based on the novel by Ernest K Gann. Cinematographer: William C. Mellor. Editor: Sally Forrest.

Cast: Anne Baxter (Lucille Stewart), William Holden (Colin McDonald), William Bendix (Porkie), Sonny Tufts (Roland McDonald), Sterling Hayden (Tad McDonald)

Paramount. 90 minutes. B&W, 35mm.

Calcutta (1947)

Director: John Farrow. Producer: Seton I. Miller. Screenplay: Miller. Art directors: Hans Dreier, Franz Bachelin. Cinematographer: John Seitz. Editor: Archie Marshek.

Cast: Alan Ladd (Neale Gordon), Gail Russell (Virginia Moore), William Bendix (Pedro Blake), June Duprez (Marina Tanev), Lowell Gilmore (Eric Lasser)

Paramount. 83 minutes. B&W, 35mm.

The Big Clock (1948)

Director: John Farrow. Producer: Richard Maibaum. Screenplay: Jonathan Latimer. Based on the novel by Kenneth Fearing. Art Directors: Hans Dreier, Roland Anderson. Cinematographer: John Seitz. Editor: Gene Ruggiero.

Cast: Ray Milland (George Stroud), Charles Laughton (Earl Janoth), Maureen O'Sullivan (Georgette Stroud), George Macready (Steven Hagen), Rita Johnson (Pauline York)

Paramount. 95 minutes. B&W, 35mm.

Beyond Glory (1948)

Director: John Farrow. Producer: Robert Fellows. Screenplay: Jonathan Latimer, Charles Marquis Warren, William Wister Haines. Cinematographer: John Seitz. Editor: Eda Warren.

Cast: Alan Ladd (Rockwell "Rocky" Gilman), Donna Reed, (Ann Daniels), George Macready (Maj. Gen. Bond), George Coulouris (LewProctor), Harold Vermilyea (Raymond Denmore, Sr.)

Paramount. 82 minutes. B&W, 35mm.

The Night Has a Thousand Eyes (1948)

Director: John Farrow. Producer: Endre Bohem. Screenplay: Barre Lyndon, Jonathan Latimer. Based on the novel by Cornell Woolrich. Art Directors: Hans Dreier, Franz Bachelin. Cinematographer: John F. Seitz. Editor: Eda Warren.

Cast: Edward G. Robinson (John Triton), Gail Russell (Jean Courtland), John Lund (Elliott Carson), Virginia Bruce (Jenny), William Demarest (Lt. Shawn)

Paramount. 80 minutes. B&W, 35mm.

Alias Nick Beal (1949)

Director: John Farrow. Producer: Endre Bohem. Screenplay: Jonathan Laumer. Based on a story by Mindret Lord. Art Directors: Hans Dreier, Franz Bachelin. Cinematographer: Lionel Lindon. Editor: Eda Warren.

Cast: Ray Milland (Nick Beal), Audrey Totter (Donna Allen), Thomas Mitchell (Joseph Foster), Geraldine Wall (Martha Foster), George Macready (Rev. Thomas Gaylord)

Paramount. 92 minutes. B&W, 35mm.

Red, Hot and Blue (1949)

Director: John Farrow. Producer: Robert Fellows. Screenplays: Farrow, Hagar Wilde. Based on a story by Charles Lederer. Art Directors: Hans Dreier, Franz Bachelin. Cinematographer: Daniel L. Fapp. Editor: Eda Warren.

Cast: Betty Hutton (Eleanor Collier), Victor Mature (Denny James), William Demarest (Charlie Baxter), June Havoc (Sandra), Jane Nigh (No-No)

Paramount. 84 minutes. B&W, 35mm.

Copper Canyon (1950)

Director: John Farrow. Producer: Mel Epstein. Screenplay: Jonathan Latimer. Based on a story by Richard English. Art Directors: Hans Dreier, Franz Bachelin. Cinematographer: Charles B. Lang, Jr. Editor: Eda Warren.

Cast: Ray Milland (Johnny Carter), Hedy Lamarr (Lisa Roselle), Macdonald Carey (Lane Travis), Mona Freeman (Caroline Desmond), Harry Carey Jr. (Lt. Ord)
Paramount. 83 minutes. B&W, 35mm.

Where Danger Lives (1950)
Director: John Farrow. Producer: Irving Cummings, Jr. Screenplay: Charles Bennett. Based on the story by Leo Rosten. Art Directors: Albert S. D'Agostino, Ralph Berger. Cinematographer: Nicholas Musuraca. Editor: Eda Warren.
Cast: Robert Mitchum (Jeff Cameron), Faith Domergue (Margo Lannington), Claude Rains (Frederick Lannington), Maureen O'Sullivan (Julie), Charles Kemper (Police Chief)
RKO Radio Pictures. 84 minutes. B&W, 35mm.

His Kind of Woman (1951)
Director: John Farrow. Producer: Robert Sparks. Screenplay: Frank Fenton, Jack Leonard. Based on the story, "Star Sapphire," by Gerald Drayson Adams. Art Director: Albert S. D'Agostino. Cinematographer: Harry J. Wild. Editors: Eda Warren, Frederic Knudtson.
Cast: Robert Mitchum (Dan Milner) Jane Russell (Lenore Brent), Vincent Price (Mark Cardigan), Tim Holt (Bill Lusk), Charles McGraw (Thompson)
RKO Radio Pictures. 120 minutes. B&W, 35mm.

Submarine Command (1951)
Director: John Farrow. Producer: Joseph Sistrom. Screenplay: Jonathan Latimer. Based on a story by Latimer. Art Directors: Hal Pereira, Hanry Bumstead. Cinematographer: Lionel Lindon. Editor: Eda Warren.
Cast: William Holden (Cmdr. White), Nancy Olson (Carol), William Bendix (C.P. Boyer), Don Taylor (Lt. Cmdr. Peter Morris), Arthur Franz (Lt. Carlson)
Paramount. 87 minutes. B&W, 35mm.

Ride, Vaquero! (1953)

Director: John Farrow. Producer: Stephen Ames. Screenplay: Frank Fenton. Art directors: Cedric Gibbons, Arthur Lonergan. Cinematographer: Robert Surtees. Editor: Harold F. Kress.

Cast: Robert Taylor (Rio), Ava Gardner (Cordelia Cameron), Howard Keel (King Cameron), Anthony Quinn (Jose Esqueda), Kurt Kasznar (Father Antonio)

MGM. 90 minutes. Color. 35mm.

Plunder of the Sun (1953)

Director: John Farrow. Producer: Robert Fellows. Screenplay: Jonathan Latimer. Based on the novel by David Dodge. Art director: Al Ybarra. Cinematographer: Jack Draper. Editor: Harry Marker.

Cast: Glenn Ford (Al Colby), Diana Lynn (Julie Barnes), Patricia Medina (Anna Luz), Francis L. Sullivan (Thomas Berrien), Sean McClory (Jefferson)

Warner Bros. 81 minutes. B&W, 35mm.

Botany Bay (1953)

Director: John Farrow. Producer: Joseph Sistrom. Screenplay: Jonathan Latimer. Based on the novel by Charles Nordhoff and James Norman Hall. Cinematographer: John F. Seitz. Editor: Alma Macrorie.

Cast: Alan Ladd (Hugh Tallant), James Mason (CapL Gilbert), Patricia Medina (Sally Munroe), Sir Cedric Hardwicke (Gov. Phillips), Murray Matheson (Rev. Thynne)

Paramount. 93 minutes. Color. 35mm.

Hondo (1953)

Director: John Farrow. Producers: John Wayne, Robert Fellows. Screenplay: James Edward Grant. Based on the story, "The Gift of Cochise," by Louis L'Amour. Art director: Al Ybarra. Cinematographer: Robert Burke, Archie Stout. Editor: Ralph Dawson.

Cast: John Wayne (Hondo Lane), Geraldine Page (Angie), Ward Bond (Buffalo), Michael Pate (Vittoro) James Amess (Lennie).
Warner Bros. 84 minutes. Color. 35mm.

A Bullet Is Waiting (1954)

Director: John Farrow. Producer: Howard Welsch. Screenplay: Thames Williamson, Casey Robinson. Based on a story by Williamson. Cinematographer: Franz F. Planer. Editor: Otto Ludwig

Cast: Jean Simmons (Cally Canham), Rory Calhoun (Ed Stone), Stephen McNally (Sheriff Munson), Brian Aheme (David Canham).
Columbia. 83 minutes. Color. 35mm.

The Sea Chase (1955)

Director: John Farrow. Producer: John Farrow. Screenplay: James Warner Bellah, John Twist. Based on the novel by Andrew Geer. Art Director: Franz Bachelin. Cinematographer: William Clothier. Editor: William Ziegler.

Cast: John Wayne (Capt. Karl Erlich), Lana Turner (Elsa Keller), Lyle Bettger (Krichner), David Farrar (Comdr. Napier), Tab Hunter (Cadet Wesser)
Warner Bros. 117 minutes. Color 35mm.

Back from Eternity (1956)

Director: John Farrow. Producer: John Farrow. Screenplay: Jonathan Latimer. Based on a story by Richard Carroll. Cinematographer: William Mellon. Editor: Eda Warren.

Cast: Robert Ryan (Bill), Anita Ekberg (Rena), Rod Steiger (Vasquez), Phyllis Kirk (Louise), Keith Andes (Joe)
RKO Radio Pictures. 97 minutes. B&W, 35mm.

The Unholy Wife (1957)

Director: John Farrow. Producer: John Farrow. Screenplay: Jonathan Latimer. Based on a story by William Durkee. Art

Directors: Albert D'Agostino, Franz Bachelin. Cinematographer: Lucien Ballard. Editor: Eda Warren.

Cast: Diana Dors (Phyllis Hochen), Rod Steiger (Paul Hocken), Tom Tryon (San), Beulah Bondi (Emma Hochen), Marie Windsor (Gwen)

RKO Radio Pictures-Treasure, Universal. 94 minutes. Color. 35mm.

John Paul Jones (1959)

Director: John Farrow. Producer: Samuel Bronston. Screenplay: Farrow, Jesse Lasky Jr. Based on the story, "Nor'wester" by Clements Ripley. Art Director: Franz Bachelin. Cinematographer: Michel Kelber. Editor: Eda Warren.

Cast: Robert Stack (John Paul Jones), Bette Davis (Catherine the Great), Marisa Pavan (Aimee de Tellison), Charles Coburn (Benjamin Franklin), Erin O'Brien (Dorothea Danders)

Warner Bros. 126 minutes. Color. 35mm.

John Farrow Bibliography

The Bad One (New York: A.L. Burt Co., 1930)—novel

Laughter Ends (New York: Harcourt, Brace, 1933)—novel

Damien the Leper (New York: Sheed and Ward, 1937)—biography of Father Damien

The Royal Canadian Navy 1908–1940 (Canadian Printing and Lithographing Company, 1940)—history

Pageant of the Popes (New York: Sheed and Ward, 1942)—history of the papacy

Seven Poems in Pattern (Cambridge: Rampant Lions Press, 1955)—collection of poetry

The Story of Sir Thomas More (New York: Sheed and Ward, 1954)—biography of Thomas More

John Farrow Awards

Knight Grand Cross of the Order of the Holy Sepulchre by Pope Pius XI in 1937.

Order of the Holy Sepulchre of Jerusalem, 1940.

Gallery of Living Catholic Authors Award for *Pageant of the Popes,* 1943.

Order of St John of Jerusalem, 1951. (The honor was bestowed in recognition of Farrow's outstanding charitable and religious work).

Knights of Malta Honors, 1959–1961.

Legion of Honor, Croix de Guerre, 1954. (for volunteer work during the war).

Loyola University of Los Angeles, California, Honorary Degree, 1943, 1949

New York Film Critics Award for *Wake Island,* 1942

Honorary Commander in the Canadian Navy, 1943.

Honorary Commander of the Order of the British Empire (CBE), 1953.

Maureen O'Sullivan Filmography

Song o' My Heart (1930)

Director: Frank Borzage. Story: Tom Barry. Adaptation: Sonya Levien. Art Director: Harry Oliver. Cinematographer: Chester Lyons. Editor: Jack Murray.

Cast: John McCormack (Sean O'Carolon), Alice Joyce (Mary O'Brien), Maureen O'Sullivan (Eileen O'Brien), Tommy Clifford (Tad O'Brien), J. M. Kerrigan (Peter Conlon).

Fox Film Corp. 90 minutes. B&W.

So This Is London (1930)

Director: John Blystone. Scenarist: Sonya Levien. Editor: Jack Dennis. Music and Lyrics: James F Hanley, Joseph McCarthy.

Cast: Will Rogers (Hiram Draper), Irene Rich (Mrs. Hiram Draper), Frank Albertson (Junior Draper), Maureen O'Sullivan (Elinor Worthing), Lumsden Hare (Lord Percy Worthing).

Fox Film Corp. 92 minutes. B&W.

Just Imagine (1930)

Director: David Butler. Story-Dialogue by B. G. De Sylva, Lew Brown, Ray Henderson. Art Director: Stephen Goosson, Ralih Hammeras. Cinematographer: Ernest Palmer. Editor: Irene Morra.

Cast: El Brendel (Single O), Maureen O'Sullivan (LN-18), John Garrick (J-21), Marjorie White (D-6), Frank Albertson (RT-42).

Fox Film Corp. 108 minutes. B&W.

The Princess and the Plumber (1930)

Director: Alexander Korda. Story: Alice Doer Miller. Screenplay: Dialogue: Howard J. Green. Cinematographer: L William O'Connell, Dave Ragin. Editor: Margaret V Clancey.

Cast: Charles Farrell (Charlie Peters), Maureen O'Sullivan (Princess Louise), H. B. Warner (Prince Conrad), Joseph Cawthorn (Merkll), Bert Roach (Albert Bowers).

Fox Film Corp. 72 minutes. B&W.

A Connecticut Yankee (1931)

Director: David Butler. Adaptation and dialogue: William Conselman. Cinematographer: Ernest Palmer. Editor: Irene Morra. Based on the novel *"A Connecticut Yankee in King Arthur's Court"* by Mark Twain

Cast: Will Rogers (Hank Martin/Sir Boss), William Farnum (Inventor/King Arthur), Maureen O'Suffivan (Alisande), Myrna Loy (Queen Morgfan), Frank Albertson (Clarence/Emile le Poulet).

Fox Film Corp. 96 minutes. B&W.

Skyline (1931)

Director: Sam Taylor. Associate Producer: John W Considine, Jr. Story-Dialogue: Kenyon Nicholson and Dudley Nichols. Cinematographer: John Mescall. Based on the novel *"East Side, West Side"* by Felix Riesenberg.

Cast: Thomas Meighan (Gordon A. McClellan), Hardie Albright (John Breen), Maureen O'Sullivan (Kathleen Kearny), Myrna Loy (Paula Lambert), Stanley Fields (Captain Breen).

Fox Film Corp. 68 minutes. B&W.

The Big Shot (1931)

Director: Ralph F. Murphy. Associate Producer: Harry Joe Brown. Story: George Dronigold and Hal Conklin. Screenplay: and Dialogue: Earl Baldwin and Joseph Fields. Cinematographer: Arthur Miller. Art Director: Carroll Clark, Editor: Charles Craft.

Cast: Cast: Eddie Qufflan (Ray Smith), Maureen O'Sullivan (Doris Thompson), Mary Nolan (Fay Turner), Roscoe Ates (Rusty), Belle Bennett (Mrs. Isabel Thompson).

RKO Pathe Pictures, Inc. 66 minutes. B&W.

The Silver Lining (1932)

Director: Alan Crosland. Producer: Emil Jensen. Story: Hal Conklin. Adaptation and Dialogue: Gertrude Orr. Cinematographer: Robert Planck. Art Director: Jack Schultze. Editor: Doris Drought.

Cast: Maureen O'Sullivan (Joyce Moore/Mary Kane), Betty Compson (Kate Flynn), John Warburton (Larry Clark), Montagu Love (Michael Moore), Mary Doran (Doris Lee).

Atlantic Pictures Corp. 75 minutes. B&W.

Tarzan, The Ape Man (1932)

Director: W. S. Van Dyke. Producer: Bernard H. Hyman. Adaptation: Cyril Home. Dialogue: Ivor Novéllo. Cinematographer: Harold Rossrin and Clyde de Vinna. Editors: Ben Lewis and Tom Held. Art Director: Cedric Gibbons. Based upon the characters created by Edgar Rice Burroughs.

Cast: Johnny Weissmuller (Tarzan), Maureen O'Sullivan (Jane Parker), Neil Hamilton (Hary Holt), C. Aubrey Smith (James Parker), Doris Lloyd (Mrs. Cutten).

MGM. 99 minutes. B&W.

The Information Kid (1932)

Director: Kurt Neumann. Producer: Carl Laemmle, Jr. Screenplay: Earle Snell. Story: Gerald Beaumont and Charles Logue. Cinematographer: Arthur Edeson. Art Director: Stanley Fleischer. Editor: Philip.

Cast: Tom Brown (Marry Black), James Gleason (Silk Henleji), Maureen O'Sullivan (Sally), Andy Devine (Information Kid), Mickey Rooney (Midge)

Universal Pictures. 71 minutes. B&W.

Strange Interlude (1932)

Director: Robert Z. Leonard. Dialogue and Continuity: Bess Meredyth and C. Gardner Sullivan. Cinematographer: Lee Garmes. Art Director: Cedric Gibbons. Editor: Margaret Booth. Based on the play *"Strange Interlude"* by Eugene ONeiIIO'Neill.

Cast: Norma Shearer (Nina Leeds [Evans]), Clark Gable (Dr. Ned Darrell), Alexander Kirkland (Sam Evans), Robert Young (Gordon), Maureen O'Sullivan (Madeleine).

MGM. 110 minutes. B&W.

Skyscraper Souls (1932)

Director: Edgar Selwyn. Dialogue and Continuity: Elmer Harris. Adaptation: C. Gardner Sullivan. Cinematographer: William Daniels. Art Director: Cedric Gibbons. Editor: Tom Held. Based on the novel *"Skyscraper"* by Faith Baldwin.

Cast: Warren William (David Dwight), Maureen O'Sullivan (Lynn Harding), Anita Page (Jenny), Verree Teasdale (Sarah Dennis), Norman Foster (Tom Shepherd).

MGM. 99 minutes. B&W.

Okay, America (1932)

Director: Tay Garnett. Producer: Carl Laemmle Jr. Original Story and Screenplay: William Anthony McGuire. Cinematographer: Arthur Miller. Editor: Ted Kent.

Cast: Lew Ayres (Larry Wayne), Maureen O'Sullivan (Sheila Barton), Louis Calhern ("Mileaway" Russell), Edward Arnold ("Duke" Morgan), Walter Catlett (City editor "Lucille").

Universal Pictures. 80 minutes. B&W.

Payment Deferred (1932)

Director: Lothar Mendes. Screenplay: Ernest Vajda and Claudine West. Cinematographer: Merritt B. Gerstad. Art Director: Cedric Gibbons. Editor: Frank Sullivan. Based on the play *"Payment Deferred"* by Jeffrey E. Dell and the novel by E. M. Forster.

Cast: Charles Laughton (William Marble), Maureen O'Sullivan (Winnie Marble), Dorothy Peterson (Annie Marble), Verree Teasdale (Mme. Collins), Ray Milland (James Medland).

MGM. 80 minutes. B&W.

Robbers' Roost (1933)

Director: Louis King. Screenplay: Dudley Nichols. Cinematographer: George Schneiderman. Art Director: Joseph Wright. Based on the novel *"Robbers' Roost"* by Zane Grey.

Cast: George O'Brien (Jim Wall), Maureen O'Sullivan (Helen Herrick), Walter McGrail (Brad), Maude Eburne (Aunt Ellen), Reginald Owen (Cecil Herrick).

Fox Film Corp. 64 minutes. B&W.

The Cohens and Kellys In in Trouble (1933)

Director: George Stevens. Producer: Carl Laemmle, Jr. Screenplay: Albert Austin and Fred Guiol. Story: Homer Croy and Vernon Smith. Cinematographer: Len Powers. Art Director: Stanley Fleischer. Editor: Robert Carlisle.

Cast: George Sidney (Nathan Cohen), Charles Murray (Captain Patrick Kelly), Maureen O'Sullivan (Molly Kelly), Frank Albertson (Bob Graham), Andy Devine (Andy Anderson).

Universal Pictures. 69 minutes. B&W.

Tugboat Annie (1933)

Director: Mervyn LeRoy. Associate Producer: Harry Rapf. Adaptation: Zeida Sears and Eve Greene. Cinematographer: Gregg Toland. Art Director: Merrill Pye. Editor: Blanche Sewell. Based on the "Tugboat Annie" short stories by Norman Reilly.

Cast: Marie Dressler (Annie Brennan), Wallace Beery (Terrj Brennan), Robert Young (Alec Brennan), Maureen O'Sullivan (Pat Severn), Willard Robertson (Red Severn).

M-G-M . 87 minutes. B&W.

Stage Mother (1933)

Director: Charles Brabin. Screenplay: John Meehan and Bradford Ropes. Cinematographer: George Folsey. Art Director: Stanwood Rogers. Editor: Frank Hull. Based on the novel *"Stage Mother"* by Bradford Ropes.

Cast: Alice Brady (Kitty Lorraine), Maureen O'Sullivan (Shirley Lorraine), Franchot Tone (Warren Foster), Phillips Holmes (Lord Aylesworth, Ted Healy (Ralph Martin).

MGM. 85 minutes. B&W.

Tarzan and His Mate (1934)

Director: Cedric Gibbons (uncredited direction by Jack Conway). Producer: Bernard H. Hyman. Screenplay: James Kevin McGuinness. Adaptation: Howard Emmett Rogers and Leon Gordon. Cinematographer: Charles G. Clarke and Clyde de Vinna. Editor: Tom Held. Art Director: Arnold Gillespie. Based upon the characters created by Edgar Rice Burroughs.

Cast: Johnny Weissmuller (Tarzan), Maureen O'Sullivan (Jane), Neil Hamilton (Harry Holt), Paul Cavanagh (Martin Arlington), Forrester Harvey (Beamish).

MGM. 116 minutes at preview, 95 minutes in general release.

The Thin Man (1934)

Director: W S. Van Dyke II. Producer: Hunt Stromberg. Screenplay: Albert Hackett, Frances Goodrich. Cinematographer: James Wong Howe. Art Directors: Cedric Gibbons, David Townsend. Editor: Robert J. Kern. Based on the novel *"The Thin Man"* by Dashiell Hammett.

Cast: William Powell (Nick Charles), Myrna Loy (Nora Charles), Maureen O'Sullivan (Dorothy Wynant), Nat Pendleton (Lieutenant John Guild), Minna Gombell (Mimi Wjnant).

MGM. 91 minutes. B&W.

Hide-Out (1934)

Director: W S. Van Dyke II. Producer: Hunt Stromberg. Screenplay: Frances Goodrich and Albert Hackett. Story: Mauri Grashin. Cinematographer: Ray June and Sidney Wagner. Art Director: Cedric Gibbons. Editor: Basil Wrangell.

Cast: Robert Montgomery (Lucky Wilson), Maureen O'Sullivan (Pauline Miller), Edward Arnold (Lieutenant MacCarthy), Elizabeth Patterson (Ma Miller), Whitford Kane (Pa Miller).

MGM. 82 minutes. B&W.

The Barretts of Wimpole Street (1934)

Director: Sidney Franklin. Producer: Irving G. Thalberg. Screenplay: Ernest Vajda, Claudine West and Donald Ogden Stewart. Cinematographer: William Daniels. Art Director: Cedric Gibbons. Editor: Margaret Booth. Based on the play *"The Barretts of Wimpole Street"* by Rudolf Besier.

Cast: Norma Shearer (Elizabeth Barrett), Fredric March (Robert Browning), Charles Laughton (Edward Barrett), Maureen O'Sullivan (Henrietta Barrett), Katharine Alexander (Anabel Barrett).

MGM. 111 minutes. B&W.

David Copperfield (1935)

Director: George Cukor. Producer: David O. Se]lznick. Adaptation: Hugh Walpole. Screenplay: Howard Estabrook. Cinematographer: Oliver T. Marsh. Art Director: Cedric Gibbons. Editor: Robert J. Kern. Based on the novel by Charles Dickens.

Cast: W C. Fields (Wilkins Micawber), Lionel Barrymore (Mr. Peggott), Maureen O'Sullivan, (Dora Spenlow), Madge Evans, (Agnes Wickfield), Edna May Oliver (Aunt Betsey Trotwood).

MGM. 133 minutes. B&W.

West Point of the Air (1935)

Director: Richard Rosson. Producer: Monta Bell. Screenplay: Frank Wead and Arthur J. Beckhard. Story: James K. McGuinness and John Monk Saunders. Cinematographer: Clyde DeVinna. Art Director: Cedric Gibbons. Editor: Frank Sullivan.

Cast: Wallace Beery ("Big Mike" Stone), Robert Young ("Little Mike" Stone), Lewis Stone (General Carter), Maureen O'Sullivan (his daughter "Skip"), Rosalind Russell (Dare Marshall).

MGM. 88 minutes. B&W.

Cardinal Richelieu (1935)

Director: Rowland V. Lee. Associate Producers: William Goetz and Raymond Griffith. Screenplajy: Maude Howell. Adaptation: Cameron Rogers. Dialogue: W. P. Lipscomb. Cinematographer: Peverell Marley. Art Director: Richard Day. Editor: Sherman Todd. Based on the play *"Richelieu"* by Sir Edward Bulwer-Lytton.

Cast: George Arliss (Cardinal Richelieu), Maureen O'Sullivan (Lenore), Edward Arnold (Louis XIII), Cesar Romero (Andre de Pons), Douglass Dumbrille (Baradas).

MGM. 82 minutes. B&W.

The Flame Within (1935)

Director/Producer: Edmund Goulding. Screenplay: Edmund Goulding. Cinematographer: James Wong Howe. Art Director: Cedric Gibbons. Editor: Blanche Sewell. Music composed by Jerome Kern.

Cast: Ann Harding (Dr. Mary White), Herbert Marshall (Dr. Gordon Phillips), Maureen O'Sullivan (Lillian Belton), Louis Hayward (Jack Kerry), Henry Stephenson (Dr. Jock Fragier).

MGM. 75 minutes. B&W.

Woman Wanted (1935)

Director: George B. Seitz. Screenplay: Leonard Fields and Dave Silverstein. Cinematographer: Charles Clarke. Art Director: Cedric Gibbons. Editor: Ben Lewis.

Cast: Maureen O'Sullivan (Ann Gray), Joel McCrea (Tony Baxter), Lewis Stone (District Attorney Martin), Louis Calhern (Smiley), Edgar Kennedy (Sweeney).

M-G-M . 70 minutes. B&W.

Anna Karenina (1935)

Director: Clarence Brown. Producer: David O. Selznick. Screenplay: Clemence Dane and Salka Viertel. Dialogue Adaptation: S. N. Behrman. Cinematographer: William Daniels.

Art Director: Cedric Gibbons. Editor: Robert J. Kern. Based on the novel *"Anna Karenina"* by Leo Tolstoy.

Cast: Greta Garbo (Anna Karenina), Fredric March (Count Vronsky), Freddie Bartholomew (Sergei), Maureen O'Sullivan (Kitty), May Robson (Countess Vronsky).

MGM. 93 minutes. B&W.

The Bishop Misbehaves (1935)

Director: E. A. Dupont. Screenplay: Leon Gordon. Cinematographer: James Van Trees. Art Director: Cedric Gibbons. Editor: James E. Newcom, Based on the play *"The Bishop Misbehaves"* by Frederick Jackson.

Cast: Edmund Gwenn (James, Bishop of Broadminster), Maureen O'Sullivan (Hester Grantham), Lucile Watson (Lady Emily), Reginald Owen (Guy Wailer), Dudley Digges ("Red").

MGM. 86 minutes. B&W.

The Voice of Bugle Ann (1936)

Director: Richard Thorpe. Producer: John W. Considine Jr. Screenplay: Harvey Gates and Samuel Hoffenstein. Cinematographer: Ernest Haller. Art Director: Cedric Gibbons. Editor: George Boemler. Based on the novel *"The Voice of Bugle Ann"* by MacKinlay Kantor.

Cast: Lionel Barrymore (Springfield Davis), Maureen O'Sufflvan (Camden Terp), Eric Linden (Benjy Davis), Spring Byington (Ma Davis).

MGM. 70 minutes. B&W.

Hollywood—The Second Step (1936)

Director: Felix E. Feist. Producer: Jack Chertok. Screenplay: Mauri Grashin.

Cast: Carey Wilson (Narrator), Jane Barnes (Jane Barnes), Maureen O'Sullivan (Maureen O'Sullivan), Francis X. Bushman Jr. (Billy Grady [as Ralph Bushman], Chico Marx (Chico Marx).

MGM. 11 minutes. B&W.

241

The Devil-Doll (1936)

Director: Tod Browning. Producer: Edward J. Mannix. Screenplay: Garrett Fort, Guy Endore and Erich Von Stroheim. Story: Tod Browning. Cinematographer: Leonard Smith. Art Director: Cedric Gibbons. Editor: Fredrick Y. Smith. Based on the novel *"Burn, Witch, Burn!"* by Abraham Merritt.

Cast: Lionel Barrymore (Paul Lavond [aka Madame Mandelip), Maureen O'Sullivan (Lorraine Lavond), Frank Lawton (Toto), Rafaela Ottiano (Malita), Robert Greig (Coulvet).

M-G-M . 79 minutes. B&W.

Tarzan Escapes (1936)

Director: Richard Thorpe, [John Farrow (uncredited), James C. McKay (uncredited)], Associate Producer: Sam Zimbalist. Screenplay: Cyril Hume. Art Director: Elmer Sheeley. Cinematographer: Leonard Smith. Editor: W. Donn Hayes. Based upon the characters created by Edgar Rice Burroughs.

Cast: Johnny Weissmuller (Tarzan), Maureen O'Sulllvan (Jane), John Buckler (Captain Fry), Benita Hume (Rita Parker), William Henry (Eric Parker).

MGM. 95 minutes. B&W.

A Day at the Races (1937)

Director: Sam Wood. Producers: Irving Thalberg and Lawrence Weingarten. Screenplay: Robert Pirosh, George Seaton and George Oppenheimer. Cinematographer: Joseph Ruttenberg. Art Director: Cedric Gibbons. Editor: Frank E. Hull.

Cast: Groucho Marx (Dr. Hugo Z. Hackenbush), Chico Marx (Tony), Harpo Marx (Stuffy), Maureen O'Sullivan (Judy Standish), Margaret Dumont (Mrs. Upjohn).

MGM. 109 minutes. B&W.

The Emperor's Candlesticks (1937)

Director: George Fitzmaurice. Producer: John W. Considine, Jr. Screenplay: Monckton Hoffe, Harold Goldman. Cinematographer: Harold Rosson. Montage: Slavko Vorkapich. Art

Director: Cedric Gibbons. Editor: Conrad A. Nervig. Based on the novel *"The Emperor's Candlesticks"* by Baroness Orczy.

Cast: William Powell (Baron Stephan Wolensky), Luise Rainer (Countess Olga Mironova), Robert Young (Grand Duke Peter), Maureen O'Sullivan (Maria Orlech), Frank Morgan (Colonel Baron Suroff).

MGM. 89 minutes. B&W.

Between Two Women (1937)
Director: George B. Seitz. Screenplay: Frederick Stephani and Marion Parsonnet. Original Story: Erich von Stroheim. Cinematographer: John Seitz. Art Director: Cedric Gibbons. Editor: W Donn Hayes.

Cast: Franchot Tone (Dr. Allen Meighan), Maureen O'Sullivan (Claire Donahue), Virginia Bruce (Patricia Sloan), Leonard Penn (Dr. Tony Wolcott), Cliff Edwards (Snoopy).

MGM. 89 minutes. B&W.

My Dear Miss Aldrich (1937)
Director: George B. Seitz. Original Story and Screenplay: Herman J. Mankiewicz. Cinematographer: Charles Lawton, Jr. Art Director: Cedric Gibbilns. Editor: William S. Gray.

Cast: Edna May Oliver (Mrs. Lou Atherton), Maureen O'Sullivan (Martha Aldrich), Walter Pidgeon (Ken Morley), Rita Johnson (Ellen Warfield), Janet Beecher (Mrs. Sinclair).

MGM. 73 minutes. B&W.

A Yank at Oxford (1938)
Director: Jack Conway. Producer: Michael Balcon. Screenplay: Malcolm Stuart Boylan, Walter Ferris and George Oppenheimer. Original story: Leon Gordon, Sidney Gilliatt and Michael Hogan. Based on an idea by John Monk Saunders. Contributors to screen construction: Frank Wead and F. Scott Fitzgerald. Cinematographer: Harold Rosson. Art Director: L. P. Williams. Editor: Charles Frend.

Cast: Robert Taylor (Lee Sheridan), Lionel Barrymore (Dan Sheridan), Maureen O'Sullivan (Molly Beaumont), Vivien Leigh (Elsa Craddock), Edmund Gwenn (Dean of Cardinal).
MGM. 103 minutes. B&W.

Port of Seven Seas (1938)

Director: James Whale. Producer: Henry Henigson. Screenplay: Preston Sturges. Cinematographer: Karl Freund. Art Director: Cedric Gibbons. Editor: Frederick Y. Smith.

Cast: Wallace Beery (Cesar), Frank Morgan (Panesse), Maureen O'Sullivan (Madelon), John Beal (Marias), Jessie Ralph (Honorine).
MGM. 81 minutes. B&W.

Hold That Kiss (1938)

Director: Edwin L. Mann. Producer: John W Considine, Jr. Original slong and Screenplay: Stanley Rauh. Cinematographer: George Folsey. Art Director: Cedric Gibbons. Editor: Ben Lewis.

Cast: Maureen O'Sullivan (Jane Evans), Dennis O'Keefe (Tommy Bradford), Mickey Rooney (Chick Evans), George Barbier (Mr J. Westley Piermont), Jessie Ralph (Aunt Lucy).
MGM. 79 minutes. B&W.

The Crowd Roars (1938)

Director: Richard Thorpe. Producer: Sam Zimbalist. Screenplay: Thomas Lennon, George Bruce, George Oppenheimer. Cinematographer: John Seitz. Art Director: Cedric Gibbons. Editor: Conrad A. Nervig.

Cast: Robert Taylor (Tommy McCoy), Edward Arnold (Jim Cain), Frank Morgan (Brian McCoy), Maureen O'Sullivan (Sheila Carson), William Gargan (Johnny Martin).
MGM. 92 minutes. B&W.

Spring Madness (1938)

Director: S. Sylvan Simon. Associate Producer and Screenplay: Edward Chodorov. Cinematographer: Joseph Ruttenberg. Art Director: Cedric Gibbons. Editor: Conrad A. Nervig. Based on the play *"Spring Dance"* by Philip Barry.

Cast: Maureen O'Sullivan (Alexandra Benson), Law Ayres (Sam Thatcher), Ruth Hussey (Kate McKim), Burgess Meredith (Lippencott), Ann Morriss (Frances).

MGM. 67 minutes. B&W.

Let Us Live (1939)

Director: John Brahm. Producer: William Perlberg. Screenplay: Anthony Veiller and Allen Rivkin. Story: Joseph F Dinneen. Cinematographer: Lucien Ballard. Art Director: Lionel Banks. Editor: Al Clark.

Cast: Maureen O'Sullivan (Mary Roberts), Henry Fonda ("Brick" Tennant), Ralph Bellamy (Lieutenant Everett), Alan Baxter (Joe Linden), Stanley Ridges (District Attorney).

MGM. 68 minutes. B&W.

Tarzan Finds a Son (1939)

Director: Richard Thorpe. Producer: Sam Zimbalist. Screenplay: Cyril Hume. Art Director: Cedric Gibbons. Cinematographer: Leonard Smith. Editors: Frank Sullivan and Gene Ruggiero.

Cast: Johnny Weissmuller (Tarzan), Maureen O'Sullivan (Jane), Johnny Sheffield (Boy), Ian Hunter (Austin Lancing), Henry Stephenson (Sir Thomas Lancing).

MGM. 95 minutes. B&W.

Pride and Prejudice (1940)

Director: Robert Z. Leonard. Producer: Hunt Stromberg. Screenplay: Aldous Huxley and Jane Murfin. Cinematographer: Karl Freund. Art Director: Cedric Gibbons. Editor: Robert J. Kern. Based on the novel *"Pride and Prejudice* by Jane Austen."

Cast: Greer Garson (Elizabeth Bennet), Laurence Olivier (Mr. Darcy), Maureen O'Sullivan (Jane Bennet), Mary Boland (Mrs. Bennet), Edna May Oliver (Lady Catherine de Bourgh).
MGM. 117 minutes. B&W.

Sporting Blood (1940)

Director: S. Sylvan Simon. Producer: Albert E. Levoy. Screenplay: Lawrence Hazard, Albert Mannheimer and Dorothy Yost. Original story: Grace Norton. Cinematographer: Sidney Wagner. Art Director: Cedric Gibbons. Editor: Frank Sullivan.

Cast: Robert Young (Myles Vanders), Maureen O'Sullivan (Linda Lockwood), Lewis Stone (Davis Lockwood), William Gargan (Duffy), Lynne Carver (Joan Lockwood).
MGM. 85 minutes. B&W.

Maisie Was a Lady (1941)

Director: Edwin L. Mardi. Producer: J. Walter Ruben. Screenplay: Betty Reinhardt, Mary C. McCall, Jr.. Onginal stoyOriginal story: Reinhardt and Myles Connolly. Cinematographer: Charles Lawton. Editor: Frederick Y Smith. Art Director: Cedric Gibbons. Based on the character created by Wilson Collinson.

Cast: Ann Sothern (Maisie), Lew Ayres (Bob Rawlston), Maureen O'Sullivan (Abby Rawlston), C. Aubrey Smith (lWalpole), Edward Ashley (Link Phillps).
M-G-M 78 minutes. B&W.

Tarzan's Secret Treasure (1941)

Director: Richard Thorpe. Producer: B. P. Fineman. Screenplay: Myles Connolly and Paul Gangelin. Cinematographer: Clyde de Vinna. Art Director: Cedric Gibbons. Editor: Gene Ruggiero. Based upon the characters created by Edgar Rice Burroughs.

Cast: Johnny Weissmuller (Tarzan), Maureen O'Sullivan (Jane), Johnny Sheffield (Boy), Reginald Owen (Professor Elliot), Barry Fitzgerald (O'Doul).
MGM. 81 minutes. B&W.

Tarzan's New York Adventure (1942)

Director: Richard Thorpe. Producer: by Frederick Stephani. Screenplay: William R. Lipman and Myles Connolly. Story: Myles Connolly. Cinematographer: Sidney Wagner. Art Director: Cedric Gibbons. Based upon the characters created by Edgar Rice Burroughs. Editor: Gene Ruggiero.

Cast: Johnny Weissmuller (Tarzan), Maureen O'Sullivan (Jane), Johnny Sheffield (Boy), Virginia Grey (Connie Beach), Charles Bickford (Buck Rand).

MGM. 71 minutes. B&W.

The Big Clock (1948)

Director: John Farrow. Producer: Richard Maibaum. Screenplay, Jonathan Latimer. Cinematographer: John F Seitz. Art Directors, Hans Dreier, Roland Anderson, Albert Nozaki. Editor: Eda Warren.

Based on the novel *"The Big Clock"* by Kenneth Fearing.

Cast: Ray Milland (George Stroud), Charles Laughton (Earl Janoth), Maureen O'Sullivan (Georgette Stroud), George Macready (Steve Hagen), Rita Johnson (Pauline York).

Paramount Pictures, Inc. 95 minutes. B&W.

Where Danger Lives (1950)

Director: John Farrow. Producer: Irving Cummings, Irwin Allen. Screenplay: Charles Bennett. Story, Leo Rosten. Cinematographer: Nicholas Musuraca. Art Directors: Albert S. D'Agustino, Ralph Berger. Editor: Eda Warren.

Cast: Robert Mitchurn Mitchum (Dr. Jeff Cameron), Faith Domergue (Margo), Claude Rains (Mr. Lannington), Maureen O'Sullivan (Julie Dorn), Charles Kemper (police chief).

RKO Radio Pictures. 84 minutes. B&W.

Bonzo Goes to College (1952)

Director: Frederick de Cordova. Producer: Ted Richmond. Screenplay: Leo Lieberman, Jack Henley. Story: Leo Leiberman.

Cinematographer: Carl Guthrie. Art Directors: Bernard Herzbrun, Hilyard Brown. Editor: Ted Kent.

Cast: Maureen O'Sullivan (Marion Drew), Charles Drake (Malcolm Drew), Edmund Gwenn (Pop Drew), Gigi Perreau (Betsy Drew), Gene Lockhart (Clarence B. Gateson).

Universal-International Pictures. 78 minutes. B&W.

Ellis in Freedomland (1952)

Director: Abby Berlin, Producers: Roland D. Reed, Guy V. Thayer Jr., Story: Arthur Hoerl, Cinematographer: Walter Strenge, Editor: S. Roy Luby, Fred Maguire.

Cast: Betty Furness, Edward Arnold (The Range voice), James Mason (The Refrigerator voice), Jerry Colonna (The Waste-away voice), Lucille Ball (The Laundromat voice), Maureen O'Sullivan (The Dishwasher voice).

Roland Reed Productions. 82 minutes. Color.

All I Desire (1953)

Director: Douglas Sirk. Producer: Ross Hunter. Screenplay: James Gunn, Robert Blees. Adaptation: Gina Kaus. Cinematographer: Carl Guthrie. Art Directors: Bernard Herabrun, Alexander Golitzen. Editor: Milton Carruth. Based on the novel *"Stopover"* by Carol Brink.

Cast: Barbara Stanwyck (Naomi Murdoch), Richard Carlson (Henry Murdoch), Maureen O'Sullivan (Sara Harper), Lyle Bettger (Dutch Heinemann), Marcia Henderson (Joyce Murdoch).

Universal-International Pictures. 79 minutes. B&W.

Mission Over over Korea (1953)

Director: Fred F. Sears. Producer: Robert Cohn. Screenplay: Jesse L. Lasky Jr., Eugene Ling, Martin M. Cinematographer: Sam Leavitt. Art Director: George Brooks. Editor: Henry Batista.

Cast: John Hodiak (Capt. George Slocum), John Derek (Lt. Pete Barker), Audrey Totter (Kate), Maureen O'Sullivan (Nancy Slocum), Harvey Lembeck (Sgt. Maxie Steiner).

Columbia Pictures. 86 minutes. B&W.

Duffy of San Quentin (1954)

Director: Walter Doniger. Screenplay: Walter Doniger. Story: Berman Swarttz, Walter Doniger. Cinematographer: John Alton. Art Director: Daniel Hall. Editor: Edward Sampson.

Cast: Louis Hayward (Edward "Romeo" Harper), Joanne Dru (Anne Halsey, Paul Kelly (Warden Clinton T. Duffy), Maureen O'Sullivan (Gladys Duffy), George Macready (Winant).

Swarttz-Doniger Productions. 78 minutes. B&W.

The Steel Cage (1954)

Director: Walter Doniger. Producers: Berman Swarttz, Walter Doniger. Cinematographer: John Alton. Art Director: Charles D. Hall. Editors: Chester Schaeffer, Everett Dodd.

Cast: Paul Kelly (Warden Clinton T. Duffy), Maureen O'Sullivan (Gladys Duffy), Walter Slezak (Louis), John Ireland (Al), Lawrence Tierney (Chet Harmon).

Phoenix Films, Inc. 80 minutes. B&W.

The Tall T (1957)

Director: Budd Boetticher. Producers: Harry Joe Brown and Randolph Scott. Screenplay: Burt Kennedy. Cinematographer: Charles Lawton Jr. Art Director: George Brooks. Editor: Al Clark. Based on the Elmore Leonard novella, "*The Captive.*"

Cast: Randolph Scott (Pat Brennan), Richard Boone (Frank Usher), Maureen O'Sullivan (Doretta Mims), Arthur Hunnicutt (Ed Rintoon), Skip Homeier (Billy Jack).

Scott-Brown Production/ Columbia Pictures. 78 minutes. Technicolor.

Wild Heritage (1958)

Director: Charles Haas. Producer: John E. Horton. Screenplay: Paul King, Joseph Stone. Story: Steve Frazee. Cinematographer:

Philip Lathrop. Art Directors, Alexander Golitzen, Robert Boyle. Editor: Edward Mann.

Cast: Will Rogers Jr. (Judge Copeland), Maureen O'Sullivan (Emma Breslin), Rod McKuen (Dirk Breslin), Casey Tibbs (Rusty), Troy Donahue (Jesse Bascomb).

Universal-International Pictures. 78 minutes. CinemaScope, Eastmancolor.

Never Too Late (1965)
Director: Bud Yorkin. Producer: Norman Lear. Screenplay: Sumner Arthur Long. Cinematographer: Philip Lathrop. Art Director: Edward Carrere. Editor: William Ziegler.

Cast: Paul Ford (Harry Lambert), Maureen O'Sullivan (Edith Lambert), Jim Hutton (Charlie Clinton), Connie Stevens (Kate Clinton), Jane Wyatt (Grace Kimbrough).

Warner Bros. Pictures. 105 minutes. Color.

The Phynx (1970)
Director: Lee H. Katzin. Producers: Bob Booker, George Foster. Written by Stan Cornyn. Cinematographer: Michel Hugo. Editor: Dann Cahn.

Cast: Lou Antonio (Corrigan), Mike Kellin (Bogey), Michael Ansara (Col. Rostinov), George Tobias (Markevitch,) Maureen O'Sullivan (cameo).

Cinema Organization/Warner Brothers. 91 minutes. Color.

The Crooked Hearts (1972—TV)
Director: Jay Sandrich. Executive Producer: Lee Rich. Producer: Allen S. Epstein. Teleplay: A. J. Russell. Cinematographer: Joseph Biroc. Editor: Gene Fowler Jr. Art Director: Jan Scott.

Cast: Rosalind Russell (Laurita Dorsey), Douglas Fairbanks Jr. (Rex Willoughby), Maureen O'Sullivan (Lillian Stanton), Ross Martin (Sergeant Daniel Shane), Michael Murphy (Frank Adamic).

ABC/Lorimar Productions. 90 minutes. Color.

The Great Houdini (1976—TV)

Cast: Paul Michael Glaser (Harry Houdini), Sally Struthers (Bess Houdini), Ruth Gordon (Cecilia Weiss), Maureen O'Sullivan (Lady Conan Doyle), Peter Cushing (Arthur Conan Doyle).

Director: Melville Shavelson. Story: Melville Shavelson. Cinematographer: Arch R. Daltzell. Editor: John M. Woodcock. Production Designer: Tracy Bousman

ABC Circle Films. 100 minutes. Color.

One Who Was There (1979)

Director: Donald Hughes. Producer: Edgar A. Gossard. Screenplay: Donald Hughes, Suzy Loftis. Cinematographer: Bill Godsey.

Cast: Maureen O'Sullivan (Old Mary Magdalene), Tisa Farrow (Young Mary Magdalene), Gregory Abels, Victor Arnold, Robert Dryden.

United Methodist Communications. 36 minutes. Color.

Mandy's Grandmother (1979)

Director: Andrew Sugerman. Producer: Andrew Sugerman. Screenplay: Mary Munisteri. Cinematographer: Charlie Clifton. Editor: Julie Sloane.

Cast: Maureen O'Sullivan (Grandmother), Amy Levitan (Mandy), Kathryn Walker (Susan), Philip Carlson (Mandy's Father), Christopher Erickson (Paulie).

Walt Disney Films. 30 minutes. Color.

Morning's at Seven (1982—TV)

Director: Vivian Matalon. Producer: Bill Siegler. Writer: Paul Osborn. Editor: Jerry Newman.

Cast: Maurice Copeland (Theodore Swanson), King Donovan (Carl Bolton), Robert Moberly (Homer Bolton), Charlotte Moore Moore (Myrtle Brown), Maureen O'Sullivan (Esther Crampton).

Showtime. 120 minutes. Color.

Too Scared to Scream (1984)

Director: Tony Lo Bianco. Producer: Mike Connors. Screenplay: Neal Barbera, Glenn Leopold. Cinematographer: Larry Pizer. Editor: Ed Beyer.

Cast: Mike Connors (Lt. Alex Dinardo), Anne Archer (Kate Bridges), Leon Isaac Kenned (Frank), Ian McShane (Vincent Hardwick), Maureen O'Sullivan (Inez Hardwick)

International Film Marketing. 100 minutes. Color.

Hannah and Her Sisters (1986)

Director: Woody Allen. Producer: Robert Greenhut. Cinematographer: Carlo Di Palma. Editor: Susan E. Morse. Production Designer, Stuart Wurtzel.

Cast: Woody Allen (Mickey Sachs), Michael Caine (Elliot), Mia Farrow (Hannah), Barbara Hershey (Lee), Maureen O'Sullivan (Norma), Lloyd Nolan (Evan).

Orion Pictures Corporation. 107 minutes. Color.

Peggy Sue Got Married (1986)

Director: Francis Coppola. Producer: Paul R. Gunan. Screenplay: Jerry Leichtling and Ariene Sarner. Cinematographer: Jordan Cronenweth. Editor: Barry Malkin. Production Designer: Dean Tavoularis. Art Director: Alex Tavoularis.

Cast: Kathleen Turner (Peggy Sue Bodell), Nicolas Cage (Charlie Bodell), Maureen O'Sullivan (Elizabeth Alvorg), Leon Ames (Barney Alvorg), Helen Hunt (Beth Bodell).

Tri-Star. 105 minutes. Color.

Stranded (1987)

Director: Tex Fuller. Producer: Mark Levinson. Screenplay: Alan Castle. Cinematographer: Jeffrey Jur. Production Design: Lisette Thomas.

Cast: lone Skye (Deirdre), Joe Morton (Sheriff McMahon), Maureen O'Sullivan (Grace Clark), Susan Barnes (Helen Anderson), Cameron Dye (Lt. Scott).

New Line Cinema. 81 minutes. Color.

The River Pirates (1988)

Director: Tom G. Robertson, Producers: Peggy Doyle, Mary Kelly. Screenplay: Paul W. Cooper. Cinematographer: Ilie Agopian. Art Director: Taylor Morrison. Editor: Jim Krob.

Cast: Richard Farnsworth (Percy), Ryan Francis (Willie), Gennie James (Rivers Applewhite), Douglas Emerson (Spit), Maureen O'Sullivan (Aunt Sue).

Multimedia Entertainment Inc. 108 minutes. Color.

With Murder in Mind (1992—TV)

Director: Michael Tuchner. Producer: Robert Huddleston. Teleplay: Daniel Freudenberger. Cinematographer: William Wages. Editor: David Campling. Production Designer: Patricia Van Ryker.

Cast: Elizabeth Montgomery (Gayle Wolfer), Robert Foxworth (Bob Sprague), Howard Rollins Jr. (Samuel Carver), Maureen O'Sullivan (Aunt Mildred), Lee Richardson (John Condon).

CBS Television. 100 minutes. Color

The Habitation of Dragons (1992—TV)

Director: Michael Lindsay-Hogg. Producer: Donald P. Borchers. Teleplay: Horton Foote (based on his play). Cinematographer: Paul Laufer. Production Designer: Vaughan Edwards. Editor: Claudia Finkle.

Cast: Frederic Forrest (Leonard Tollivar), Jean Stapleton (Leonora Tollivar), Brad Davis (George Tollivar), Hallie Foote (Margaret Tollivar), Maureen O'Sullivan (Helen Taylor).

Turner Pictures. 94 minutes. Color.

Hart to Hart: Home Is Where the Hart Is (1994—TV)

Director: Peter Roger Hunt. Producers: Stefanie Powers, James Polster. Teleplay: Lawrence Hertzog. Based on characters created by Sidney Sheldon. Cinematographer: Roy H. Wagner. Editor: Andrew Cohen. Production Designer: Peter M. Wooley.

Cast: Robert Wagner (Jonathan Hart), Stefanie Powers (Jennifer Hart), Maureen O'Sullivan (Eleanor Biddlecomb), Lionel Stander (Max), Alan Young (Charley Loomis).

NBC/Columbia. 100 minutes. Color.

Mia Farrow Filmography

John Paul Jones (1959)

Minor Role (uncredited) *Director:* John Farrow. Producer: Samuel Bronston. Screenplay: John Farrow, Jesse Lasky Jr. Based on the story, "Nor'wester," by Clements Ripley. Art Director: Franz Bachelin. Cinematographer: Michel Kelber. Editor: Eda Warren.

Cast: Robert Stack (John Paul Jones), Bette Davis (Catherine the Great), Marisa Pavan (Aimee de Tellison), Charles Coburn (Benjamin Franklin), Erin O'Brien (Dorothea Danders).

Warner Bros. 126 minutes. Color.

Guns at Batasi (1964)

Director: John Guillermin. Producer: George H. Brown. Screenplay: Robert Holles, Leo Marks, Marshall Pugh. Art Director: Maurice Carter. Cinematographer: Douglas Slocombe. Editor: Max Benedict.

Cast: Richard Attenborough (Regimental Sgt. Major Lauderdale), Flora Robson (Miss Barker-Wise), Jack Hawkins (Colonel Deal), John Leyton (Private Wilkes), Mia Farrow (Karen Eriksson).

20th Century Fox. 103 minutes. B&W.

Johnny Belinda (1967—TV)

Director: Paul Bogart. Producer: David Susskind. Teleplay: Allan Sloane. Editor: Jack Shultis.

Cast: Mia Farrow (Belinda MacDonald), Ian Bannen (Dr. Jack Richardson), David Carradine (Locky), Barry Sullivan (Black MacDonald), Ruth White (Aggie MacDonald).

Talent Associates, ABC, Rediffusion Television. 90 minutes. Color.

A Dandy in Aspic (1968)

Director: Anthony Mann. Producer: Anthony Mann. Screenplay: Derek Marlowe. Art Director: Carmen Dillon,

Patrick McLoughlin. Cinematographer: Christopher Challis. Editor: Thelma Connell.

Cast: Laurence Harvey (Krasvenin), Tom Courtenay (Gatiss), Mia Farrow (Caroline), Harry Andrews (Fraser), Peter Cook (Prentiss).

Columbia British Productions. 107 minutes. Color.

Rosemary's Baby (1968)

Director: Roman Polanski. Producer: William Castle. Screenplay: Roman Polanski. Story: Ira Levin. Art Director: Joel Schiller. Cinematographer: William Fraker. Editors: Sam O'Steen, Robert Wyman.

Cast: Mia Farrow (Rosemary Woodhouse), John Cassavetes (Guy Woodhouse), Ruth Gordon (Minnie Castevet), Sidney Blackmer (Roman Castevet), Ralph Bellamy (Dr. Sapirstein).

William Castle Enterprises. 137 minutes. Color.

Secret Ceremony (1968)

Director: Joseph Losey. Producer: John Heyman, Norman Priggen. Screenplay: George Tabori. Story: Marco Deveni. Art Director: John Clark Cinematographer: Gerry Fisher. Editor: Reginald Beck.

Cast: Elizabeth Taylor (Leonora), Robert Mitchum (Albert), Mia Farrow (Cenci), Peggy Ashcroft (Hannah), Pamela Brown (Hilda).

World Film Services. 109 minutes. Color.

John and Mary (1969)

Director: Peter Yates. Producer: Ben Kadish. Screenplay: John Mortimer. Story: Mervyn Jones. Cinematographer: Gayne Rescher. Editor: Frank P. Keller.

Cast: Dustin Hoffman (John), Mia Farrow (Mary), Michael Tolan (James), Sunny Griffin (Ruth), Tyne Daly (Hilary).

Debrod Productions. 92 minutes. Color.

Goodbye, Raggedy Ann (1971—TV)

Director: Fielder Cook. Producer: Jack Sher. Teleplay: Jack Sher. Cinematograper: Earl Rath. Editord: Philip W. Anderson, Gene Fowler Jr.

Cast: Mia Farrow (Brooke Collier), Hal Holbrook (Harlan Webb), John Colicos (Paul Jamison), Marlene Warfield (Louise Walters), Ed Flanders (David Bevin)

Metromedia Productions. 90 minutes. Color.

See No Evil (1971)

Director: Richard O. Fleischer . Producers: Martin Ransohoff, Leslie Linder. Screenplay: Brian Clemens. Art Director: John Hoesli. Cinematographer: Gerry Fisher. Editor: Thelma Connell.

Cast: Mia Farrow (Sarah), Dorothy Alison (Betty Rexton), Robin Bailey (George Rexton), Diane Grayson (Sandy Rexton), Brian Rawlinson (Barker).

Genesis Productions, Ltd., Filmways, Inc. 89 minutes. Color.

The Public Eye (1972)

Director: Carol Reed. Producer: Hal B. Wallis. Screenplay: Peter Shaffer. Art Director: Robert Cartwright. Cinematographer: Christopher Challis. Editor: Anne V. Coates.

Cast: Mia Farrow (Belinda), Topol (Julian Cristoforou), Michael Jayston (Charles), Margaret Rawlings (Mrs. Sidley), Annette Crosbie (Miss Framer).

Hal Wallis Productions, Universal Pictures, Ltd. 95 minutes. Color.

Scoundrel in White (1972)

Director: Claude Chabrol. Producer: Jean-Paul Belmondo, Andre Genoves. Screenplay: Hubert Monteilhet. Production Designer: Guy Littaye. Cinematographer: Jean Rabier. Editor: Jacques Gaillard.

Cast: Jean-Paul Belmondo (Dr. Paul Simay), Mia Farrow (Christine Dupont), Laura Antonelli (Martine Dupont), Daniel Lecourtois (Le professeur), Marlene Appelt (L'Infirmiere Carole).

Les Films de la Boetie, Cerito Films, Rizzoli Film. 95 minutes. Color.

The Great Gatsby (1974)

Director: Jack Clayton. Producer: David Merrick. Screenplay: Francis Ford Coppola. Story: F. Scott Fitzgerald. Production Designer: John Box. Cinematographer: Douglas Slocombe. Editor: Tom Priestley.

Cast: Robert Redford (Jay Gatsby), Mia Farrow (Daisy Buchanan), Bruce Dern (Tom Buchanan), Karen Black (Myrtle Wilson), Sam Waterson (Nick Carraway).

The Newdon Company. 148 minutes. Color.

Peter Pan (1976—TV)

Director: Dwight Hemion, Teleplay: Andrew Birkin, Jack Burns. Producer: Dwight Hemion. Art Director: David Chandler.

Cast: Mia Farrow (Peter Pan), Danny Kaye (Captain Hook), Paula Kelly (Tiger Lily), Lynsey Baxter (Jane), John Gielgud (Narrator).

Associated Television, Hallmark Hall of Fame Productions, NBC. 120 minutes. Color.

The Haunting of Julia (1977)

Director: Richard Loncraine. Producer: Peter Fetterman. Screenplay: Dave Humphries. Story: Peter Straub. Production Designer: Brian Morris. Cinematographer: Peter Hannan. Editor: Ron Wisman.

Cast: Mia Farrow (Julia Lofting), Kier Dullea (Magnus Lofting), Tom Conti (Mark Berkeley), Jill Bennett (Lily Lofting), Robin Gammell (David Swift).

Canadian Film Development Corporation. 98 minutes. Color.

Avalanche (1978)

Director: Corey Allen. Producer: Roger Corman. Screenplay: Gavin Lambert, Corey Allen. Story: Frances Doel. Production Designer: Sharon Compton. Cinematographer: Pierre-William Glenn. Editors: Stuart Schoolnik, Larry Bock.

Cast: Rock Hudson (David Shelby), Mia Farrow (Caroline Brace), Robert Forster (Nick Thorne), Jeanette Nolan (Florence Shelby), Rick Moses (Bruce Scott).

New World Pictures. 91 minutes. Color.

A Wedding (1978)

Director: Robert Altman . Producer: Robert Altman. Screenplay: John Considine, Patricia Resnick, Allan Nicholls, Robert Altman. Art Director: Dennis J. Parrish. Cinematographer: Charles Rosher. Editor: Tony Lombardo.

Cast: Desi Arnaz Jr. (Dino Corelli), Carol Burnett (Tulip Brenner), Paul Dooley (Snooks Brenner), Amy Stryker (Muffin Brenner), Mia Farrow (Buffy Brenner).

Lion's Gate Films. 125 minutes. Color.

Death on the Nile (1978)

Director: John Guillermin. Producer: John Brabourne, Richard Goodwin. Screenplay: Anthony Shaffer. Story: Agatha Christie. Production Designer: Peter Murton. Cinematographer: Jack Cardiff. Editor: Malcolm Cooke.

Cast: Peter Ustinov (Hercule Poirot), Mia Farrow (Jacqueline De Bellefort), Simon MacCorkindale (Simon Doyle), Jane Birkin (Louise Bourget), Lois Chiles (Linnet Ridgeway).

Mersham Productions Ltd. 140 minutes. Color.

Hurricane (1979)

Director: Jan Troell. Producer: Dino De Laurentiis. Screenplay: Lorenzo Semple Jr. Story: James Normal Hall. Production Designer: Danilo Donati. Cinematographer: Sven Nykvist. Editor: Sam O'Steen.

Cast: Jason Robards (Capt. Charles Bruckner), Mia Farrow (Charlotte Bruckner), Max von Sydow (Dr. Danielsson), Trevor Howard (Father Malone), Dayton Ka'ne (Matangi).

Famous Films Productions N.V. 120 minutes. Color.

The Last Unicorn (1982)

Directors: Arthur Rankin Jr., Jules Bass. Producers: Arthur Rankin Jr., Jules Bass. Screenplay: Peter S. Beagle. Production Designer: Arthur Rankin Jr. Editor: Tomoko Kida.

Cast (voice): Alan Arkin (Schmendrick), Jeff Bridges (Prince Lir), Mia Farrow (Unicorn), Angela Lansbury (Momma Fortuna), Tammy Grimes (Molly Grue).

iTC Films, Inc., Rankin/Bass. 85 minutes. Animated. Color.

A Midsummer Night's Sex Comedy (1982)

Director: Woody Allen. Producer: Robert Greenhut. Screenplay: Woody Allen. Production Designer: Mel Bourne. Cinematographer: Gordon Willis. Editor: Susan E. Morse.

Cast: Woody Allen (Andrew), Mia Farrow (Ariel), Jose Ferrer (Leopold), Julie Hagerty (Dulcy), Tony Roberts (Maxwell).

Orion Pictures. 89 minutes. Color.

Sarah and the Squirrel (1982)

Director: Yoram Gross. Producer: Yoram Gross. Screenplay: Yoram Gross, Elizabeth Kata. Editor: Lindy Trost.

Cast: Mia Farrow (Narrator (live action segments) / Sarah (animated segments) (voice), Joan Bruce, John Faasen, Ron Haddrick, Shane Porteous.

Yoram Gross Films. 60 minutes. Animated. Color.

Zelig (1983)

Director: Woody Allen. Producer: Robert Greenhut. Screenplay: Woody Allen. Production Designer: Mel Bourne. Cinematographer: Gordon Willis. Editor: Susan E. Morse.

Cast: Woody Allen (Leonard Zelig), Mia Farrow (Dr. Eudora Nesbit), Patrick Horgan (The Narrator (voice), John Buckwalter (Dr. Sindell), Marvin Chatinover (Glandular Diagnosis Doctor). Orion Pictures, Warner Bros. 79 minutes. B&W/Color.

Supergirl (1984)

Director: Jeannot Szwarc. Producer: Timothy Burrill. Screenplay: David Odell. Production Designer: Richard MacDonald. Cinematographer: Alan Hume. Editor: Malcolm Cooke.

Cast: Faye Dunaway (Selena), Helen Slater (Supergirl), Peter O'Toole (Zaltar), Mia Farrow (Alura), Brenda Vaccaro (Bianca). Artistry Limited. 124 minutes. Color.

Broadway Danny Rose (1984)

Director: Woody Allen. Producer: Robert Greenhut. Screenplay: Woody Allen. Production Designer: Mel Bourne. Cinematographer: Gordon Willis. Editor: Susan E. Morse .

Cast: Woody Allen (Danny Rose), Mia Farrow (Tina Vitale), Nick Apollo Forte (Lou Canova), Sandy Baron, Corbett Monica. Orion Pictures. 84 minutes. B&W.

The Purple Rose of Cairo (1985)

Director: Woody Allen. Producer: Robert Greenhut. Screenplay: Woody Allen. Production Designer: Stuart Wurtzel. Cinematographer: Gordon Willis. Editor: Susan E. Morse.

Cast: Mia Farrow (Cecilia), Jeff Daniels (Tom Baxter), Danny Aiello (Monk), Irving Metzman (Theater Manager), Stephanie Farrow (Cecilia's Sister). Orion Pictures. 82 minutes. B&W/Color.

Hannah and Her Sisters (1986)

Director: Woody Allen. Producer: Robert Greenhut . Screenplay: Woody Allen. Production Designer: Stuart Wurtzel. Cinematographer: Carlo Di Palma. Editor: Susan E. Morse.

Cast: Woody Allen (Mickey), Michael Caine (Elliot), Mia Farrow (Hannah), Dianne Wiest (Holly), Barbara Hershey (Lee). Orion Pictures. 107 minutes. Color.

September (1987)

Director: Woody Allen. Producer: Robert Greenhut. Screenplay: Woody Allen. Production Designer: Santo Loquasto. Cinematographer: Carlo Di Palma. Editor: Susan E. Morse.

Cast: Denholm Elliott (Howard), Mia Farrow (Lane), Elaine Stritch (Diane), Dianne Wiest (Stephanie), Sam Waterston (Peter).

Rollins-Joffe Productions. 82 minutes. Color.

Radio Days (1987)

Director: Woody Allen. Producer: Robert Greenhut. Screenplay: Woody Allen. Production Designer: Santo Loquasto. Cinematographer: Carlo Di Palma. Editor: Susan E. Morse.

Cast: Mia Farrow (Sally White), Dianne Wiest (Bea), Danny Aiello (Rocco), Jeff Daniels (Bill Baxter), Helen Miller (Mrs. Needleman)

Orion Pictures. 88 minutes. Color.

Another Woman (1988)

Director: Woody Allen. Producer: Robert Greenhut. Screenplay: Woody Allen. Production Designer: Santo Loquasto. Cinematographer: Sven Nykvist. Editor: Susan E. Morse.

Cast: Gena Rowlands (Marion), Mia Farrow (Hope), Ian Holm (Ken), Blythe Danner (Lydia), Gene Hackman (Larry). Orion Picutres. 81 minutes. Color.

New York Stories (1989)

Directors: Woody Allen, Francis Ford Coppola, Martin Scorsese. Producer: Robert Greenhut. Screenplay: Woody Allen, Francis Ford Coppola, Sofia Coppola, Richard Price.

Cast: Woody Allen (Sheldon), Mia Farrow (Lisa), Nick Nolte (Lionel Dobie), Rosanna Arquette (Paulette), Mae Questel (Mother).

Touchstone Pictures (The Walt Disney Company). 120 minutes. Color.

Crimes and Misdemeanors (1989)

Director: Woody Allen. Producer: Robert Greenhut. Screenplay: Woody Allen. Production Designer: Santo Loquasto. Cinematographer: Sven Nykvist. Editor: Susan E. Morse.

Cast: Woody Allen (Cliff Stern), Martin Landau (Judah Rosenthal), Claire Bloom (Miriam Rosenthal), Anjelica Huston (Dolores Paley), Mia Farrow (Halley Reed).

Jack Rollins & Charles H. Joffe Productions. 104 minutes. Color.

Alice (1990)

Director: Woody Allen. Producer: Robert Greenhut. Screenplay: Woody Allen. Cinematographer: Carlo Di Palma. Editor: Susan E. Morse. Production Designer: Santo Loquasto.

Cast: Mia Farrow (Alice), William Hurt (Doug), Joe Mantegna (Joe), June Squibb (Hild), Marceline Hugot (Monica).

Jack Rollins & Charles H. Joffe Productions. 106 minutes. Color.

Shadows and Fog (1992)

Director: Woody Allen. Producer: Robert Greenhut. Screenplay: Woody Allen. Production Designer: Santo Loquasto. Cinematographer: Carlo Di Palma. Editor: Susan E. Morse.

Cast: Woody Allen (Kleinman), Mia Farrow (Irmy), Michael Kirby (Killer), David Ogden Stiers (Hacker), James Rebhorn (Vigilante).

Jack Rollins & Charles H. Joffe Productions, Orion Pictures. 85 minutes. Color.

Husbands and Wives (1992)

Director: Woody Allen. Producer: Robert Greenhut. Screenplay: Woody Allen. Production Designer: Santo Loquasto. Cinematographer: Carlo Di Palma. Editor: Susan E. Morse.

Cast: Woody Allen (Gabe Roth), Mia Farrow (Judy Roth), Sydney Pollack (Jack), Judy Davis (Sally), Juliette Lewis (Rain).

TriStar Pictures (Sony Pictures Entertainment, Inc.). 107 minutes. Color.

Widows' Peak (1994)

Director: John Irvin. Producers: Jo Manuel, Steven D. Mackler. Screenplay: Hugh Leonard. Production Designer: Leo Austin. Cinematographer: Ashley Rowe. Editor: Peter Tanner.

Cast: Joan Plowright (Mrs. Doyle-Counihan), Mia Farrow (Miss Katherine O'Hare), Natasha Richardson (Mrs. Edwina Broome), Adrian Dunbar (Godfrey Doyle-Counihan), Jim Broadbent (Con Clancy).

British Screen Productions. 98 minutes. Color.

Miami Rhapsody (1995)

Director: David Frankel. Producers: Barry Jossen, David Frankel. Screenplay: David Frankel. Production Designer: J. Mark Harrington. Cinematographer: Jack Wallner. Editor: Steven Weisberg.

Cast: Sarah Jessica Parker (Gwyn), Gil Bellows (Matt), Antonio Banderas (Antonio), Mia Farrow (Nina), Paul Mazursky (Vic).

Hollywood Pictures. 95 minutes. Color.

Reckless (1995)

Director: Norman René. Producer: Amy Kaufman. Screenplay: Craig Lucas. Production Designer: Andrew Jackness. Cinematographer: Frederick Elmes. Editor: Michael Berenbaum.

Cast: Mia Farrow (Rachel), Tony Goldwyn (Tom), Mary-Louise Parker (Pooty), Deborah Rush (Trish), Scott Glenn (Lloyd).

Playhouse International Pictures. 92 minutes. Color.

Angela Mooney (1996)
Director: Tommy McArdle. Producer: Samuel Benedict. Production Designer: Sinead Clancy. Cinematographer: Seamus Deasy. Editor: Ron Davis.

Cast: Mia Farrow (Angela Mooney), Brendan Gleeson (Barney Mooney), Alan Devine (Young Malone), Patrick Bergin (Older Malone), Lesley Conroy (Nancy).

Merlin Films. 86 minutes. Color.

Private Parts (1997)
Director: Betty Thomas. Producer: Ivan Reitman. Screenplay: Len Blum, Michael Kalesniko. Story: Howard Stern. Production Designer: Charles Rosen. Cinematographer: Walt Lloyd. Editor: Peter Teschner.

Cast: Howard Stern (Self), Mary McCormack (Alison Stern), Robin Quivers (Self), Fred Norris (Self), Mia Farrow (uncredited).

Paramount Pictures. 109 minutes. Color.

Forget Me Never (1999—TV)
Director: Robert Allan Ackerman. Producer: Samuel Benedict. Teleplay: H. Haden Yelin, Renee Longstreet. Cinematographer: Mike Fash. Art Director: James Phillips. Film Editor: Scott Vickrey.

Cast: Mia Farrow (Diane McGowin), Martin Sheen (Jack), Colm Feore (Albert), Ingrid Veninger (Ginny), Kyra Harper (Paula).

Alliance Atlantis Communications, Citadel Entertainment, Storyline Entertainment. 95 minutes. Color.

Coming Soon (1999)
Director: Colette Burson. Producers: Beau Flynn, Stefan Simchowitz, Keven Duffy. Screenplay: Colette Burson, Kate

Robin. Production Designer: Anne Stuhler. Cinematographer: Joaquin Baca-Asay. Editor: Norman Buckley.

Cast: Tricia Vessey (Nell Kellner), Gaby Hoffmann (Jenny Simon), Bonnie Root (Stream Hodsell), Mia Farrow (Judy Hodsell), Bridget Barkan (Polly).

Key Entertainment, Bandeira Entertainment. 95 minutes. Color.

A Girl Thing (2001—TV Miniseries)

Director: Lee Rose. Writer: Lee Rose. Producer: Cydney Bernard. Cinematograper: Eric Van Haren Noman. Art Director: Eija Johnson. Film Editors: William Marrinson, Christopher Rouse.

Cast: Kate Capshaw (Casey Montgomery), Stockard Channing (Dr. Beth Noonan), Rebecca De Mornay (Kim McCormack), Mia Farrow (Betty McCarthy), Elizabeth Franz (Josephine McCormack).

Hallmark Channel, Showtime Networks. 237 minutes. Color.

The Secret Life of Zoey (2002—TV)

Director: Robert Mandel. Producer: Richard Davis. Teleplay: Betty Goldberg. Cinematographer: Norayr Kasper. Art Director: Kathryn Hatton. Editor: Benjamin A. Weissman.

Cast: Mia Farrow (Marcia), Julia Whelan (Zoey), Cliff De Young (Larry), Andrew McCarthy (Mike Harper), Caroline Aaron (Mimi).

Once and Future Films, Patricia Clifford Productions, Viacom Productions. 92 minutes. Color.

Purpose (2002)

Director: Alan Ari Lazar. Producer: Michael S. Murphey, Ronnie Apteker, Alan Ari Lazar. Screenplay: Ronnie Apteker, Alan Ari Lazar, Saki Missaikos. Production Designer: Franco-Giacomo Carbone. Cinematographer: John Peters. Editor: Lawrence A. Maddow.

Cast: Mia Farrow (Anna Simmons), John Light (John Elias), Elena Evangelo (Claire), Ismael East Carlo (Fisherman), Chris Howell (Ted Oits).

Earth Magic Pictures. 96 minutes. Color.

Julie Lydecker (2002—TV)

Director: Jerry Zaks. Producers: Jennifer Crittenden, Phil Rosenthal. Teleplay: Jennifer Crittenden.

Cast: Mary McCormack (Julie Lydecker), Bryan Cuprill (Josh), Amy Farrington, Mia Farrow, Sean O'Bryan.

CBS, Paramount Television. Unaired. Color.

An American Girl Holiday (2004—TV)

Director: Nadia Tass. Teleplay: Marsha Norman. Cinematographer: David Parker. Editor: Susan Shipton. Adapted from the "Samantha" stories from the "The American Girl Collection."

Cast: Mia Farrow (Grandmary Edwards), AnnaSophia Robb (Samantha Parkington), Kenner Ames (Mr. O'Malley), Stewart Arnott (The Doctor), Olivia Ballantyne (Jenny O'Malley).

Red Om Films, Revolution Studios, Sam Films. 86 minutes. Color.

The Ex (original title *"Fast Track"*) (2006)

Director: Jesse Peretz. Producers: Anthony Bergman, Anne Carey, Ted Hope. Screenplay: David Guion, Michael Handelman. Production Designer: John Paino. Cinematographer: Tom Richmond. Editors: Tricia Cooke, John Michel, Jeff McEvoy.

Cast: Zach Braff (Tom Reilly), Amanda Peet (Sofia Kowalski), Jason Bateman (Chip Sanders), Charles Grodin (Bob Kowalski), Mia Farrow (Amelia Kowalski).

This is That/2929 Productions. 89 minutes. Color.

The Omen (2006)

Director: John Moore. Producers: Glenn Williamson, John Moore. Screenplay: David Seltzer. Production Designer:

Patrick Lumb. Cinematographer: Jonathan Sela. Editor: Dan Zimmerman.

Cast: Julia Stiles (Katherine Thorn), Liev Schreiber (Robert Thorn), Mia Farrow (Mrs. Baylock), David Thewlis (Keith Jennings), Seamus Davey-Fitzpatrick (Damien).

Twentieth Century Fox. 110 minutes. Color.

Arthur and the Invisibles (2006)
Director: Luc Besson. Producer: Luc Besson. Screenplay: Celine Garcia. Story: Luc Besson. Production Designer: Hugues Tissandier. Cinematographer: Thierry Arbogast. Editor: Karin Benhammouda, Yann Herve, Vincent Tabaillon.

Cast: Freddie Highmore (Arthur), Mia Farrow (Granny), Madonna (Princess Selenia), Ron Crawford (Archibald), Penny Balfour (Arthur's Mother).

EuropaCorp/Avalanche Productions. 94 minutes. Color. Animated/Live Action.

Be Kind Rewind (2008)
Director: Michel Gondry. Producer: Michel Gondry, Julie Fong, Georges Bermann. Screenplay: Michel Gondry. Production Designer: Dan Leigh. Cinematographer: Ellen Kuras. Editor: Jeff Buchanan.

Cast: Jack Black (Jerry), Mos Def (Mike), Danny Glover (Mr. Fletcher), Mia Farrow (Miss Falewicz), Melonie Diaz (Alma).

Partizan Films. 102 minutes. Color.

Arthur and the Revenge of Maltazard (2009)
Director: Luc Besson. Producers: Luc Besson, Emmanuel Prevost. Screenplay: Luc Besson, Patrice Garcia. Production Designer: Hugues Tissandier. Cinematographer: Thierry Arbogast. Editor: Julien Rey.

Cast: Freddie Highmore (Arthur), Selena Gomez (Selenia [voice]), Snoop Dogg (Max [voice]), Logan Miller (Jake), Mia Farrow (Granny).

EuropaCorp. 107 minutes. Color. Animated/Live Action.

Arthur 3: The War of the Two Worlds (2010)

Director: Luc Besson. Producers: Luc Besson, Emmanuel Prevost. Screenplay: Luc Besson, Patrice Garcia. Production Designer: Hugues Tissandier. Cinematographer: Thierry Arbogast. Editor: Julien Rey.

Cast: Mia Farrow (Granny), Ron Crawford (Archibald), Penny Balfour (Rose), Robert Stanton (Armand), Richard Davis (M).

EuropaCorp. 101 minutes. Color. Animated/Live Action.

Dark Horse (2012)

Director: Todd Solondz. Producers: Ted Hope, Derrick Tseng. Screenplay: Todd Solondz. Production Designer: Alex Digerlando. Cinematographer: Andrij Parekh. Editor: Kevin Messman.

Cast: Justin Bartha (Richard), Selma Blair (Miranda), Mia Farrow (Phyllis), Christopher Walken (Jackie), Jordan Gelber (Abe).

This is That, Double Hope Films. 85 minutes. Color.

BIBLIOGRAPHY

Allen, Woody. *Apropos of Nothing*. New York: Arcade Publishing, 2020.

Anger, Kenneth. *Hollywood Babylon*. New York: Bantam Books/Bantam Dell Publishing Corporation, 1975.

Anonymous. *The Mia Farrow Story/The Woody Allen Story*. He Said She Said Comics, vol. 2. New York: First Amendment Publishing, 1993.

Barton, Ruth. *Hedy Lamarr: The Most Beautiful Woman in Film*. Lexington: University Press of Kentucky, 2010.

Basinger, Janine. *The Star Machine*. New York: Vintage, 2008.

Behlmer, Rudy. *Inside Warner Bros. (1935–1951)*. New York: Simon & Schuster, Inc., New York, 1985.

Berg, A. Scott. *Kate Remembered*. New York: G.P. Putnam's Sons, 2003,

Bogdanovich, Peter. *Who the Hell Made It: Conversations With Legendary Film Directors*. New York: Ballantine Books, 1997.

Bogdanovich, Peter. *Who the Hell's In It: Conversations With Hollywood's Legendary Actors*. New York: Ballantine Books, 2004.

Bordwell, David. *Reinventing Hollywood: How 1940s Filmmakers Changed Movie Storytelling*. Chicago and London, The University of Chicago Press, 2017

Bruns, Prudence Farrow. *Dear Prudence: The Story Behind the Song*. North Charleston: Create Space Independent Publishing Platform, 2015.

Cameron, Ian, and Douglas Pye, eds. *The Book of Westerns.* New York: Continuum, 1996.

Caruth, Cathy. *Unclaimed Experience: Trauma, Narrative, History.* Baltimore and London: The Johns Hopkins University Press, 1996.

Cavell, Stanley. *The Hollywood Melodrama of the Unknown Woman.* Chicago and London: University of Chicago Press, 1996.

Coleman, Herbert. *The Man Who Knew Hitchcock: A Hollywood Memoir.* Lanham, Toronto, Plymouth, U.K.: Scarecrow Press, 2007.

Cook, David A., *A History of Narrative Film.* New York and London: W.W. Norton & Company, 1981.

Davis, Bette. *The Lonely Life, An Autobiography.* New York: G.P. Putnam's Sons, 1962.

Eelis, George. *Robert Mitchum: A Biography.* New York: Franklin Watts, 1984.

Epstein, Edward Z., and Joe Morella. *Mia: The Life of Mia Farrow.* New York: Delacorte Press, 1991.

Evans, Robert. *The Kid Stays in the Picture.* New York: Hyperion, 1994.

Farmer, Manny. *Negative Space.* New York: Praeger, 1971.

Farrow, Mia. *What Falls Away: A Memoir.* New York: Doubleday, 1997.

Farrow, Moses. "A Son Speaks Out." May 23, 2018. http://mosesfarrow.blogspot.com/.

Fleischer, Richard. *Just Tell Me When to Cry: A Memoir.* New York: Carroll & Graf Publishers, Inc., 1993.

Fury, David. *No Ordinary Jane: The Life of Maureen O'Sullivan.* New York: Scribners, 2009.

Gabler, Neal. *An Empire of Their Own: How the Jews Invented Hollywood.* New York: Anchor Books, 1989.

Gaines, Jane. *Classical Hollywood Narrative: The Paradigm Wars.* Durham and London: Duke University Press, 1992.

Goodrich, David, L., *The Real Nick and Nora: Frances Goodrich and Albert Hackett, Writers of Stage and Screen Classics.* Carbondale and Edwardsville: Southern Illinois University Press, 2001.

Graham, Sheilah. *The Garden of Allah.* New York: Crown Publishers, 1970.

Groteke, Kristie. *Mia and Woody, Love and Betrayal.* New York: Carroll & Graf Publishers, 1994.

Higham, Charles. *Bette: The Life of Bette Davis.* New York: MacMillan, 1981.

Hodel, Steve. *Black Dahlia Avenger II.* Studio City: Thoughtprint Press, 2014.

Kelley, Kitty. *His Way.* New York: Bantam, 1986.

Keenan, Vince, "The Catholic Noir of John Farrow," *Noir City,* 29, (2020): 117–121.

Kipen, David, ed. *Dear Los Angeles: Los Angeles City in Diaries and Letters, 1542 to 2018.* New York: Random House, 2018.

Levin, David, ed. *Hollywood and the Great Fan Magazines.* New York: Arbor House, 1970.

Levy, Shawn, *Rat Pack Confidential: Frank, Dean, Sammy, Peter, Joey and the Last Great Show Biz Party.* New York: Crown Publishing Group, 1999.

Marx, Groucho, and Richard Anobile. *The Marx Brothers Scrapbook. New York:* Darien House, 1963.

McGilligan, Patrick. *Nicholas Ray: The Glorious Failure of an American Director.* New York: HarperCollins, 2011.

Meade, Marion. *The Unruly Life of Woody Allen.* London: Orion Books, 2000.

Milland, Ray. *Wide-Eyed in Babylon: An Autobiography.* New York: William Morrow & Company, Inc., 1974.

Miller, Patsy Ruth. *My Hollywood, When Both of Us Were Young: The Memories of Patsy Ruth Miller.* Albany, Georgia: BearManor Media, 1995.

Mitchell, Lee Clark. *Westerns: Making the Man in Fiction and Film.* Chicago: The University of Chicago Press, 1996.

Moss, Marilyn Ann. *Raoul Walsh: The True Adventures of Hollywood's Legendary Director.* Lexington: University Press of Kentucky, 2011.

Munn, Michael. *John Wayne: The Man Behind the Myth.* New York: New American Library, 2003.

Murray, Scott. "John Farrow." Cinema Papers, No. 77 (January 1990).

Pinkerton, Nick, *"The Original Sinner."* May 28, 2020. *Nickpinkerton.substack.com.*

Polanski, Roman. *Roman, by Polanski.* New York: William Morrow and Company, Inc., 1984.

Pomerance, Murray. "Down and Away to Botany Bay." *Sight & Sound, Australia.*

Price, Victoria, *Vincent Price: A Daughter's Biograph.* New York: St. Martin's Press, 1999.

Ricciardi, Alessa. *The Ends of Mourning: Psychoanalysis, Literature, Film.* Stanford: Stanford University Press, 2003.

Rubin, Sam, and Richard Taylor. *Mia Farrow: Flowerchild, Madonna, Muse.* New York: St. Martin's Press, 1989.

Server, Lee. *Ava Gardner: Love Is Nothing.* New York: St. Martin's Press, 2006.

———. *Robert Mitchum: Baby, I Don't Care.* New York: St. Martin's Press, 2001.

Silver, Alain, and James Ursani. *Gangster Film Reader.* Pompton Plains, New Jersey: Limelight Editions, 2007.

Silver, Alain, and James Ursani. "John Farrow: Anonymous Noir," in *Film Noir Reader*, edited by Alain Silver and James Ursani, 145–159, New York: Limelight Edition, 1996.

Slide, Anthony. *Inside the Hollywood Fan Magazine: A History of Star-Makers, Fabricators, and Gossip Mongers.* Jackson: University Press of Mississippi, 2010.

———. *They Also Wrote for the Fan Magazines: Film Articles by Literary Giants from e.e. cummings to Eleanor Roosevelt, 1920–1931.* Jefferson, North Carolina and London: McFarland & Company, Inc., 1992.

Smith, Cynthia. *What Has She Got? Women Who Attract Famous Men—And How They Did It.* New York: D.I. Fine, 1991, 9–26.

Staiger, Janet, ed. *The Studio System.* New Brunswick: Rutgers University Press, 1995.

Thomson, David. *Warner Bros: The Making of an American Movie Studio.* New Haven and London: Yale University Press, 2017.

Weissmuller Jr., Johnny. *Tarzan My Father.* Toronto: ECW Press, 2002.

Wills, Garry. *John Wayne's America.* New York: Touchstone Books, 1998.

Youngerman, Joseph, *My Seventy Years at Paramount Studios and the Directors Guild of America*, Los Angeles: Directors Guild of America, 1996.

NOTES

CHAPTER ONE

1. *The Hollywood Reporter,* "Golden Globes: Woody Allen to Receive Cecil B. Demille Award," September 2013.
2. Tab Hunter with Eddie Muller, *Tab Hunter Confidential: The Making of a Movie Star.* Chapel Hill, NC: Algonquin Books, 2005, 105.
3. Rubin, Sam, and Richard Taylor, *Mia Farrow: Flowerchild, Madonna, Muse.* New York: St. Martin's Press, 1989, 9.

CHAPTER TWO

1. John Villiers Farrow, https://libraries.catholic.edu/special-collections /archives/collections/finding-aids/finding-aids.html?file=farrow; Hazlehurst, Cameron, Australian Dictionary of Biography, https: //adb.anu.edu.au/biography/farrow-john-villiers-10158; Garry Maddox, "New documentary to reveal the forgotten life of Australian film maker John Farrow," *Sunday Morning Herald,* August 5, 2017, https://www.smh.com.au/entertainment/movies/new-documentary -to-reveal-the-forgotten-life-of-australian-filmmaker-john-farrow -20170802-gxnxlw.html
2. Cameron Hazlehurst, *Australian Dictionary of Biography,* https: //adb.anu.edu.au/biography/farrow-john-villiers-10158.
3. Cameron Hazlehurst, *Australian Dictionary of Biography*
4. Barrie Pattison, "Ray Milland" (Part 2), *Australian Film Guide,* edited by John Howard Reid, Vol. 1, No. 10, xxii–xxiii.
5. Winifred Van Duzer, King Features, "Romance of the 'Little Red Devil' and the Roving Lord: Parents Snubbed Him, Police Arrested Him, His Captain Jailed Him, His Own Consul Called Him Bogus—And Still She Loved Him Madly," *Evening Independent,* August 16, 1924, 13.
6. Photo caption, *Telegraph-Herald,* June 20, 1924, 3.

7. Van Duzer, "Romance of the 'Little Red Devil," 13.

8. *Variety,* September 14, 1927, 46.

9. *Los Angeles Times*, "Farrow Faces Inquisition," February 8, 1933, A3.

10. *Modern Screen*, July 1933, 109.

11. Marilyn Ann Moss, *Raoul Walsh: The True Adventures of Hollywood's Legendary Director*, Lexington: University Press of Kentucky, 110.

12. *Variety,* "Picture Upstarts of '27," January 4, 1928, 29.

13. *Motion Picture News,* "New Writers Join Staff at Paramount Scenarists," February 11, 1928, 435.

14. *Exhibitors Herald and Motion Picture World,* "Music Has Big Part in Paramount Film," September 29, 1928, 34.

15. *Variety,* January 2, 1929, 174.

16. *Barrier Miner,* "Secret Marriage Denial," October 25, 1932, 1.

17. John Farrow, *The Bad One*, New York: A.L. Burt Company, 1930, 5.

18. Katherine Alpert, "What's Wrong with Hollywood Love?," *Modern Screen Magazine,* 1930, reprinted in Martin Levin, *Hollywood and the Great Fan Magazines,* New York: Arbor House, 1970.

19. Joseph Youngerman, *My Seventy Years at Paramount Studios and the Directors Guild of America*, Los Angeles: Directors Guild of America, 1996, 59.

20. Maureen O'Sullivan friend Mark Montgomery, interview with author, February 2021.

21. Cable, John Farrow to William Wellman, 1927. Given to the author by Kevin Brownlow from personal collection.

22. *Los Angeles Times*, "Wider Drive to Bar Hollywood Aliens" January 29, 1933, N1.

23. John Villiers Farrow, Catholic Authors, http://www.catholicauthors .com/farrow.html.

24. *Los Angeles Times,* "New Counts to Be Faced by Farrow," February 4, 1933, 12.

25. Dennis Sprague, "Laird of the Blue Lagoon," *World Magazine,* February 1945, 96.

26. *Motion Picture Daily,* July 18, 1934, 2.

27. *Motion Picture Daily,* September 12, 1934, 6.

28. Dennis Sprague, "Laird of the Blue Lagoon," 55.

29. Barrie Pattison, "Ray Milland" (Part 2), in John Howard Reid (ed.), *Australian Film Guide,* Vol. 1, No. 10, xxii–xxiii.

30. Dennis Sprague, "Laird of the Blue Lagoon," 55.

31. Victoria Price, *Vincent Price: A Daughter's Biography*, New York: St. Martin's Press, 1999, 150.

32. Herbert Coleman, *The Man Who Knew Hitchcock: A Hollywood Memoir*, Lanham, MD: Scarecrow Press, 2003, 128.

33. Herbert Coleman, *The Man Who Knew Hitchcock: A Hollywood Memoir*, 128.

CHAPTER THREE

1. Associated Press, "Maureen O'Sullivan," *Hutchinson* (KS) *News*, May, 1961, 12.

2. *Motion Picture News*, "Janet Gaynor Is Contrite, Awaits Sheehan Pardon," July 12, 1930, 24.

3. *The Irish Times*, "From Roscommon to Hollywood—The Story of Maureen O'Sullivan," November 26, 2019, https://www.irish-times.com/life-and-style/abroad/from-roscommon-to-hollywood-the-story-of-maureen-o-sullivan-1.4094481.

4. Marilyn Ann Moss, *Raoul Walsh: The True Adventures of Hollywood's Legendary Director*, 327.

5. Johnny Weissmuller, Jr., *Tarzan My Father*, Toronto: ECW Press, 2002, 38.

6. Marsha Hunt/Roger Memos interview with the author, January 15, 2021.

7. David Fury, *Maureen O'Sullivan: "No Average Jane"*, 17.

8. David Fury, *Maureen O'Sullivan: "No Average Jane"*, 20.

9. David Fury, *Maureen O'Sullivan: "No Average Jane"*, 14

CHAPTER FOUR

1. David Fury, *Maureen O'Sullivan: "No Average Jane"*, 94.

2. "Beautiful Australian Girl Arrives: Antipodean Prize Winner Comes to Woo Fame as Picture Actress," *Los Angeles Times*, June 14, 1927, A8

3. "Society of Cinemaland," *Los Angeles Times*, Nov. 20, 1927, C24.

4. *Variety*, January 4, 1928.

5. *Motion Picture News*, February 11, 1928.

6. Sheilah Graham, *The Garden of Allah*, New York: Crown Publishers, 1970, 53.

7. Sheilah Graham, *The Garden of Allah*. 64; Marion Marx acquaintance Robert Bader in conversation with author, September 10, 2022.

8. Grace Kingsley, "Open House in Hollywood," *Screenland*, March, 1929, 30, 94.

9. Grace Kingsley, "All These Hollywood Folks," *Los Angeles Times*, December 8, 1929, H7.

10. Grace Kingsley, "Edith Mayer's Wedding is One of the Highlights of the Cinema Social Season," *Los Angeles Times*, May 11, 1930, H4.

11. "Affairs of the Heart: Film folk who are saying 'We Will!'—'We do!'—'We're through!' *Talking Screen*, September, 1930, 39.

12. Betty Boone, "Maureen from Dublin," *Screenland*, October, 1930, 66.

13. "Affairs of the Heart: Film folk who are saying 'We Will!'—'We do!'—'We're through!' *Talking Screen*, 39.

14. "Film Gossip of the Month," *Screen Magazine*, November 1930, 11.

15. *The Modern Screen Magazine*, November 1930, 14.

16. "Two Stars Fight Back to Health," *Los Angeles Times*, December 8, 1930, 1.

17. *Screenland*, January 1931, 99.

18. *Silver Screen*, August 1931, 42.

19. "The Love Fever Chart of Hollywood," *Movie Mirror*, April 1932, 35.

20. Patsy Ruth Miller, *My Hollywood, When Both of Us Were Young: The Memories of Patsy Ruth Miller* (Albany, GA: BearManor Media, 1995), 156–157.

21. "Looking Them Over," *Movie Classic*, June 1932, 182.

22. *Movie Classic*, March 1933. 50.

23. "Lila Lee's Marriage to Director Will End Four-Cornered Romance," *Movie Classic*, March 1933, 33.

24. William J. Mann, *Kate: The Woman Who Was Katharine Hepburn*, London: Faber and Faber, 2006, 185.

25. A. Scott Berg, *Kate Remembered*, New York: Berkley Publishing Group, 2004, 210.

26. *Screenland*, April, 1933, 70.

27. *Modern Screen*, August 1933, 24.

28. *Screenland*, October 1933, 69.

29. *Los Angeles Times*, December 11, 1933, A6.

30. William H. McKegg, "Maureen Laughs It Off," *Picture Play Magazine*, December 1933, 39.

31. William H. McKegg, "Maureen Laughs It Off," 39.

32. William H. McKegg, "Maureen Laughs It Off," 39.

33. William H. McKegg, "Maureen Laughs It Off," 39, 58.

34. William H. McKegg, "Maureen Laughs It Off," 38–39, 58–59.

35. *Modern Screen*, January 1934, 126.

36. *Variety*, April 3, 1934, 60.

37. Read Kendall, "Around and About in Hollywood," *Los Angeles Times*, June 15, 1934, 15.

38. Alma Whitaker, "Maureen O'Sullivan's Long Betrothal Baffles Filmdom," *Los Angeles Times*, July 29, 1934, A3.

39. *Pittsburgh Post-Gazette*, August 11, 1934, 1.

40. "John Farrow's Divorce in Way of Church Wedding," *Boston Globe*, August 11, 1934.

41. "Maureen Still Single on Her Canada Arrival," *Los Angeles Times*, Sept. 20, 1934, 1.

42. "Tie To Wait Papal Visa: Maureen O'Sullivan Admits Marriage to John Farrow Matter of Time," *Los Angeles Times*, September 28, 1934, A3.

43. *Movie Mirror*, October 1934, 14.

44. "Cal York Announcing the Monthly Broadcast of Hollywood's Goings-On!," *Photoplay*, January 1935, 86.

45. Read Kendall, "Around and About in Hollywood," *Los Angeles Times*, February 4, 1935, 16.

46. Read Kendall, "Around and About in Hollywood," *Los Angeles Times*, October 12, 1935, 11.

47. "Irish Actress Gets License. Wedding Notice Filed by Maureen O'Sullivan and John Farrow," *Los Angeles Times*, September 6, 1936, 1.

CHAPTER FIVE

1. David Fury, *Maureen O'Sullivan: "No Average Jane"*, 326.

2. *Los Angeles Times*, "'Mrs. Tarzan' Devotes Time Now To New Interest," June 22, 1939, 8.

3. *Los Angeles Times*, "John Farrow's Son Christened," June 13, 1939, A16.

4. *Los Angeles Times*, "Mrs. Tarzan Devotes Time Now to New Interest," 8.

5. *New York Times*, "Actress Sails to Make Film in London After Assurances on Situation Abroad," August 24, 1939, 13.

6. John Farrow, letter to Maureen O'Sullivan, August 30, 1939.

7. John Farrow, letter to Maureen O'Sullivan, August 31, 1939.

8. John Farrow, letter to Maureen O'Sullivan, September 2, 1939.
9. John Farrow, letter to Maureen O'Sullivan, September 7, 1939.
10. *Los Angeles Times*, "Actress Flies From London, Maureen O'Sullivan Comes Home When War Halts Film Work Aboard," September 17, 1939, A1.
11. *The Advertiser*, Adelaide, Australia, November 8, 1939.
12. John Farrow to Maureen O'Sullivan, Western Union Telegram, April 2 1940, 2:45 a.m.
13. John Farrow to Michael Farrow, postal telegraph, May 12,1940 1:02 a.m.
14. Letter from John Farrow to Maureen O'Sullivan, Department Of National Defence, Ottawa, Canada, May 14, 1940.
15. Letter from John Farrow to Maureen O'Sullivan, Department Of National Defence, Ottawa, Canada, May 24, 1940.
16. Jimmie Fidler, "Jimmie Fidler In Hollywood," *Los Angeles Times*, December 23, 1940, 11.
17. *Los Angeles Times*, "Lieut. John Farrow on Duty at Sea: Maureen O'Sullivan, Wife, Back in Hollywood," February 6, 1941, 4.
18. *Los Angeles Times,* "Farrow Home From War Duty," May 10, 1941, A1.
19. May Driscoll, "How Tarzan Saved Maureen O'Sullivan," *Hollywood*, April 1942, 36.
20. "Commander Hollywood," CFB Esquimalt Naval Military Museum, https://navalandmilitarymuseum.org/article/john-farrow.
21. "Commander Hollywood," CFB Esquimalt Naval Military Museum.

CHAPTER SIX

1. *The Advertiser*, December 17, 1932, 9.
2. *John Farrow, Hollywood's Man in the Shadows*, directed by Frans Vandenburg and Claude Gonzalez, 1:36.
3. "Director Tells Psychology of Direction," *Los Angeles Times*, July 13,1938,12.
4. Thomas M. Pryor, "A Director Talks of Writers," *New York Times,* October 13, 1946, 67.

CHAPTER SEVEN

1. *Los Angeles Examiner*, December 11, 1942.
2. *Hollywood Talk* syndicated column, Louella Parsons, *Pittsburgh Post-Gazette*, August 18, 1960, 47.
3. Dennis Sprague, "Laird of the Blue Lagoon," 97

4. *John Farrow: Hollywood's Man in the Shadows.*

5. *John Farrow: Hollywood's Man in the Shadows.*

6. Steve Hodel, *Black Dahlia Avenger II,* Studio City, Ca: Thoughtprint Press, 2014, 42–45.

7. Hedda Hopper letter to Francis Sill Wickware, June 16, 1944, Academy of Motion Picture Arts and Sciences Margaret Herrick Library.

8. Howard da Silva interview with film historian Frank Thompson, May 1984.

9. Film historian Frank Thompson interview with author, February 18, 2021.

10. Mia Farrow, *What Falls Away: A Memoir,* New York: Doubleday, 1997, 27

11. Mia Farrow, *What Falls Away: A Memoir,* 1–6.

12. Mia Farrow, *What Falls Away: A Memoir,* 27.

13. *John Farrow: Hollywood's Man in the Shadows.*

14. "Maureen Mother Award," *New York Daily News,* April 24, 1981, 34.

15. Dinitia Smith, "Picking Up the Legos and the Pieces, *New York Times*, May 8, 1994, Section 2, 1.

16. Dinitia Smith, "Picking Up the Legos and the Pieces," Section 2, 1.

17. Prudence Farrow Bruns, *Dear Prudence: The Story Behind the Song*, North Charleston, SC: Create Space Independent Publishing Platform, 2015, 48.

18. Prudence Farrow Bruns, *Dear Prudence: The Story Behind the Song,* 53.

19. Joseph Youngerman, *My Seventy Years at Paramount Studios and the Directors Guild of America,* 143–146.

20. Richard Maibaum, "'Great Gatsby' Employs Two Generations of Farrows: Gatsby Employs Farrow Family," *Los Angeles Times,* July 15, 1973, 15.

21. Joseph Youngerman, *My Seventy Years at Paramount Studios and the Directors Guild of America,* 59.

22. Joseph Youngerman, *My Seventy Years at Paramount Studios and the Directors Guild of America,* 60.

23. George Eelis, *Robert Mitchum: A Biography,* New York: Franklin Watts, 1984, 150–151.

24. Lee Server, *Robert Mitchum: Baby I Don't Care,* New York: St. Martin's Press, 2001, 208.

25. Lee Server, *Robert Mitchum: Baby I Don't Care,* 208.

26. Lee Server, *Robert Mitchum: Baby I Don't Care,* 208–209.

27. George Eelis, *Robert Mitchum: A Biography,* New York: Franklin Watts, 1984, 150.

28. George Eelis, *Robert Mitchum: A Biography,* 150–151.

29. George Eelis, *Robert Mitchum: A Biography,* 204.

30. Jane Russell interview with author, June 2010.

31. Lee Server, *Robert Mitchum: Baby I Don't Care,* 209–211.

32. Server, *Robert Mitchum: Baby I Don't Care,* 219.

33. Server, *Robert Mitchum: Baby I Don't Care,* 215.

34. Judy Klemesrud, "Being Mia's Sister Was Tisa's Burden," *New York Times,* January 8, 1970, 36.

35. Judy Klemesrud, "Being Mia's Sister Was Tisa's Burden," 36.

36. Lee Server, *Ava Gardner: Love Is Nothing,* New York: St. Martin's Press, 2006, 243.

37. "Wayne Talks Tough: An Interview by Joe McInerney," *Film Comment,* 1972, 52–55.

38. Edward Z. Epstein and Joe Morelia, *Mia: The Life of Mia Farrow,* New York: Delacorte Press, 1991, 42.

39. Tab Hunter with Eddie Muller, *Tab Hunter Confidential: The Making of a Movie Star,* 105.

40. Charles Higham, *The Life of Bette Davis,* New York: Macmillan, 1981, 249–250.

41. Prudence Farrow Bruns, *Dear Prudence: The Story Behind the Song,* 63.

42. Letter, May 29, 1958, John Farrow Collection, Catholic University.

43. *Los Angeles Times,* "Maureen O'Sullivan Son Killed," October 30, 1958, 1.

44. *Los Angeles Times,* "Maureen O'Sullivan Attends Rites for Son," November 5, 1958, 6.

45. Mia Farrow, *What Falls Away: A Memoir,* 54.

46. Mia Farrow, *What Falls Away: A Memoir,* 54.

47. Prudence Farrow Bruns, *Dear Prudence: The Story Behind the Song* 101–102.

48. Mia Farrow, *What Falls Away: A Memoir,* 35–36.

49. Mia Farrow, *What Falls Away: A Memoir,* 35–36.

50. Mia Farrow, *What Falls Away: A Memoir,* 17.

51. Prudence Farrow Bruns, *Dear Prudence: The Story Behind the Song,* 112.

52. Prudence Farrow Bruns, *Dear Prudence: The Story Behind the Song,* 112.

53. David Fury, *Maureen O'Sullivan: "No Average Jane"*, 326.

54. Film Historian Frank Thompson, taped interview with Julie Barton, 1984, given to author.

55. Film Historian Frank Thompson interview with author, February 2021.

56. Tab Hunter with Eddie Muller, *Tab Hunter Confidential: The Making of a Movie Star*, 105

57. Mia Farrow, *What Falls Away: A Memoir*, 77.

58. Mia Farrow, *What Falls Away: A Memoir*, 61

59. Prudence Farrow Bruns, *Dear Prudence: The Story Behind the Song*, 112.

60. Prudence Farrow Bruns, *Dear Prudence: The Story Behind the Song*, 112–113.

61. George Stevens Jr., correspondence with author, May 2022.

62. Prudence Farrow Bruns, *Dear Prudence: The Story Behind the Song*, 112–114

63. Prudence Farrow Bruns, *Dear Prudence: The Story Behind the Song*, 112–114.

64. Gaby Wood, "I've always had a sense of the unworthiness of myself," *The Guardian*, January 28, 2006, https://www.theguardian.com/film/2006/jan/29/2.

65. David Fury, *Maureen O'Sullivan: "No Average Jane"*, 347.

CHAPTER EIGHT

1. "Actress' Son Convicted," *Des Moines Register*, March 26, 1963, 2; "Son of Actress Fined on Narcotics," *Fort Worth Star-Telegram*, April 24, 1963, 19.

2. *Rutland Herald*, Patrick Villiers Farrow obituary, June 20, 2009, https://www.legacy.com/obituaries/rutlandherald/obituary.aspx?n=patrick-villiers-farrow&pid=128650348.

3. "Girl Defects From Convent," AP story, *Gettysburg Times*, October 24, 1967, 5.

4. Oliver Trager, *The American Book of the Dead*, New York: Simon & Schuster, 1997, 90.

5. "Mia's Brother Is Acquitted on Marijuana," *Daily Independent Journal*, August 10, 1967, 11.

6. *San Bernardino County Sun*, August 6, 1970, 28; "Actress' Brother Exonerated," 40.

7. Julia Marsh, "How I Was Almost the Manson Family's 6th Victim," *New York Post*, August 8, 2014, https://nypost.com/2014/08/08/i-would-have-been-the-manson-familys-6th-victim/.

8. Ava Roosevelt, "The Racing Heart" https://www.theracingheart .com/about-the-author-2/.

9. "Edgewater Man Accused of Sexually Abusing 2 Boys," *Baltimore Sun,* Nov. 16, 2012, A4.

10. Judy Klemesrud, "Being Mia's Sister Was Tisa's Burden," 36.

11. *Colorado Springs Gazette,* "Excuse Me, But You Must Be Mia Farrow's Sister," 49.

12. "That's Earl for Today," Earl Wilson syndicated column, August 17, 1970.

13. *Syracuse Herald American,* July 17, 1977, 168.

14. *Globe and Mail,* February 5, 2000, R.9.

15. *New York Times,* "Stephanie Farrow Married to Jim Kronen, an Artist," September 14, 1970, 49.

16. *New York Post,* "Woman who inspired The Beatles' 'Dear Prudence' once dated Robert Durst," March 28, 2015, https: //nypost.com/2015/03/28/woman-who-inspired-the-beatles-dear -prudence-once-dated-robert-durst/.

17. Robert D. McFadden, "Robert Durst, Scion and Killer Made for the Tabloids, Dies at 78," *New York Times,* January 11, 2022, A1.

18. Robin Adams Sloan, King Features Syndicate, "The Gossip Column," September 14, 1979.

19. Kristie Groteke, *Mia and Woody, Love and Betrayal, New* York: Carroll & Graf Publishers, 1994, 185

20. Kristie Groteke, *Mia and Woody, Love and Betrayal,*185.

21. Emily Cutts, "Farrow Gallery Is Put Up for Sale," *Rutland Daily Herald,* May 30, 2015, A1.

22. Gordon Dritschilo, "Farrow Left Mark on Region," *Rutland Daily Herald,* June 18, 2009, A1–A2.

23. *Huffington Post,* https://www.huffpost.com/entry/mia-farrows-brother -a-sui_b_216995.

24. David Olinger, "The battle within," *Denver Post,* August 24, 2008, https://www.denverpost.com/2008/08/24/the-battle-within/.

25. "Mia Farrow's brother found dead in Vt. art gallery," Associated Press, June 17, 2009, https://www.benningtonbanner.com/local -news/mia-farrows-brother-found-dead-in-vt-art-gallery/article _ae8de0cd-a716-5466-9584-0be9b86383a4.html.

26. Greg Mitchell, "Mia Farrow's Brother, a Suicide, Had Slammed Iraq War After Nephew Died," *Huffington Post,* July 18, 2009, updated May 25, 2011.

27. Gordon Dritschilo, "Farrow Left Mark on Region," A1–A2.

28. Patrick Villiers Farrow Obituary, *Rutland Daily Herald*, June 20, 2009, B2.

29. "Mia Farrow blames brother's suicide on death of soldier nephew," NewsHub.com, March 7, 2009 https://www.newshub.co.nz /entertainment/mia-farrow-blames-brothers-suicide-on-death-of -soldier-nephew-2009070316.

30. "Edgewater Man Accused of Sexually Abusing 2 Boys," *Baltimore Sun*, Nov. 16, 2012, A4.

31. "Mia Farrow's sex abuse silence," *Salon*, February 4, 2014, https: //www.salon.com/2014/02/04/mia_farrows_sex_abuse_silence/

32. "Mia Farrow's Brother Sentenced for Child Sex Abuse," NBC, October 28, 2013, https://www.nbcwashington.com/news/local /mia-farrows-brother-to-be-sentenced-for-sex-abuse/1957532/.

33. "Mia Farrow's Child Molester Brother Was Paroled 3 Years Early," February 20, 2021, Showbiz411, https://www.showbiz411.com /2021/02/20/mia-farrows-child-molester-brother-was-paroled-3 -years-early-prosecutor-says-took-advantage-of-boys-in-particularly -horrible-way.

34. David Evanier, *Woody: The Biography*, New York: St. Martin's Press, 2015, 336.

35. *New York Post*, "Woman Who Inspired The Beatles' 'Dear Prudence' Once Dated Robert Durst," March 28, 2015, https: //nypost.com/2015/03/28/woman-who-inspired-the-beatles-dear -prudence-once-dated-robert-durst/.

CHAPTER NINE

1. Cynthia S. Smith, *What Has She Got: Women Who Attract Famous Men—And How They Did It*, New York: D.I. Fine, 1991, 15.

2. Author interview with writer, director, and film historian C. Courtney Joyner, February 2022.

3. Levy, Shawn, *Rat Pack Confidential: Frank, Dean, Sammy, Peter, Joey and the Last Great Show Biz Party*, New York: Crown Publishing Group, 1999, 213.

4. Kitty Kelley, *His Way*, New York: Bantam, 1986, 346.

5. Kristie Groteke, *Mia and Woody, Love and Betrayal*, 34.

6. Kristie Groteke, *Mia and Woody, Love and Betrayal*, 54.

7. Roman Polanski, *Roman, by Polanski*, New York: William Morrow, 1984, 274.

8. Maureen Orth, "Momma Mia!," *Vanity Fair*, 3–4.

9. "Momma Mia!," 3.

CHAPTER TEN

1. Orson Welles to Peter Bogdanovich recounted by Bogdanovich in *The Last Picture Show: A Look Back*, directed by Laurent Bouzereau, 1999, Columbia Tr-Star Home Video.
2. Marion Meade, *The Unruly Life of Woody Allen*, London: Phoenix Books, 2000, 27.
3. Mia Farrow, *What Falls Away: A Memoir*, 226.

CHAPTER ELEVEN

1. Andrew M. Coleman, *Oxford Dictionary of Psychology*, Fourth Edition, Oxford: Oxford University Press, 2015.
2. Author interview with Jayson Mystkowsky, PhD, cognitive psychologist, September 1, 2022.
3. Mark Twain, *Adventures of Huckleberry Finn*, Boston and New York: Bedford Books of St. Martin's Press, 1995, 27.
4. Cathy Caruth, *Unclaimed Experience: Trauma, Narrative, History*, Baltimore: The Johns Hopkins University Press, 1996, 2.
5. Cathy Caruth, *Unclaimed Experience: Trauma, Narrative, History*, 2.
6. Moses Farrow, "A Son Speaks Out," May 23, 2018, http://moses-farrow.blogspot.com/2018/05/a-son-speaks-out-by-moses-farrow.html.
7. Woody Allen, *Apropos of Nothing*, New York: Arcade Publishers, 2020, 223–224.
8. Amelia McDonell-Parry, "Soon-Yi Previn Speaks Out About Woody Allen Marriage, Mia Farrow," *Rolling Stone*, September 17, 2018, https://www.rollingstone.com/culture/culture-news/soon-yi-woody-allen-marriage-mia-farrow-724957/.
9. Amelia McDonell-Parry, "Soon-Yi Previn Speaks Out About Woody Allen Marriage, Mia Farrow."
10. Moses Farrow, "A Son Speaks Out."
11. Woody Allen, *Apropos of Nothing*, 222–223.
12. Ben Smith, "Is Ronan Farrow Too Good to Be True?" *New York Times*, https://www.nytimes.com/2020/05/17/business/media/ronan-farrow.html.
13. "Matt Lauer Lashes Out at Ronan Farrow in Wake of New York Times critique," Associated Press, May 19, 2020, https://www.theguardian.com/media/2020/may/19/matt-lauer-lashes-out-at-ronan-farrow-in-wake-of-new-york-times-critique.

APPENDICES

1. Mia Farrow, *What Falls Away: A Memoir*, 20.
2. Dennis Sprague, "Laird of the Blue Lagoon," 55.
3. Dan Knapp, "From Whence They Came," March 29, 2005, https://news.usc.edu/23510/From-Whence-They-Came/.
4. J. Emmett Winn, "Targeting Alien Filmmakers in 1930s Hollywood," *Kinema: A Journal for Film and Audiovisual Media*, Fall 2010, https://openjournals.uwaterloo.ca/index.php/kinema/article/download/1215/1520?inline=1#ViewNotes_122.
5. *Los Angeles Times*, "New Alien Drive Round-Up Near," January 28, 1933, A1.
6. *Los Angeles Times*, "New Counts to Be Faced by Farrow," February 4, 1933, 12.
7. *Los Angeles Times*, "Alien Entry Case Aimed at Farrow," February 9, 1933, A1.
8. *Los Angeles Times*, "Alien Entry Case Aimed at Farrow," A1
9. *Los Angeles Times*, "Screen Writer Wins Probation," March 28, 1933, A16.
10. *Los Angeles Times*, "Farrow Found Not Guilty," January 10, 1934, A10.
11. J. Emmett Winn, "Targeting Alien Filmmakers in 1930s Hollywood,"
12. Sheila Weller, "Uncovering the Secrets of the Black Dahlia Murder," DuJour News, https://dujour.com/news/uncovering-the-secrets-of-the-black-dahlia-murder/).
13. Steve Hodel, *Black Dahlia Avenger II*, 43.
14. *John Farrow: Hollywood's Man in the Shadows*, 2021.
15. Steve Hodel, *Black Dahlia Avenger II*, 44.
16. Steve Hodel, *Black Dahlia Avenger II*, 44.
17. *Motion Picture*, November 1930, 113.
18. *Screenland*, February 1931, 31.
19. *Screenland*, April 1931, 95.
20. *Screenland*, May 1933, 79.
21. *Screenland*, July 1933, 19.
22. William H. McKegg, "Maureen Laughs It Off," 38–39, 58–59.
23. Alma Whitaker, *Los Angeles Times*, July 29, 1934, A3.

INDEX